When Blood and Bones Cry Out

When Blood and Bones Cry Out

Journeys through the Soundscape of Healing and Reconciliation

JOHN PAUL LEDERACH

ANGELA JILL LEDERACH

OXFORD
UNIVERSITY PRESS

Oxford University Press, Inc., publishes works that further
Oxford University's objective of excellence
in research, scholarship, and education.

Oxford   New York
Auckland   Cape Town   Dar es Salaam   Hong Kong   Karachi
Kuala Lumpur   Madrid   Melbourne   Mexico City   Nairobi
New Delhi   Shanghai   Taipei   Toronto

With offices in
Argentina   Austria   Brazil   Chile   Czech Republic   France   Greece
Guatemala   Hungary   Italy   Japan   Poland   Portugal   Singapore
South Korea   Switzerland   Thailand   Turkey   Ukraine   Vietnam

Copyright © John Paul Lederach and Angela Jill Lederach, 2010. All rights reserved.
Foreword © Judy Atkinson 2010

First published by University of Queensland Press,
PO Box 6042, St. Lucia, Queensland 4067, Australia.

Published by Oxford University Press, Inc.
198 Madison Avenue, New York, New York 10016

www.oup.com

Oxford is a registered trademark of Oxford University Press

All rights reserved. No part of this publication may be reproduced,
stored in a retrieval system, or transmitted, in any form or by any means,
electronic, mechanical, photocopying, recording, or otherwise,
without the prior permission of Oxford University Press.

Library of Congress Cataloging-in-Publication Data
Lederach, John Paul.
When blood and bones cry out : journeys through the soundscape of healing and reconciliation / John Paul Lederach and Angela Jill Lederach.
    p. cm.
Includes bibliographical references and index.
ISBN 978-0-19-983710-6   1. Peace-building.
2. Mediation.   3. Reconciliation.   4. Forgiveness.   5. Conflict
management.   I. Lederach, Angela Jill.   II. Title.   III. Title: Journeys through
the soundscape of healing and reconciliation.
HM1126.L435 2010a
327.1'72—dc22   2011009171

For Tom Cauuray, whose life and words inspired our writing, and for his family in the Falui Poets Society who faced the horrors of unfettered violence with the prophetic imagination of memory and hope;

For the family of Efraín Arenas and Doris Berrio and the more than four million displaced and disappeared in the Colombian wars;

For Morris Matadi and the thousands of child combatants on the journey to find their way home;

For Kadiatu Koroma and women everywhere who have the courage to give voice to the unspeakable devastation of sexual violence.

Contents

Foreword		ix
Preface		xv
Introduction: social healing in the age of the unspeakable		1
SECTION I	**NARRATIVE REFLECTIONS**	15
CHAPTER 1	Drums and gardens	17
CHAPTER 2	The wandering elders	23
CHAPTER 3	The Women of Liberia Mass Action for Peace Campaign	28
CHAPTER 4	The bones with no name	34
CHAPTER 5	Shifting metaphors	41
SECTION II	**THE SONICS OF HEALING**	73
CHAPTER 6	Sonic survival	75
CHAPTER 7	The Tibetan singing bowl	89
CHAPTER 8	Following the healing muse	111
SECTION III	**THE WOMB OF CHANGE**	145
CHAPTER 9	When mothers speak	147
CHAPTER 10	The poetry of social healing	170
SECTION IV	**THEORY, IMPLICATIONS AND CONCLUSIONS**	195
CHAPTER 11	The resonating echo of social healing	197
CHAPTER 12	Conclusions	225

Acknowledgements	235
Endnotes	239
References	241
Index	251

Foreword

When I first read the book *Moral Imagination: The art and soul of building peace* by John Paul Lederach, I felt the pull towards a kindred spirit, someone who knew something about where I had been and what I was doing in my life and work. John Paul had written in a way that connected with me. I felt he knew the landscape, often a rough, harsh terrain, over which I had been walking, and sometimes a moisture-rich valley of sounds, calling me to places where people desired to sit in the *Dadirri*[1] circle, listening to and learning from each other.

Later, when he sent me the draft manuscript for *When Blood and Bones Cry Out: Journeys through the soundscape of healing and reconciliation,* as I read, page by page, slowly, taking time to think, reflect, and reconnect where I had been, I felt and heard that kindred soul speaking to me on another level.

John Paul observed that this writing project with his daughter Angie is 'one of the most beautiful experiences a father could have'. Perhaps even more so is to work with your children on things that matter. *When Blood and Bones Cry Out* links John Paul's work in many places, but for this book, violence in Colombia links with that of his daughter Angie's work with child soldiers in West Africa, coming home from their childhood war zone experiences.

John Paul writes about what he calls a neglected aspect of healing and reconciliation. We too often write about it as a linear process. Of course it is not. And yet as John Paul points out we say 'healing is not a linear process', and then in the next sentence, as I have done many times, write about the stages and steps of healing.

So, within *When Blood and Bones Cry Out*, the imagery created, for example, of the Tibetan singing bowl, with the circular process, and the sound, both moving deep into the bowl and upwards in a shared space, provides a visual element, producing for those who have been there the acknowledgement: 'Yes, I know that space – this is how it is!' The process is both personal and social healing, as voices mingle, join and resonate with each other.

Within the academy, this creates problems. Personal healing, for them, suggests therapy. Professional skills development is about education, they would perceive, and you cannot mix them. Education, within the western construct, is an intellectual pursuit. Other Indigenous models of 'education' – or, as we call it at Gnibi,[2] 'educaring' – can provide both and, I would argue, are necessary when working within the field of historic, social trauma and generational community social healing.

I would argue that when working with people who have been through layered experiences of generational trauma, the only ethical approach is to allow both deep personal inner work within the context of social healing, and the development of skills to continue the work with others. In the last month I have seen this possibility while working with my own people in Australia; Aboriginal Australians; and with our brothers and sisters we could call our near neighbours, in Papua New Guinea and in Timor Leste.

In September 2009, I was invited by Peter and Lydia Kailap of Kaugere, a settlement on the edge of Port Moresby, the government centre of Papua New Guinea, to run a five-day workshop with a focus on human rights in relationship to family and community violence. Because there is no school in Kaugere for the children, Peter and Lydia had established the Children's University of Music and Arts (CUMA), with volunteer workers using music and art to teach children who are eager to learn. Often the only meal the children will receive for the day is at the school. For the five days we were there, the school became an adult learning centre – a 'university'. Each day 75 men and women, parents of the 70 children who attend the school, sat together to consider the United Nations Declaration of the Rights of the Child (1959), the United Nations Declaration of Human Rights (1948) and the United Nations Declaration on the Rights of Indigenous Peoples (2007) in relationship to the violence they live with on a daily basis. Starting with what happens to children when they witness and hence experience violence, the men and the women – at first in separate gender groups, and then together – worked to develop a community development approach to their needs, which would allow healing to occur across generations. As I think back to those five days I see the metaphor of the bowl taking shape.

In the first round people began to feel safe, so that they could listen and learn together. Once they felt comfortable, not threatened by what they were learning, they went deeper into the bowl, inwards, looking at themselves. And in the circular process of listening and learning together, as their voices grew strong and powerful, the sound rose up, and in the process talking became music, shared between them, and with us, the visitors, a social healing. On the last day, in what they called a *celebration of change*, they sang us a farewell song. A young man, Emmanuel Mailau, sang his song 'Children'. Ceremonies can often be rituals of grieving, and the song 'Children' is a lament for the lives of children who are crying and dying on the hills outside Port Moresby.

From the first day in Kaugere, I kept thinking of John Paul and Angie's metaphor, and the need for a metaphor shift. As they write, healing is aural. And sound is not linear. Sound rises and falls in joy and in sorrow, in loss and in triumph, in fear and in courage.

These are human experiences and they validate our humanness. The song 'Children' locates us in a place where children see much violence, where children are hungry because their parents have no money to buy food, and where children die early from diseases that are preventable. As Emmanuel says: 'I live in a settlement. The song is about all the children that I see everyday living such hard lives of poverty, the orphans that roam the streets in the settlement – it is an emotional song.' Yet every morning in Kaugere we also hear the voices of children who attend CUMA, singing their joyful morning songs, showing that while violence in its varied shapeshifting forms is remarkably resilient, so are children, as they reach beyond themselves engaging in celebration – ceremonies of healing, each morning in this small classroom without walls. They teach us how to be human.

And as I left Papua New Guinea to travel to Timor Leste, to deliver the last unit in the Diploma of Community Recovery,[3] I carried with me the draft manuscript of *When Blood and Bones Cry Out*. Each night I would read again pages I had previously read, and each day in class we would explore the need for men and women to heal from the multiple human rights violations that have been part of the historical, social trauma of Timor Leste. There is, within this small island, the world's youngest democracy, the human will to find a better way to live together, a resonance that rises from working in conflict transformation and peacebuilding, in healing from trauma.

'In Timor,' the students said, 'we must all be responsible for rebuilding our country. No one person created our violence. We now must find a way to heal, men and women, separately, and together, always placing our children in the centre of our circle.' They painted as they talked together in the classroom, a circle dance on canvas, with children surrounded by their families and communities. As I sat back listening and watching them talk and work together, the canvas moved and danced and sang to me. They discussed culture as a changing, moving entity, and yet under the intellectual discussions, at their core, they drew on the strength of their resilience and resonance, both separate yet interdependent qualities in the work of community peacebuilding. They taught me.

In Timor, completing my day's work, I retired to my room to read *When Blood and Bones Cry Out*, as if it were written for this country, for these people.

This is my third reading. Each reading has taken place in a location that has meaning: in Tasmania, Australia, with its history of genocide, talking with people about their proposal to build a healing centre. In Papua New Guinea, where orphaned children starve, yet each morning children sing songs in their university of music and arts. And in Timor Leste, where the film *Balibo* has just been released, and my students are all members of families who have, in various ways, survived the genocide of multiple colonisations and invasions. The students all work with people who have suffered torture trauma, and where *blood and bones cry out*. These students inspire me with their capacity to laugh, sing, cry and be heartbreakingly real as we go about our studies. In Timor, while I am there, there is always a celebration – a birth, a marriage, the commemoration of the Santa Cruz massacre this last time. They gather to dance and sing in celebration of their survival, of the great genocide that is their history. Here students asked me, 'What is the difference between political trauma, historical trauma, and social trauma? Can you explain the difference between loss and grief, victimisation, and traumatisation?' Their challenge to me is my challenge to myself, to get it right.

As John Paul and Angie have written, violence displaces people at multiple levels, fracturing their sense of safety in the world. The key to health and being well is both immediate and transgenerational, essentially at the same time. It is also about healing, in education or educaring. Education is healing, yet our policy makers do not yet understand that. The process will never be linear, just as songs are circular, transcending time and space, linking people – in sound, space and words – to each other.

Let me go back to the beginning. When John Paul said that writing this book was 'one of the most beautiful experiences a father could have', he did not say that he and his daughter could not have written *When Blood and Bones Cry Out*, a beautiful, heart wrenching, inspirational song, without first working together. That is obvious, however.

They set an example for us all. Only we can raise our individual voices to make a collective song of healing. Only we can choose to sit in circles and listen and learn together. Only we can put into action what we have learned, knowing that as we nurture spaces for healing and reconciliation, we do so from our own experiences and a longing for a renewed world, in which humans live and work together with mutual care and respect for each other and the lifeworld in which we all live.

Dadirri – listening to one another.

Judy Atkinson
Head of Gnibi, the College of Indigenous Australian Peoples
Southern Cross University
Lismore, Australia

Preface

A book always grows out of curiosity, care and experience. This one has perhaps undergone the process at a deeper level. It has taken a while for us to pull these pages together and the process was an unusual gift in the relationship between father and daughter. While a generation separates us in age, our experiences bind us together.

As the reader will find in the coming pages a lifetime of experience has touched us at the level of our family. Many of the most formative moments in pursuing peacebuilding have had direct ripple effects in our family life. Angie was a young child when our paths moved in the war-torn regions of Central America. The impact of a car accident in the Basque country caught us all up short. Shared and independent relationships and experiences we have had with colleagues and friends so hard hit by violence in places like Somalia, West Africa and Colombia have made untold contributions to our lives. The faces and love of these people have never left our consciousness or our hearts. As a family we have hosted and been hosted by people from all those locations, sat together around tables, listened to people, shared experiences, felt the trauma and seen resilient hope.

Over the years our paths at times separated as we individually moved into peacebuilding research and practice in different locations. Coming back together, sharing our experiences, at times our traumas, and certainly our ideas, we intuited that aspects of our experiences were converging and leading to interesting insights and understandings. This volume represents an effort to share those conversations, ideas, insights and understandings with a much wider audience.

We have co-authored this book, though at times we knew we had to provide space to speak from our individual voice and experience. We hope readers can follow the unfolding without confusion. The first and last sections of the book were written together. However, in Section II John Paul, as the primary author, follows his deep interest in the sonics of healing, starting with personal stories that were lived in flesh and bone. In Section III Angie reflects on her multiple visits and stays in West Africa that began when she accompanied her father on trips to the region, and continued when she returned later on her own to pursue research and to work with people in communities affected by violence. In each of those sections the voice at times moves to first person even though we have contributed ideas and suggestions to each other's writing.

As a final note we must thank the readers who will permit us to share these stories and musings. We experienced, much as we describe in the book, a healing wave as we remembered and found hope in the telling and exploration of our inner and collective voice that mixed our experiences with the stories of those whose lives of courage and resiliency have enriched and blessed us across the years.

John Paul Lederach
Angela Jill Lederach

Others simply love and respect us. These are true leaders of humanity, descendants in a direct spiritual line from one or other of the great teachers. They can be recognized by their amazing generosity in both giving and receiving unconditional love.
Adam Curle

When Blood and Bones Cry Out

Introduction: social healing in the age of the unspeakable

'Speaking the unspeakable.' With three words poet Robert Pinsky (2008) frames his *New York Times* review of Kathryn Harrison's book *While they slept* (2008). Her study follows the lives of the survivor sister and her perpetrator brother across several decades in the tragic multi-member Gilley family murder that stunned the small town of Medford, Oregon in 1984. Harrison recounts the night a troubled and routinely physically abused teenager pounded his father–abuser, his mother and his sister to death with a baseball bat. Two children survived – one a sister who hid in the closet and one the teenage brother who more than 25 years later still sits in prison. His lawyer has recently asked for a legal review of his case, based on the argument that the young perpetrator was a victim–offender. Even legal language has had to invent categories to describe the ambiguities of the unimaginable. The two siblings have not spoken a word to each other in the past two and a half decades.

Unspeakable. How do people express and then heal from violations that so destroy the essence of innocence, decency and life itself that the very experience penetrates beyond comprehension and words? It takes a poet to situate what may otherwise appear in news media as a sensational anomaly in the context of this longstanding human inquiry, which remains for the most part unanswered. Pinsky (2008, p. 1) opens his review by looking back to mythology and the classics of literature, the literature before and beyond what he calls the 'the Freudian cure' and the 'too mild and cool' notion of the 'therapeutic'. He brings forward the figure of Philomena, her tongue torn from her mouth, who transforms into a nightingale in order to 'sing' the accusations against her rapist. He cites the narrator's lament from Sophocles's *Oedipus Tyrannus* that 'it cannot speak' and is forced to look away, unable to absorb the tragedy heaped upon the destroyed yet living Oedipus: 'I would speak, ponder, question if I were able'. He returns as far as Genesis and the story of the first murder where Abel's voice was silenced and his blood had to 'cry out from the ground' (Pinsky 2008, pp. 1, 10).

What happened in microcosm in Medford in 1984 has unravelled at macro levels in untold numbers – from Rwanda to Liberia, Bosnia to Colombia blood has cried from the ground. Minow (1998) refers to these unspeakable macro-tragedies in a variety of ways – 'mass', 'collective' or 'societal-level violence', all clearly creating the image of whole communities and nations facing violation. Atkinson (2002) refers aptly to the impact of arriving coloniser violence on the Aboriginal experience in Australia as 'trauma trails' that cross and transfer to whole generations of people. Hayner (2002), in her early and comprehensive review of truth commissions in the aftermath of two decades of civil war, chose the title *Unspeakable truths*.

We return to the question: How do people with collective experiences of violence reconcile and heal from experiences that penetrate below and beyond words?

Over the past fifteen years, with an increase in peace agreements that purport to end, or at least hold hopes for a conclusion to civil war, the literature and programmatic interest in reconciliation has exploded. What the term *reconciliation* has gained in broad popular coinage it seems to have lost in definitional value, to the degree that recent overviews and essays note as a standard starting point the variety and lack of common definitions (Bloomfield et al. 2003; Kaimal 2008). Once the primary territory of religious concern and to a lesser degree, of social psychology, reconciliation has increasingly emerged as a political category (Abu-Nimer 2001; Barkan 2000; Biggar 2003; Minow 1998, 2002; Philpott 2006; Schapp 2005). On a regular basis our news media report on the need for political, national, inter-religious or inter-ethnic reconciliation. The word has increasingly become a buzzword for politicians wishing to end wars they no longer seem interested in supporting. The political arena in particular seems to treat the word as synonymous with some form of enmity accommodation, a coexistence necessary to control the bitterness of entrenched divisions in favour of a reasoned peace, or what political philosopher David Crocker (1999, p. 60) has called a 'thin' rather than a 'thick' understanding of reconciliation. Political analyst Ignatieff called this a 'cold peace' when he observed that politically it is possible to 'coexist with people without forgetting or forgiving their crimes against you' (Ignatieff 2003).

In the mix of this varied multidisciplinary, academic, self-help and media-driven literature we find a remarkable absence of agreement on what exactly reconciliation represents and even less consensus about what the term means or how it best should be used, though some important efforts have helped clarify the range of understandings and definitions (Bloomfield et al. 2006; Villa-Vicencio & Doxtader 2004; Kaimal 2008; van der Mark 2007). The most significant volume of case studies is the book *Peacebuilding in traumatized societies* in which Barry Hart (2008) facilitates the gathering of experiences that explicitly link the wider approaches of conflict transformation and peace strategies with the challenging concern about trauma. The range and depth of articles testifies to the creativity required, the diversity of ideas and approaches, and the wisdom emerging from these hard-won efforts. Hart (2008, p. viii) suggests that among the key challenges are the questions of how to address those elements that are intangible and hidden below the surface but which so significantly affect healing and reconciliation, themes that we explore in the following pages. In recent years we have witnessed an extraordinary explosion of programs and initiatives that purport to pursue and deliver reconciliation – that much-sought-after concept – in what appear to be far more random applications, often only loosely referring to reconciliation. Smith (2004), for example, in the review of expenditures of major donor programs and categories reported that reconciliation is among the top four international funding categories: it ranks third behind political development and socioeconomic assistance, and one ahead of security. This interest in reconciliation points to the fact that something resonates deeply in the human soul about the need to find our way towards healthier human relationships and the forging of what Martin Luther King Jr referred to as the 'beloved community'. But at the same time, the multi-varied understandings and particularly the political use and manipulation of the word 'reconciliation' show how far we fall short of King's vision of authentic community.

Within this wide-ranging and contested literature two points of consensus seem to hold about the concept of reconciliation.

One point of consensus is the idea that reconciliation begins from and solidifies around a relational focus (Assefa 1993; Bloomfield et al. 2003; Bloomfield et al. 2006; Helmick & Peterson 2001; Lederach 1997, 1999; McSpadden 2000; Schreiter 1998; Volf 1996). As a relationally based and nuanced construct this view of reconciliation is guided by a *spatial* metaphor of *encounter*, an understanding that suggests places for the estranged to meet, exchange, engage and even embrace; where they create and re-create common ground in contested histories embedded in their social and physical geographies. The spatial encounter motif involves a repetitious back and forth, the circling if you will, that relationships in real life actually represent.

v) Another point of consensus is the widely embraced notion that reconciliation is best understood as a process involving some form of movement as in a developmental progression. Movement as metaphor has had two distinct, at times seemingly contradictory, perspectives. On the one hand quite a number of authors posit the notion that reconciliation and healing involve cyclical or circular movements (Assefa 1993; Atkinson 2002; Bloomfield et al. 2003; Botcharova 2001; Hart 2008; Helmick & Peterson 2001; Kraybill 1995; Pranis et al. 2003; Yoder 2005). These are literally drawn out as images with circles, often in the form of a single iteration that seems to suggest the beginning of a spiral, the end point of the circle being somewhat higher than the beginning point. In addition, an emerging trend in recent years has documented the important contributions, perspectives and practices of indigenous peoples that focus much more directly on the importance of *circle* per se, on native understandings of restoration and change, and on approaches based on ceremony and ritual (Atkinson 2002; McCaslin 2005; Pranis 2005).

Invariably those who describe reconciliation and healing as cyclical in nature also suggest the processes follow a *linear* progression. Here they identify discernible stages, phases or steps (Botcharova 2001; Herman 1992; Kraybill 1995; Yoder 2005). This description responds to the *analytical* need to identify patterns that emerge when considering many cases of how healing and reconciliation function. In this latter metaphor most authors recognise the inherent tension between the movement images that hold the circular and linear. Ironically, however, as Bloomfield and his co-authors (2003) noted, while analysts argue that reconciliation is not a linear process they then proceed to suggest in almost the same breath the stages it follows. Overridingly in seeking to create scientific and pragmatically useful categories and meaning the academic literature has tended to pass over this inherent tension. While reconciliation and healing have risen to greater prominence as political categories integrated into peacebuilding – with corresponding investment in research and program development – a paradigm deeply guided by a metaphor structure of linearity, with its sequential notion of social change and progression in time, has become increasingly prevalent. Though not always explicit, the underlying meaning arising from this structure suggests that reason, maturity and individual and social health develop towards the latter stages of the sequential progression, whereas unhealthy patterns of reactivity, denial, being stuck, repetitiousness and irrationality are prevalent in the earlier stages. Thus, while the literature acknowledges the spatial and cyclical metaphors, the bulk of the writing seems to accept as necessary the notion that linearity forms a foundation for understanding, agency and application. Few authors who explore the merits of *spatial* and *movement* metaphors do not give way to the pressures of sequential linearity. In this book we explore these more hidden aspects of healing and reconciliation in contexts of protracted, violent and deep-rooted conflict.

As a starting point we propose a more direct exploration of the underlying metaphoric structure rising from the experience of healing and reconciliation. Our purpose focuses on the development of the concept of *social healing* as an intermediary phenomenon located between micro-individual healing and wider collective reconciliation. The phrase *social reconciliation* is better known in the literature (Bronkhorst 1995; Kaimal 2008; Schreiter 1998). Though not a new term, the topic used in this book, *social healing*, has not been as fully explored or developed, though examples do exist. O'Dea (2004) on the website of the Institute of Noetic Sciences suggests social healing is 'an emerging field that seeks to deal with wounds created by conflict, collective trauma and large-scale oppression'. Thompson (2005, p. 7) frames social healing as 'justice-making' and 'as a matter of addressing and healing social wounds, not punishing human evil'. In her recent essay Paula Green has provided the most specific definition when she suggests that social healing 'can broadly be defined as the reconstruction of communal relations after mass violence'. She goes on to suggest that social healing precedes reconciliation after open warfare, asking only that 'postwar communities begin the process of restoring relations so that they can coexist, make decisions together and rebuild their destroyed commons. Often a prelude to reconciliation and forgiveness, social healing can emerge through initiatives that rehumanise broken relations, rebuild trust, normalise daily life and restore hope' (Green 2009, p. 77).

In our concluding speculations on theory we propose a definition of social healing based primarily on an aural understanding of change and movement, a context that requires a metaphor shift away from linearity. We suggest that social healing requires a focus on the local community that takes seriously their lived experience in settings of protracted conflict, with their inevitable need to survive and locate both the individual and the collective voice. Voice suggests a notion of movement that is both internal, within an individual, and external, taking the form of social echo and resonance that emerges from collective spaces that build meaningful conversation, resiliency in the face of violence and purposeful action. These terms suggest an important metaphor shift with reference to how we understand individual and social processes, a shift based on an understanding of change that reflects the nature and movement of sound. It is this underlying metaphor shift we wish to explore in greater depth in this book.

Across the wider literature on reconciliation, trauma healing and peacebuilding we find three elements that are often mentioned as important caveats but are rarely explored in depth on their own merits and which form the particular challenges of our approach. These elements create both the opportunity and the challenge faced by this volume, precisely because our interest lies in finding creative ways to lift out those hidden but very real aspects of social healing that seem least attended to in the literature.

First, as described in the opening of this introduction, time and again authors note a fundamental dilemma around the issues of justice and reconciliation. On the one hand they are keenly cognisant that gross human rights violations and collective violence in protracted conflict must be addressed. At the same time they recognise that words inadequately express the depth of tragedy of this lived experience (Atkinson 2002; Biggar 2003; Hayner 2002; Minow 1998, 2002). Perhaps Minow (1998) articulated this human dilemma most succinctly in her early volume *Between vengeance and forgiveness*. She writes (1998, p. 5) that collective violence poses the challenge that 'closure is not possible. Even if it were, any closure would insult those whose lives are forever ruptured. Even to speak, to grope for words to describe horrific events, is to pretend to negate their unspeakable qualities and effects. Yet silence is also an unacceptable offense, a shocking implication that the perpetrators in fact succeeded...' Our challenge in this book is to open some pathways into the exploration of the unspeakable that are not dependent primarily on the spoken and explanatory word, a challenge to say the least, when approaching this through the written medium.

Second, numerous authors discuss the idea that reconciliation and healing are inadequately understood exclusively as linear processes, though most offer frameworks that provide a structure of change as passing through phases or stages (Botcharova 2001; Kraybill 1995; Yoder 2005). Our interest lies in the less explored aspect of this affirmation, namely that linearity is not adequate on its own to fully penetrate the nature of social healing. Our challenge is to find ways to guide the conversation towards other metaphors that are not linear in nature but which, by their very structure, provide insight and contribute to our understanding of the multifaceted nature of reconciliation and social healing. Here we must envision elements of movement metaphors – for example, repetitiousness or circularity – as contributive and positive components of change, rather than as negative components that are stagnating, reactive or detrimental.

Third, we find that many authors acknowledge the extraordinary complexity of healing and reconciliation whether at personal, community or national levels (Bloomfield et al. 2003; Hamber & Kelly 2005; Hart 2008; Lederach 1997). Of particular note is the basic idea that complexity functions by way of *temporal simultaneity* of processes and experiences. Simultaneity in the midst of complexity suggests that many things happen at once. For political reconciliation this complexity refers to major events and programmatic needs in the post-agreement phase of implementation. We propose to study the metaphoric structure of spatial simultaneity more carefully than that of directional sequentiality. We explore social healing through its metaphoric structure, with an emphasis on examples that address the simultaneity of temporal experience; of how we as humans construct meaning around our response to past, present and future, not as a linear concept but as lived multiple realities that are simultaneously present in the ways we make sense of our lives, our place and our purpose, particularly in the context of protracted conflict.

The focus on social healing also requires us to narrow the discussion of reconciliation to several focal points or boundaries. Three specific limitations delineate our inquiry. First, we emphasise *lived experience* and place particular importance on *local communities* affected by violence and faced with a need to address grievances and deep loss in the presence of their enemies. We propose a *preferential option for the local community* within the rubric of categories for locating reconciliation. We believe that social healing is best understood and explored at the level of real-life, face-to-face relationships. Following one of the spatial metaphors, we explore in much greater detail how the local community provides a container that holds the unique capacity and potential to both experience and create echoes. These echoes are the ripples of vibration that touch and are felt by people and that move out into a wider context and which offer at least one way to bridge the intriguing but theoretically difficult chasm that separates micro and macro approaches to both healing and social change. The local community as locus emphasises a social unit that includes but goes beyond individual processes of healing, while at the same time it provides a context of more direct, accessible experience than is commonly experienced in national processes.

Second, we direct our inquiry towards the phenomenon of healing as seeking good health that can include but does not require a vigorous expression of forgiveness and reparations in broken relationships. Here we must explore the nature of healing as a *permanently dynamic* aspect of ongoing life when in fact the possibilities of a far more vigorous reconciliation may be partial and incomplete, remote or even impossible. As such we propose to de-link social healing from politically expedient notions of reconciliation as a one-time event. Health-as-metaphor suggests not a one-time event but a daily presence that necessarily entails a constancy of vigilance, with ups and downs, prevention and cure, and which is present in the everydayness of people's lives. In contexts of violence communities that provide the space for individual and social processes of health must face and engage with the unpredictable nature of historically patterned and immediately dynamic situations, with many variables that lie beyond their direct control. In other words, healing while facing the continued threat of violence represents simultaneous aspects of a complex reality; aspects that are rarely experienced in a neat, sequential order.

This approach requires us to ground our exploration of social healing in the context of what we believe is best described as the *midst and aftermath* of open violence. Combining these temporal terms affirms the idea that contexts of sustained and systematic violence continuously offer up extraordinary challenges *before, during and after* spikes of violence and/or the signing of peace agreements, independent of whether these are adhered to or broken. In recent years, the increase in literature about the *aftermath* of armed strife has highlighted the multifaceted experiences war and peace create for those who must survive and rebuild after the guns fall silent, even though the deep patterns of violence keep re-emerging (Brison 2002; Herman 1992; Meintjes et al. 2001; Stolen 2007; Terry 2005; Webster 1998). In other words, analogous to the discussion of healing and reconciliation, violence itself shows a remarkable capacity for repetitious circularity and rarely follows patterns easily described as linear.

Our interest in social healing has been sparked by the resiliency of people and communities who in the extended and unremitting midst and aftermath of open violence must make sense of their lives and build a way forward, while still living in the presence of their enemies and all that makes their suffering vivid, painful and difficult. We propose that social healing cannot be understood as a phenomenon that emerges exclusively after violence ends, in large part because in so many places it simply does not end and it finds ever new forms by which to express itself locally. We suggest that social healing creates and rises from a fragile though dynamic space with a *seed-like quality* that simultaneously is both birth and fruit and that by this very nature requires a more intentional reflection on important aspects of reconciliation that do not neatly fit a linear metaphor.

Third, to explore this seed-like quality of social healing we propose to follow our intuition that a significant starting point requires serious engagement with metaphor. Our approach suggests and unpacks a series of phenomena as metaphors – some of which may seem far-fetched to the pragmatic reader – that by their very nature distinctively display the character of circularity and multi-layered simultaneity and provide insight into processes of healing and reconciliation. In this sense, our purpose in exploring these concepts is not to propose a progression or even a process as is typically conceptualised by common usage of scientific method, the accepted categories of the social sciences, or the pragmatic demands of program-driven peacebuilding and conflict resolution agency, agendas and time frames. Rather, we wish to give ourselves permission to enter and explore healing and reconciliation as spaces of human interaction that have qualities of deepening and expanding, though they rarely move uni-directionally with clear sequential or intentionally purposeful logics. Through exploration of metaphor–phenomena like sound, music, poetry and mothering, we watch for ideas, suggestions and qualities that stimulate the imagination about the challenges and mechanisms by which social healing may be observed and perhaps understood.

We do not propose a forced choice between circular and linear views of movement in processes of reconciliation. But we do propose to describe with greater intentionality and depth what is often mentioned in passing, and what remains mostly unexplored in the literature: the constructive elements of healing that are circular and which, envisioned through the lens of a metaphoric structure, are not dependent on sequential linearity.

Finally, it should be noted that we are proposing an empirical journey both intuitively adventurous and experimental in nature.

From the empirical standpoint, our points of reference are rooted in contexts where we have worked, practised and directly observed. These are decidedly well within the description of contexts characterised as resurgent in the midst and aftermath of open violence.

Specifically these include contexts such as Colombia, Somalia and West Africa.

Methodologically in working with stories, observations and metaphoric structure we build from what could be understood as a phenomenological approach. Phenomenology in its classic application, particularly from the perspectives of authors like Berger and Luckman (1966) and Schutz (1967) provides a focus on a two-fold understanding of how things *appear* in the social world.

First, phenomenology attends to how something appears, as in how it arrives in the world; the process of giving birth to something. We are interested here in a range of issues that include, among others, how violence and response to violence creates the need for people to locate themselves and name the realities that surround them. Australian Aboriginals, for example, locate their place and themselves through songs – the songlines function like maps of geography that are simultaneously attending to more than one aspect of their lived reality, and in so doing provide a sense of location, name and meaning. Or, the common phraseology of 'internally displaced persons' provides a deeply metaphoric structure at numerous levels, from forced physical departure, to feeling lost, to attempting to relocate a sense of place and purpose in a context where few things make sense and must constantly be negotiated. Displacement functions simultaneously as individual and social processes that can legitimately perhaps best be defined and explored in spatial terms, with significant circular, repetitious and even sonic points of reference in everyday language. Displacement therefore requires metaphoric structures that reflect the complexity of creating and bringing into existence social realities, rather than the assumption that these are predetermined – a category created by and useful to the outside observer.

At a second level phenomenology focuses on how things appear once they are noticed, as in what meaning people attach to things in the social world of intersubjective shared human experience. In our particular case, we are interested in how communities negotiate meaning in contexts of violence. At the same time, we are curious about metaphors that seem to parallel this experience and which function as archetypical spatial understandings that touch aspects of human experience not easily understood through paradigms that focus on change and which are attached to logical progression and analytically defined categories. For example, the fundamental category alluded to by many authors, that the experience of violence creates an experience of unspeakable depths, suggests that words alone attend to only a small portion of the deeper process.

We wish to write from an intuitively adventurous and experimental standpoint that breaks away from the most common vantage points from which studies and essays on reconciliation have approached the subject matter of social change. With somewhat wild abandon our chapters explore phenomena like sound, music, the poetry of presence, mothering and the too-oft neglected shifts that come with deeper understandings of a gender lens. Chapters on a Tibetan singing bowl, the music of Van Morrison, the ways of mothers in West Africa, or the poetry of life in a community stand as experiments that seek to discover and follow metaphors on their own merits, metaphors not commonly found in the literature. We hope that their weaving together provides a fabric of thought, proposal and insight that may, in some ways, deepen the theoretical exploration that appears overly driven by short-term political objectives and the predetermined needs of social programs. This weaving of approaches also includes a speculative theoretical fabric, the suggestion of how such a range of ideas may come together into a common framework where key aspects of widely diverse inquiries may converge and how, following the metaphor of sound in particular, these ideas provide insight into the nuances and potential of community-based social healing.

SECTION I

NARRATIVE REFLECTIONS

I will tell you something about stories.
They aren't just entertainment.
Don't be fooled.
They are all we have,
All we have to fight off illness and death.
You don't have anything if you don't have stories.
Leslie Marmon Silko

CHAPTER 1

Drums and gardens

'I was thirteen when the rebels came. My father, a local farmer, made me hide under the table. I never saw the rebels kill him, but I saw them through the window, blood was dripping from the knife. I will never forget the blood on the knife.'

A child soldier and a commander in both the Liberian and Sierra Leonean civil wars, Morris remembers all too well the day his life changed forever.

In the chaos of his father's death his older siblings fled. Morris remained frozen, crouched under the table. He waited. And waited. At such a young age – and in the midst of such trauma – he could not connect the bloodied knife with the death of his father. 'I kept thinking my father would walk through the door. But he never came, so I too fled.' Alone he found the road to look for his aunt, haunted by what had transpired at the farm. In Liberia's capital, Monrovia, he found other youngsters; some had guns for protection and soon Morris did as well. Living in the streets without a family he found comfort in their friendship and shared experience. He soon joined them at the rebel camp outside town. 'You know, people think that child soldiers are greedy for material goods or just want to do something wicked, but many of us watched our families being killed. We had nowhere to go.'

Morris and his friends were told they could fight for the death of their parents. They were told they would help bring their country to peace. They were told they would be heroes. They were given new names. New identities. New families. 'There was a whole army of us, child soldiers. We ruled the camp. And that is when it all started. That is when the real violence began. That is when I really saw killing, you know. Anything you can imagine,' he paused, his eyes drifting to another time, another place. 'They sent us back into our communities, to do these horrible things to our own people. And then one day you realise I just killed my auntie, or my sister, the woman who fed me when I was young. We had AK47s, grenades, M16s, anything you can imagine and we would shoot from the trucks through the villages, because if you didn't do it, you wouldn't survive.'

He soon moved up the ranks to become a commander. In the mid-nineties, as the war shifted in Liberia and peace seemed close, he travelled to Sierra Leone. He trained young child soldiers to fight for the Revolutionary United Front (RUF). He, too, continued fighting.

'And then I realised I couldn't do this anymore, I was just becoming something negative. I had nothing, I was nothing.'

He escaped and came to Ghana. Buduburam Refugee Camp – far away from the land of his people – became his new home.

The United Nations Refugee Agency opened Buduburam Refugee Camp in 1990 in response to the devastating violence that swept across Liberia in 1989. It holds more than 30,000 refugees who fled their homeland of Liberia in a drastic attempt to escape the war. The war, which lasted from 1989 to 2003, garnered international attention for the gross human rights abuses of child soldiering, diamonds for arms trade, and sexual violence. Although Buduburam is located only 45 minutes from Ghana's capital city of Accra, the two places are worlds apart. The camp buzzes with life. The sounds of laughter, music, chickens, and children playing fill the air in a place created as a result of devastation. Like a small city the camp holds several schools and various neighbourhoods. People live in makeshift homes that line the narrow dirt alleys which weave through the camp.

Though the fighting had ended, the violence continued to plague Morris's mind as he tried to begin a new life in the refugee camp.

'It is so hard. You have this weapon. I don't mean a weapon like just a gun, but your mind, your mind is the weapon. All you have in your mind is violence. You have been living in violence for so long and at any moment with any person you can take this weapon out. It doesn't matter where you are. It's embedded in you. And it is creative. You can do unimaginable things, terrible things with this creativity, because you have seen so much violence. It takes willpower to transform that. Some of us are working hard to change. I think about how Saul became Paul and that gives me hope. I know I can transform and maybe people will begin to accept me, forgive me. We need reintegration. We need acceptance. What we really need is forgiveness. To forgive is divine.'

Morris lives with the daily challenges countless others in his position face. He lives with the images of war, of death replete with the visions of blood. He lives with a debilitating guilt. He lives the multiple realities of child soldiering: victim and perpetrator. Morris has not stopped working towards healing. He wants transformation. He wants, like the biblical story of Saul, to find forgiveness.

In an attempt to give back to the community, Morris began gathering an army of children once again – this time to build a farm. Today, 200 child combatants have come together to grow vegetables and fruit. They work the land. They create and nurture new life. They support one another. They have found, once again, friendship in their shared experiences.

'As a group we did so many bad things, so many bad things. We were so powerful. Maybe if we bring that group together again we can have the same power, but this time we can use it to do *good* things. We want to give life back to our community, our people. They told us we were helping our people, but we were destroying them, our own people. Now we want to give back to our people.'

It has not been easy. Morris lives with stigmatisation by the community every day. The names cannot be washed off: Child soldier. Murderer. Rapist. He carries those labels with him, but continues to work – to show how he has changed, in the hope of one day finding acceptance.

'People think you will just be violent forever. There is stigma and fear. We are afraid to even share our stories because of the stigma. Facing the past is too hard. Today I still see things in the past before me, they come right here in front of me like I am there again. They always return. But with this organisation we are also trying to take away the weapons and bring all of us together. *We* are doing the disarmament. And maybe if the community sees that, they will begin accepting us.'

How are relationships restored after such devastating violence? Where is healing located in the complexity and violation of child soldiering?

Through his garden, Morris eventually met Jake.[1] A refugee and peace practitioner, William 'Jake' Jacobs was among the first young people to arrive here, almost 20 years earlier. 'There was nothing when we first arrived here. You had to fight for food, if you didn't fight, you wouldn't eat. Everything was so violent because people were trying to survive. But I am not a violent person, so I knew I had to survive some other way. That is when I started gardening. I grew and sold food. You see that coconut tree,' Jake points across the dirt road. 'I planted that tree! I planted it sixteen years ago. That is where my tent was. We didn't have these buildings then, you know, just tents.'

Jake lived in Monrovia, Liberia where he studied at university. His family lived miles away in a small village. When the war came, they separated forever – he on one side of the rebel lines, his family on another. For a year he survived, running and hiding, never knowing what day might be his last. As a last resort, he boarded a boat to Ghana and became one of the first refugees at Buduburam.

Morris has found comfort and encouragement in his relationship with Jake. He has found transformation in the cultivation of life – his garden. And he has found healing at the Buduburam cultural centre.

'Here it is,' Jake smiled as he walked into the bright orange youth cultural centre he helped design and build.

The cultural centre began as a space where children could come together. A dance troop formed as a result of the cultural centre. They now use dance, music, drumming and theatre to tell the stories of war, journeys of displacement, the too prevalent HIV/AIDS and teenage pregnancies, and the challenges child soldiers continue to face on a daily basis. Displaced for over 20 years, Jake understands the importance of connection to the homeland, to the traditions of his ancestors, for surviving life in the refugee camp. He started the cultural centre to create a bridge. The traditional Liberian practices of drumming and dancing create a link to connect lost children and their lost childhoods to their homeland. They learn the languages, tribes and traditional dancing from Liberia. They learn the songs of their grandmothers. It is a space of healing and transformation, an undeniable reality for anyone who has the privilege of stepping through the bright orange opening and onto the dirt floor of the centre.

Jake's desire to continue meeting and encouraging former child soldiers lies in his understanding of collective responsibility. He recognises that Morris was both a victim and a perpetrator of the war. 'We are all responsible, no one person created the war, we are all at fault for the war in Liberia and we all need to participate in the rebuilding of our lives and our country.' The challenge, however, of rebuilding life after devastating violence is enormous. The hope of social healing gets lost in the barriers to peace that are built into the aftermath of war, but it has not stopped Jake. He sees a new world; he sees a new hope in the young people who come to the cultural centre.

Hope is found as the *jembe* drums resonate throughout the community, their sound rising above the sound of rain falling on the tin roof. Black hands beat white cowhide and life pours out from each finger. *Jembe* literally translates as 'coming together', the drawing point where pulsating rhythms create dance, celebration and ritual (Doumbia & Doumbia 2004). Youthful black bodies bob and weave, sweating intensity from head to foot, their rhythms pound into the dirt releasing something of themselves back into the earth. These are no ordinary dancers. Their eyes have seen too much death, their hands spilt too much blood; and their feet, hardened from the miles of bush, no longer know the pathway home. Much needs to be released as the *jembes* call to these young lives, these child soldiers, living hundreds of miles from their native Liberia, far from, yet inextricably wrapped in, the mantle of the war they never started.

'You know, you see these kids and they tell you what peace is. They are so bright, and full of hope and life. That is it. That is what keeps you going. It is healing you know, to drum and dance and sing and be together.'

Jake watches the hands pound and bodies sweat. 'Sometimes I just want to cry! I think about what they have seen and lived through and I just want to cry. To see this talent and this passion. They are so beautiful. This is the hope!'

Drums and gardens.

CHAPTER 2

The wandering elders

We sat in a courtyard on the outskirts of Hargeisa. It was midway through 1990. Three of us were visiting from Europe and the United States, working on finding ways for the international community to support peace efforts in Somalia.

A year earlier longtime strongman Siad Barre had been chased from power. The fighting was intense and militias spread like wildfire. Though armed movements had taken on nationalist names, their subclan affiliations suggested the deep divisions that would continue for years to come. The groups and the fighting, while unified against Barre, soon descended into subclan fighting, animosities rising sharply between militia strongmen who wished to accede to power in the political vacuum. Exacerbating the violence and the displacement of people was one of the most severe droughts experienced in decades across this far eastern portion of the Horn of Africa. People were starving, driven by armed conflicts, fearing militias; the country was falling into chaos.

The worst of this fighting tracked towards Mogadishu, the

national capital in the south of the country. In the face of a daily televised humanitarian disaster the international community was desperate to find ways to end the fighting and provide much needed food and shelter to millions of Somalis on the brink of collapse. But as was seen over the next decades, the intensive efforts, including multiple internationally convened peace processes, hundreds of temporary ceasefires, interim governments and massive humanitarian relief deliveries, have not been able to reconstitute a stable and functioning national government in Somalia.

In the midst of this sustained violence extraordinary exceptions were found. Perhaps the most robust and comprehensive, though still poorly documented, was a process of reconciliation that was initiated in the environs of Hargeisa. It all started with some conversations. Margaret Wheatley (2002), in her book *Turning to one another*, suggests that most significant social movements can be traced to a single conversation. In this courtyard outside Hargeisa we were watching one such conversation begin.

Located in the north, a great distance from Mogadishu, Hargeisa is the largest city in the region and a historic hub of political activity. The people in the north, as longtime adversaries of Siad Barre and resistant to his autocratic rule, had suffered excessive repression from the dictator for years. Hargeisa had been air bombed into shambles. Landmines had systematically been placed around cities and towns and in the major pathways used by the nomadic tribes. Armed resistance emerged early in the north and by the time Barre fell, fighting had begun and had spread from west to east in the northern part of the country. The violence turned inwards once Barre was gone and the people of the north began to suffer the challenges of severe subclan fighting. The conversation we heard in 1990 rose out of a simple proposal. Peace was possible but only through talk. A grassroots effort was underway to build what was being called a reconciliation process. *Nabad raadin*, reconciliation, or 'let us talk', were the phrases we heard. The time had come to stop the fighting. Reconciliation required engaged dialogue. The elders proposed to travel and talk.

Across from us sat three elders, two sheiks and a sultan, in white flowing robes, prayer caps, with walking sticks in hand. They seemed to be in their seventh decade of life. Beside them, four or five younger, western-educated Somali NGO leaders served as interpreters. The elders spoke little English but some of the younger generation had sharp British accents, having recently graduated from the best universities in the United Kingdom. We inquired about their proposed process and about what we from the international community might do to help. Over sweet tea the discussion rambled across history, poetry, current situations of fighting and their pending departure and mission.

Nomadic by background, the three elders were about to embark on a rather remarkable journey. Each came from one of three subclans but were widely recognised and were among the most respected elders in the region. Following lengthy discussions within their own subclans and then together, the three were forming an *ergada*, a travelling group of elders that would venture out to meet the other warring subclan elders in an effort to persuade them to participate in a *guurti*, a gathering of elders, poets, spokespersons and chosen representatives of the various subclans (Farah 1993; Lederach 1997; Lewis 1994, 1998; Samatar 1982). As Farah (1993) has noted, they named themselves with the rather modest term, *dab damin* or fire extinguishers.

Given their culture, travel was nothing new. They would move by small convoy, and where necessary by camel and foot, from one village in the region to the next. Their proposal was to go from as far west as Boroma to the east into Sanaag and Erigavo. We asked if it was safe. They smiled and said, 'This is our place, our people. It is our duty. They will recognise us. Each of us is from one of these places. We travel together'.

In greater detail, they also noted that women had already gone ahead of them. As later documented by anthropologist Farah (1993), women had indeed prepared the way. Located as they were in cross-clan marriages, women were the informal early diplomats, travelling safely in the midst of war from their clan of marriage to their clan of birth. In the lineage culture of this northeast region, women experienced the war in a way far different from men. Their fathers and brothers were fighting their husbands and sons. In times of open fighting women traditionally could travel from their subclan of marriage back to their subclan of birth, effectively creating an informal diplomacy that appealed for violence to stop and peace negotiations to open. So, the elders explained to us 'our way has been prepared by the women'.

'What exactly would they do?' we asked. On each stop the elders would seek their counterparts and talk. 'Somalis say, "The answer to the problem is more talk"', one elder remarked. One round of talks would not be enough. It would only start the process. Few if any commitments were expected on a first conversation, except that the subclan elders they met would in turn talk among themselves. The *ergada* might grow by a member or two and would return, going back again for more talk. And again and again as necessary. As the rounds of contact and discussions coalesced some specific subclan issues would be identified and interclan, bilateral negotiations might be proposed. Reconciliation, they said, required long discussions. Many times it would take poetry to make the historical case and situate the current problems. *Akils*, the heads of *dia*-paying lineage groups, would be involved. *Dia* is payment for loss of life, so compensation would be discussed as well as immediate and future responsibilities. The elders projected that over time these rounds would bring together more and more groups until a grand *guurti* could be achieved, where many would sit together and discuss the wider issues of the region and the steps needed to end the internecine wars.

'What might we offer to help facilitate your process?' we asked. Their answer: 'Maybe some petrol and rice. But mostly, please understand that this will take time. And do not interfere.' Smiles again. And a second time, 'We don't need your help. We need to do it ourselves.'

Three years later in 1993 the elders' initiative arrived in Boroma, en masse. From February to May a grand *guurti* was held in the northwest of the region. This *guurti* is known as the Boroma conference; hundreds of delegates gathered as did thousands of observers from the subclans. The deliberations lasted for six months. Talk, poetry and song filled the days and nights. The delegates circled round and round the issues and proposals, the grievances and demands, until slowly a consensus began to form. As a proverb puts it, 'You can deny a Somali food but you can never take away his word.'

A proposal eventually emerged: the wider region declared itself independent as the Republic of Somaliland. The road to the declaration was built on hundreds of discussions; initiated, failed and re-initiated negotiations; small and larger subclan agreements; compensations and more talk. Some say it never did really end. The process was simply transferred to another level: the formation of a parliament, space for traditional leaders, local peace initiatives between the subclans still fighting.

Now nearly two decades since we talked with the three elders who wandered out to meet with their counterparts, Somaliland still claims independence, though little international recognition has come its way. However, the northwest and northeast of what was Somalia have had far less fighting than other regions to the south. The process in the early nineties, called by Farah (1993) the 'roots of reconciliation', stands as perhaps one of the most extraordinary and least documented processes of its kind.

CHAPTER 3

The Women of Liberia Mass Action for Peace Campaign

A NEW KIND OF BOLDNESS

In the midst of the brutal civil war in Liberia a few women began talking. They had watched their brothers, husbands, sons and daughters killed and raped. Innocent lives stolen for a senseless war. 'We could not sit down anymore to see this hopeless situation degenerate into a greater state of hopelessness.' And so they began organising. They met in the fish markets and refugee camps. They met in homes and on street corners. They met as Christian and Muslim women, in churches and in mosques: 'Can a bullet pick and choose? Does the bullet know Christian from Muslim?' Leymah Gbowee asked when religious differences threatened the possibility of peace (*Pray the Devil back to Hell* 2008). And slowly, the barriers of religion, class, age and ethnicity shattered in the common desire to end the war. The women were refugees, educators, politicians, police officers and market women. They were mothers, daughters, aunties, grandmothers and nieces. They were the creators of life. Women talking, mothers rising, they could not sit anymore.

The first meeting of four women soon grew to meetings of more than 500. And the Women of Liberia Mass Action for Peace Campaign was born.

As their numbers grew, so too did their actions. They organised mass protests: they danced, they sang, they wept. They began a sex strike, refusing to have sex with their husbands. Using the power they had to demand an end to the war.

But mostly they sat.

Lining the streets in bright white t-shirts they sat through rain, blazing sun, wind – sometimes with bullets and air raids whirling around them. They sat. With only one simple message: 'We Want Peace, No More War.'

William Saa,[1] a renowned Liberian peacebuilder, later reflected, 'The women's reserved energy was there for a long time. It was like a time bomb just waiting to explode.'

And explode they did. They insisted on meeting with the then president, Charles Taylor. Finally, after weeks of protest he agreed to see them. The women lined the halls of parliament in their simple white t-shirts as Leymah Gbowee presented their statement to the president: 'The women of Liberia, including the Internally Displaced People, are tired of war. We are tired of the killing of our people and we, the women of Liberia, want peace now' (*Pray the Devil back to Hell* 2008). Taylor refused to meet with the rebel factions. He ignored the women's plea for peace.

But this did not stop the women. They went to the United States Embassy and to the international press. The pressure mounted and the women did not stop until eventually, the day came when Charles Taylor could no longer ignore the power of the women who gathered. He agreed to meet for peace talks with the rebel faction, Liberians United for Reconciliation and Democracy (LURD). So the women travelled, unarmed, as mothers, into the bush. They met with the LURD warlords, delivering their message: 'The women of

Liberia want peace now.' LURD agreed to meet for peace talks and arrangements were made for the top rebel leaders of LURD to meet with Charles Taylor and his administration for peace talks in Accra, Ghana.

Despite their leadership the women were excluded from the talks. They were not invited to the negotiation table. Their voices did not count. 'What could market mothers know of negotiation?' the men asked.

But they had found a new power in their collectivity. 'We have all suffered,' Leymah said. 'If you are illiterate: you are a target of rape; if you are a market woman: you are a target of rape; if you are active in civil society and politics: you are a target of rape. We are all victims. *And we all have a voice.*' Once again, they began talking and gathering. They spread their message throughout the marketplaces. One mother to another. Their message soon reached mothers in Ghana. The Ghanaian women began gathering – in marketplaces, on street corners, in churches and mosques – and they in turn alerted their Sierra Leonean, Ivorian and Nigerian sisters. Together, they raised money and travelled to Accra. A powerful coalition of more than 200 women gathered outside the building where the political leaders who had denied them voice met. Fatura, a strong woman from the north of Ghana recalled the day, a sparkle in her eyes:

> We were dressed in our white t-shirts to show we were all women. We all wanted peace. We were Liberian Women. We were Ghanaian Women. We were Nigerian women. And we were weeping and dancing and it was raining and we were in the rain dancing and singing and weeping.

They circled the building, holding hands and dancing. Unshaken in their message, 'We Want Peace, No More War'.

While the women gathered outside the site of the peace talks in

Accra, the war in Liberia continued to spread. They received a devastating call that all-out war had erupted in Monrovia, the capital city. Charles Taylor fled the talks, hoping to save his own life. And the negotiations began to crumble. 'I was just raging inside,' Leymah said, 'so I told the women, "Sit at the door and loop arms one with the other"' (*Pray the Devil back to Hell* 2008). The women held the doors, refusing to let the men out. They would not allow anyone to leave until the peace agreement was signed.

When the men sitting behind closed doors finally realised what was happening, an announcement came through the overhead speakers: 'The peace hall has been seized by General Leymah and her troops' (*Pray the Devil back to Hell* 2008). Armed only with their tears, their song, their dance and their sisterhood, the women took control of the negotiating room. When several of the leaders attempted to escape, Leymah began stripping in front of the men – one of the greatest taboos in West African culture. Finally, the head mediator of the peace talks, General Abdulsalami Abubakar, the former head of state of Nigeria, turned to the men and said, 'I dare anyone to leave this hall until we have negotiated with these women' (*Pray the Devil back to Hell* 2008). And with that, the men went back to the negotiating table and began constructing the terms of the agreement.

Two weeks later the Comprehensive Peace Agreement between the Government of Liberia, and LURD and the Movement for Democracy in Liberia was signed.

The signing of a peace accord never ends violence. The women had much work to do, particularly with the reintegration of child soldiers. Initially the United Nations (UN) excluded the women from the disarmament process. The women sat back, helplessly, and watched. The child soldiers came, drugged and armed, and complete chaos ensued. Money for arms was not enough. Eventually, the UN turned to the women, who began their own approach to disarmament.

As victims of the war the women understood the complexity and gravity of disarmament. As mothers, they understood the suffering and needs of their children who had become machines of war. As women, they knew much more was needed than the signing of an agreement and the promise of money to sustain disarmament. 'We offered a rehumanising approach,' Leymah Gbowee explained. 'We engaged in real relationships with the child soldiers. We saw them not as perpetrators of violence, but as our *sons* and *daughters*.' They ate food together, laughed and cried together. 'We had to rehumanise them in their powerlessness. We had to take away not only their guns but also their vulnerability. We had to give them a new kind of power.' In the presence of their mothers, the children no longer found power in their guns, but in their relationships. 'We took away their fear and gave them a new kind of boldness through love.'

In one village, the women chose to create a rebirthing ritual. They wore white, a colour symbolic of childbirth and peace. From outside the villages, they took the hands of their sons and daughters and began the long walk home. Mother and Son. Grandmother and Daughter. Each woman walked, hands clasped, with one child soldier. As they walked, they sang. They sang songs of lament, songs of loss, songs of exile. And when they entered the village their voices rose in unison: jubilant songs of celebration spilled from their lips. They sang their lost children home.

As the women became more involved in leading their villages towards reconciliation, they began to realise that sustainable change could only come if their voices were represented in the political process as well. 'When I talked with the men,' Leymah Gbowee (2006) explained, 'I would tell them that you are only comfortable with empowerment and with women's leadership as long as it doesn't involve your own social structure. So during the war, women could engage in peacebuilding because it did not interfere with the immediate social structures. But, when the war ended and communities started to come back together, women recognised that they could continue leading, but that is when the men tried to take away the voice of the women again. So the question then became, do we sit down again, or do we push this leadership so that it is sustained?'

The Women of Liberia Mass Action for Peace Campaign decided that they could no longer sit down, and they began a grassroots campaign to register women to vote in the hope of electing the first woman president in Liberia, Ellen Johnson Sirleaf. They travelled door to door, village to village, to meet and talk with women from all walks of life about the power of the democratic voting process. They tended the market stands and babysat small children so that working women and mothers had the freedom to register. Woman to woman, they began once more to organise their masses, working beyond social and economic boundaries to bring democracy to Liberia. Eventually, more than 7,000 women registered to vote. And on 23 November 2005, Ellen Johnson Sirleaf became the first woman president of Liberia. The Women of Liberia Mass Action for Peace Campaign, which had contributed enormously to community reconciliation, to the signing of the Liberian Peace Accords, had now also entered the political realm. The power they found, however, did not come from traditional notions of domination – but from a profound capacity to network; from the grassroots markets to the parliamentarians, women organised and transcended the barriers of class and political party to bring a new form of leadership to their country. In desperation the women found voice. They broke the shackles of violence and exclusion placed on their hands and feet. They danced, cried and sang their country back onto the long road towards healing.

CHAPTER 4

The bones with no name

A few miles from the Venezuelan border, Maria,[1] her husband, brothers and neighbours have small coffee farms in the cool high altitudes of far northeastern Colombia. In addition to planting, pruning and picking the red berries at harvest the families have learned to live with war. With their farms located in the lower portions of the mountainsides sitting above a wide valley, local farmers have negotiated a delicate balance in their existence. It is a balance between the pressures of the leftist guerillas roaming the higher elevations along the ridgelines of the mountains and the paramilitaries who emerge from the towns below, and who are often financed by the large landowners and cattle-farming families seeking to protect their valley territories from the guerillas. In this geography of the Colombian wars the two fighting groups rarely engage each other directly. Rather, the fighting consistently focuses on the allegiances and lands of local campesinos, families like Maria's.

In early 2002 Maria's family and their neighbours experienced a systematic rise in violence. It started with selected killings and disappearances of young men and fathers. Bodies appeared by the roadsides on occasion but, more frequently, family members simply did not return at night. Arriving home from the market late one afternoon Maria found her house ransacked, chairs and clothes strewn around. Her husband was nowhere to be found, his tools spread oddly around the front porch and yard. Frantically, the family ran throughout the small farm, calling his name – up to the coffee fields, out to the few cattle, back again to the house. On the table his lunch sat untouched. As Maria would report it, he had *disappeared*, or in the language of war, he *was disappeared*. Within days they discovered two of her brothers had disappeared from the farm next door. Fearful, they stayed close to the house, no longer venturing into the fields. When some weeks had passed, Maria gathered her courage, descended the pathways off the farm and sought the authorities in the nearby city. There she faced a different mountain, the piles of papers that accumulated as she submitted the official forms notifying the government that her husband and two brothers had disappeared.

Nobody knew a thing. No leads could be offered. Nothing could be done. After many conversations with her neighbours and people along the swathe of mountain farms and the towns on the way down the valley, Maria, her family and neighbours knew that the disappearances had all the hallmarks of the paramilitaries, the Autodefensas. And everyone knew the name and whereabouts of the local commander. After a month and many difficulties she met the commander – Maria, a lone middle-aged woman, faced one of the most feared people in the country.

'I have come to ask about my husband. Where is he?'

'What makes you think I know anything about your husband?' the commander asked. 'Why don't you talk with your friends in the guerilla?'

'We have lived for more than 26 years on this farm. In all these years the guerrilla have come and gone. We never talk to them and they never talk to us. But never once did they bother us. I know you know about my husband. What I want to know is where he is, where I can find him.'

The commander denied any knowledge and then threatened her for asking and sent her home, suggesting she not pursue it further. The disappearances continued. More threats came, round after round. If a family can stay on the mountainside, it was argued, then they must be linked to the guerrilla. If you stay, then you are with them and the legitimate target of attacks. Fearing for her children and nephews, Maria and dozens of families walked down out of the mountain and into the city. *Desplazados* they now called themselves, internally displaced persons. IDPs. Forced by fear from their homes they moved into the geography of war statistics, the abyss of people with no place, neither refugee nor functioning citizen. They were added to the count: a few without-a-place families among the 4 million people forced from their homes in Colombia's wars (UNDP 2007). And the only place to be was with others like themselves, about 20 families who shared a common trail of descent that led from their farms on the mountainside to the regional capital of the province and who, whenever asked 'Who are you?' responded using the mantle that violence left them: *We are desplazados from the mountain near the border.*

Months passed into years and no news. No answer. They formed a group with the local parish. Living on handouts from relief agencies and church charities, they survived week to week. They tried to find jobs. They worked to get their children into school. They got a small loan from the church, and in the backyard of a friend they raised a few vegetables and some chickens, selling the eggs to repay the loan. They called it the Garden of Peace.

In time the government announced a new peace plan. It was not the first and it would not be the last, but this one affected them.

As a result of a negotiation with the paramilitaries, President Uribe wanted to bring the Autodefensas, the AUC, out of the bush and back into the fold. The agreements were formalised, initiating a multifaceted process of disarmament and demobilisation and, to promote reconciliation, including a national justice and reparation law focused on the victims of paramilitary violence. Criteria were established to access the reparations, including the primary gateway: it is the responsibility of the person affected to verify that they are a victim, or a dependent family member of a victim of paramilitary violence.

The people-without-a-place were frantic to find out how this would work. Would they be targeted if they spoke up? Could they expect money? Could they return to their farms? Was there a return plan? How exactly do you get yourself declared a victim? Will someone tell the truth about what happened to their loved ones? Where are they? Where are their bodies?

Just before Christmas Maria's brother-in-law took a risk. He decided to go back up to the farms and see if anything of a coffee harvest might be possible. He found the fields abandoned. The rains had long since subsided and the dry season seemed to be fracturing the unattended land. He made his way along the coffee plants the families had seeded and cared for in earlier decades. Late in the afternoon on his second day, in the portion of the field closest to Maria's home, he stopped dead in his tracks. Something was calling. His eyes riveted on a cracked area of dry ground. He was frozen for minutes and later he would say, 'His blood called my name. I heard a voice. Someone calling, like, "I am here. Get me out".'

The late afternoon sun cast shadows as he approached the clay-cracked area. Hoe in hand he scraped around one larger crack. Within a few minutes a solitary rib emerged. By then it was too dark to continue. Under a tree nearby he wrestled with sleep most of the night. At first light the next morning he dug around the opening.

A grave revealed itself and at the bottom, in a small square open box he found dry bones. On top of the bones, neatly folded, a shirt and pants retained their colour and form. He knew it was his brother-in-law.

Back in the city he waited several weeks until after the holidays of Christmas and New Year to tell Maria. She collapsed.

'I cannot go see some bones.'

Weeks later Maria's son and brother-in-law returned. They walked carefully around the farm and up to the coffee fields. When they reopened the box it took only a single glance to confirm what they knew. 'The clothes, the teeth – it is our father,' he would tell his mother.

Maria went back to the local authorities.

'We have found the remains of my husband on our farm. They are in a shallow grave and his bones and clothes are in a box. We don't want to touch them in case there is some legal problem. Can you retrieve them and verify the remains?'

'No, we cannot go up there. You must bring them here.'

After some internal family debate they returned to the farm, removed the box with the remains untouched, and brought them down the mountain to the regional capital.

'These are the clothes of my husband and his bones,' Maria handed over the box. 'I would like to be able to bury them, but first want to make sure I have your papers in order, showing that we have suffered this death and that we are victims of this paramilitary violence.'

'You say this is your husband but we cannot just accept that. We have to send these bones to Bogota for testing. And how do you know who killed him?'

The box of bones was mailed to Bogota. Dental specialists, medical doctors, coroners all took a look. A few talked to Maria when she would call. His death was traumatic. His chest had been opened from throat to stomach.

After six months the first official report returned: 'This is clearly a victim of violence, we just don't know if this box of bones is your husband. We need to verify with DNA. And your children all need to go to a dentist to see if there is any parallel structure of palate and teeth.'

Blood was taken from one daughter. Another daughter had a protruding tooth that was near exact to a small hidden tooth that had never come out in the husband's mouth. The DNA matched.

Another four months passed. By late summer the authorities finally signed a paper that said the bones were those of Maria's husband. According to the state she officially had a new status: Maria was a verified victim.

Papers in hand she started the process to receive the promised humanitarian aid and potential reparations. Several months later a letter arrived: 'Your request for aid has been denied because too many years have passed since the death of your husband.'

She went to the authorities to argue her case. 'For three years we thought he was "disappeared". Then it took forever to verify. We did not know if he was alive or dead. Now that we have the bones, we know. The verification shows this year, not some years back.'

'Go to Bogota and talk with them there. We cannot do anything here.'

A year later, a pile of paper stamped and signed, trips made to Bogota, Barranquilla and back to their local town, they reached consensus. Maria was officially a victim of violence within the defined time frame.

More than two years after the official approval Maria and her family are still waiting for compensation. The new law established that though the death was likely caused by paramilitaries – who are in the final stages of the peace process, disarming and demobilising – no one has admitted to killing her husband. Once again, time has elapsed and put her beyond the period of having rights; in this case the right to reparation.

Hardly daunted, Maria and friends continued to gather. With the small shared profits from the first loan they bought more chickens and found a bigger plot of land to plant a few vegetables. And they began to look for the other graves back on their farms.

The blood called, unexpectedly. The bones spoke, scientifically. They had a name. And by the time the state named the bones so had Maria and her friends. 'We know where we are from. We know who we are even if we have very little,' Maria says. 'And we know where the graves are located. We will find our way home.' The farmers of the mid-mountains near the border, though far from their fields, found each other, the courage to question, and with it a sense of dignity. As they did in planting the vegetables in their small Garden of Peace, they keep tilling the soil to create a way home.

CHAPTER 5

Shifting metaphors

If I make the lashes dark
And the eyes more bright
And the lips more scarlet,
Or ask if all be right
From mirror after mirror,
No vanity's displayed:
I'm looking for the face I had
Before the world was made.
WB Yeats

HIDDEN ASPECTS OF SOCIAL HEALING

The opening stories in this volume pose a daunting challenge: How are adequate platforms built to nurture personal and social healing in the midst of repeated cycles of direct and structural violence? No one story captures these challenges in full. However, by looking across these stories and those that follow in subsequent chapters with their distinct social and political landscapes, a window opens onto a number of elements that, when viewed from the perspective of local communities, are particularly relevant to our inquiry.

In this chapter we explore the nature of the underlying structure of metaphor in social healing. Several mechanisms are useful for approaching this task. First, using our interactions and work with local communities – illustrated in part by the range of stories in the opening chapters of this book – we identify framing metaphors that are prevalent in the experience and response to violence in protracted conflict, and discuss how these are mobilised and important for understanding the challenges of social healing. Second, we explore the guiding metaphor around which much of the current literature and programmatic initiatives related to peacebuilding and reconciliation organise and create meaning. Of particular note, we will discuss the role and significance of metaphor, how it works and the potentialities it offers for our wider inquiry, which in subsequent chapters we explore through a variety of lenses. Third, we highlight some of the differences and tensions that may exist between the experience-based perspective and the predominant analytical metaphor structures found in the literature. We will not exhaust or resolve the tensions between various metaphoric structures as they relate to our broad themes. Rather, we propose to lift out important differences, particularly between those found in the shift from the dominant linear movement metaphors for understanding social change and healing, and those metaphors organised around the more hidden aspects of circularity, simultaneity and multidirectionality. In other words, we wish to establish the metaphor shift that moves beyond linear sequential notions of change.

The role of metaphor – making sense of the world

Significant work has been done on the role and place of metaphor as an important, if not the key, mechanism by which we make sense of the world. Approaches to metaphor and meaning, while traditionally relevant in literature and linguistics, are also found in arenas such as philosophy and phenomenology (Kóvecses 2002; Ricoeur 1987), therapy, counselling and mediation (Burns 2001; Gordon 1978; Lawley & Tompkins 2000; Monk et al. 1997; Winslade & Monk 2000). Of particular importance to our inquiry is the seminal work of Lakoff and Johnson in *Metaphors we live by* (1980). These authors make the case that metaphors are more than just poetic devices; they are deeply related to our ways of perceiving, understanding and interpreting the world. By their very structure metaphors organise the way we understand our experience and create meaning. By definition this happens through a process of comparison, where 'one kind of thing' is understood 'in terms of another' (Lakoff & Johnson 1980, p. 5). Depending on how we use and mobilise the very structure of language and how we use metaphor we shift meaning and, through comparison, the framing of reality.

For example, in relation to the study of conflict and peacebuilding, Lakoff and Johnson tell the story of an Iranian student who, on hearing the phrase 'the solution of my problems' from his American colleagues, drew an association by way of a metaphor that was different to the one used by his American colleagues. His classmates associated the word 'solution' with a mathematical image in which 'solution' represents an 'answer' to a 'problem'. In this metaphor structure the word 'solution' is associated with an effort to locate a correct and final answer to a problem. In essence, what is sought is the completion of an equation that solves the issue at hand. When the solution to a conflict is found, the problem is over.

Unlike his colleagues, the Iranian student associated the word 'solution' with a chemical metaphor; in other words, he saw liquids mixed in a beaker, not an answer to a mathematical equation. As such, his notion of how to proceed in working on crises and conflicts was one that involved visualising the conflict as being held continuously in a liquid solution, dissolving or appearing according to other catalysts that are introduced. Lakoff and Johnson (1980, pp. 143–4) note how radically different meaning structures rise from the metaphor association of solution-as-answer and solution-as-liquid, and how those meanings lead to different ways of interacting and seeing conflicts or problems.

Our interest here is to offer what we consider to be a dominant metaphoric structure as it relates to the topics of peacebuilding, reconciliation and healing. Then, by way of contrast, we explore more carefully the experience of local communities in protracted armed conflicts and suggest other metaphor structures that rise from their everyday language and meaning creation. Several key questions help focus this approach. In contexts like those described in our opening stories, what does the challenge of violence feel like to people living within these communities? How are their responses to unfolding events, their language and organising metaphors in dealing with violence and seeking health in places like Colombia and West Africa instructive for understanding the topics of social healing and reconciliation? What are the reference points that help frame their experience and the ways they make sense of their challenges?

The power and weakness of dominant metaphors

We begin with a simple affirmation. The dominant understanding of healing and reconciliation has organised agency around the metaphoric structure of linear movement. Agency refers here to the way political and, to a large degree, non-governmental projects have viewed and developed programs to work on healing and reconciliation. By agency we refer to the conceptual categories that guide both funding and action. While conceptually people note and recognise that healing and reconciliation are not linear processes, the organisational structure, that is the agency, by which they pursue funding and action responds to a metaphoric structure guided and defined by linear movement. Projects have short time lines. Funding must respond to activities with goals and measurable outcomes. In turn, these projected goals are plotted along stages and phases of change that will unfold from the action pursued. Agency follows a linear and sequential understanding of change.

On the other hand, the closer one gets to everyday contexts of protracted conflict, individual and social healing do not follow and are rarely experienced along the 'lines' of phase-based progression. To be more precise, in community-level experience, such as that arising from most of the stories just recounted, healing and reconciliation are not easily comprehended as phenomena that *follow* the ending of violence or that *unfold* in directional movement *forward* through a staged progression.

Community people in settings of protracted conflict have no greater daily wish than to silence the guns. This was the cry of the Women of Liberia Mass Action for Peace Campaign. This was the hope of Maria and her community. They long for the day when power is not manipulated through the barrels of blackened steel that control their local events and define their shared social landscape; a power they know has rarely been gained by means of legitimate political process, authenticity of social mandate, personal integrity of shared values, or the imagining of change hoped for by those most affected by violence.

However, another reality is also present. Once armed conflict has been unleashed people in local communities experience violence in varied phoenix-like forms; negatively resilient it keeps bouncing back with new and old faces. The challenge of violence does not stop with a declared ceasefire. Healing and reconciliation therefore must take place in highly dynamic and unpredictable settings whether or not peace agreements have been signed. This requires a deeper exploration to probe into the metaphoric level.

Over the past several decades when theorists have analysed peace processes we find a commonly accepted notion that reflects the tensions between different metaphoric views of movement structures. On the one hand many authors note the cyclical nature of conflict (Curle 1971; Galtung 1975; Kriesberg 1973; Lederach 2003; Lund 1996). On the other hand, as practical applications began to emerge from the study of armed conflicts, negotiations and peace accords, an analytic construct developed that posited a linear view of conflict and peace as unfolding in categorical phases. The etymology of the word 'analysis' traces to Greek origins and essentially is about the task of breaking something apart; in the case of scientific study, to break a complex phenomenon into its component parts in order to understand more specifically particular aspects that make up the complexity. Within peacebuilding the analytical lens has focused on identifying roles and activities as the waves of violence rise and descend.

Increasingly common in peace studies has been the use of a bell-curve image that looks like a single wave and initially referred to a life cycle of conflict posed in the singular (Figure 1) (Crocker et al. 2001; Lund 1996). The wave-graph describes and tracks the evolution of conflict and change, locates patterns of escalation and de-escalation of open violence, places important events like ceasefires and signed agreements on the time line, and identifies various activities and roles needed for building peace in each of the major phases. Metaphorically, the broad categories establish a linguistic construct that follows the movement of conflict. It begins from a latent stage of pre-conflict where the conflict remains mostly hidden and invisible. Then the conflict emerges as violence, becomes more visible and escalates, often into sustained periods of open warfare. At the top end of the wave-graph we find the point at which negotiations begin and flow into signed peace accords. From this point the wave descends, with de-escalation of the open violence captured as the post-conflict phase. This tool presents the rise and descent of open violence as the defining characteristic in the cycle.

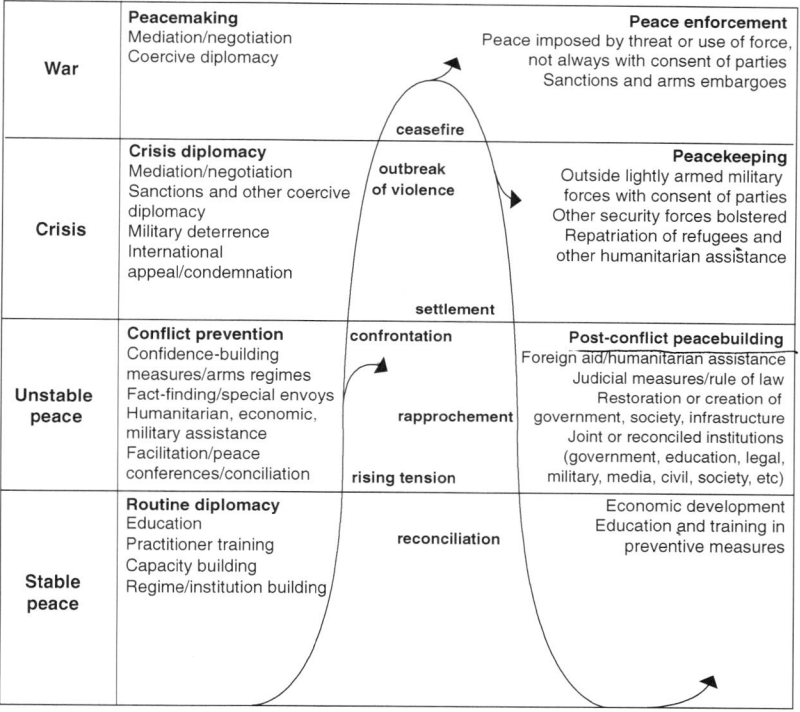

Figure 1. The life cycle of international conflict management.

In roughly the same time period that the bell curve was emerging and significant, Secretary-General of the United Nations (UN) Boutros Boutros-Ghali crafted the well-known Agenda for Peace (1992). This document uses language that was designed to sharpen the definition of the primary roles exercised by the UN in settings of civil and international warfare. Included were the notions of peacemaking, peacekeeping and, for the first time in UN documents, a category called post-conflict peacebuilding.

Since that period in the early and mid-nineties the language and terminology of post-conflict, post-violence and in some cases post-accord has become commonly accepted in the wider literature (Chetail 2009; Crocker et al. 2001; Darby & MacGinty 2003; Lund 1996). Centres and academic specialisations have emerged under the rubric of post-conflict peacebuilding. A Google search of the term 'post-conflict' reveals more than 24 million entries. An Amazon search reveals dozens of books with titles and subtitles with that phrase and the numbers move into the hundreds if titles to chapters are noted. A very recent addition is Chetail's (2009) Oxford University Press publication *Post-conflict peacebuilding: a lexicon*, which indicates the degree to which the category has developed its own sub-specialisations and language.

We emphasise our point that the metaphoric structure of this 'post' language builds around a view that conflict and peace flow in a linear and phase-based manner.

Within the wave-type graph categorisation the potential and need for healing and reconciliation are usually located in the post-conflict phase. In essence this phase, emerging around and after signed peace agreements and ceasefires, signals the end of the escalated open violence. In other words, healing and reconciliation are generally positioned as activities taking place after violence in armed conflict has for the most part subsided, and the leaders of the various sides in the conflict have reached an agreement.

Though referred to as a conflict cycle in Figure 1 and though authors go to some length to note the cyclical nature of conflict, the temporal and directional image embedded in this view is one based on seeing conflict as a forward-moving progression that fits and follows a metaphoric structure suggestive that social change is *linear and sequential*. The phase-based understanding, captured in prevalent linguistic terms like transition, pre-conflict, post-conflict, post-accord, post-violence and post-war, dominates the mainstream literature. In this widely accepted metaphoric framework, trauma healing and reconciliation become programmatically relevant tasks possible to achieve, and required to sustain wider political transition at the point a phase or stage opens with the signing of an agreement. For the purposes of this discussion let us accept the oft-used title of this phase as the 'post-conflict stage'.

We suggest this language and generally accepted terminology creates a dominant metaphoric structure in the field with a two-fold implication: CONFLICT IS LINEAR. PEACE IS SEQUENTIAL. The use of capitalisation was a tool used in describing a central metaphor structure developed by Lakoff and Johnson (1980) that we use here on occasion to lift out the underlying metaphors. In this case, the chosen language views conflict and peace as following directional and movement-based metaphors that associate change with a progressive, forward-moving understanding of transition.

Lived experience at the community level suggests something less linear and sequential, more fluid and ambiguous. Most local communities affected by decades of armed conflict do not experience violence, reconciliation or healing as having such clear frontiers of where they begin and end, as portrayed by the dominant metaphoric structure's phase-based descriptions of conflict and peace.

Hard hit by repeated waves of open warfare, people in local communities experience violence, structural and direct, as ongoing and resurgent in their midst. To develop an understanding of this we must reassert an important distinction that emerged in early peace research first and foremost from the seminal work of Johan Galtung (1975) and Adam Curle (1971). Both emphasised that violence must be understood as developing in more than one form. Galtung (1975) in particular noted the difference between direct and structural violence. Direct violence, war in its systemic expression, refers to open fighting and the active use of weapons with direct intention to kill, maim and damage the opposing enemy, though often in contemporary armed conflicts civilians find their towns, homes and lives directly impacted. Structural violence on the other hand refers to harm that happens without direct intent to hurt another and which can be detected by seeing patterns that diminish the potential to live a full and healthy life. Structural violence rises when social patterns, political structures and economic systems diminish, destroy and exclude people from access to basic life needs and greatly lower their potential for human flourishing.

A small example may be useful to emphasise this point of structural violence. We, the authors, are both citizens of the United States and in our home country the average life expectancy, while not in the top ten countries, is 78 years. Liberia, West Africa, where several of the opening stories came from, struggles to reach an average life expectancy of 46 years. That represents a 32-year difference in life expectancy. In these statistics we see a structural form of violence. From this viewpoint violence as structural injustice rises from rampant poverty, lack of access to clean water and healthcare, abuse of human rights, political exclusion and dominance by some groups. These all factor in to create violence in the form of systemic patterns that do not permit people to reach their full potential.

For our purposes the direct violence and structural violence distinction helps identify a two-fold challenge that people living in settings of protracted conflicts continuously face. When we describe violence as having resilient patterns we are suggesting that this social phenomenon has a capacity to regenerate, bounce back and take new forms that replicate old patterns. In settings of protracted armed conflict local communities face both direct and structural violence. Both forms of violence appear and reappear time and again in spite of efforts to limit, eliminate or, more typically, classify the armed portion of conflict (open violence) as officially over. We must note this cannot be explained as a form of perceptual or trauma-based paranoia in the local people who have lived through inexplicable situations. The resiliency of violence represents the dynamic legacy of centuries of structural violence and in many cases decades of armed conflict unleashed in settings where people must find ways of surviving and coping.

Returning for a moment to our stories, Maria's experience in Colombia provides an example of violence in multiple forms rising before, during and after the recent ceasefires, signed agreements and even demobilisation of paramilitaries. While she lost her husband in an act of direct violence, *disappeared* in the midst of civil war, she has also had to suffer untold threats to her life and needed to face an unresponsive bureaucracy as the years went on, even after a peace process was signed and put in place. She suffered deep violation in that she was required to prove she was in fact a victim so she could be acknowledged as such and seek redress. Yet, even after she followed the state's demands, she was left excluded, exhausted and economically broken. Maria faced and must continue to face forms of violence that were open and direct, and forms of patterned structural injustice that continue to violate her basic rights. As mentioned above, these multiple forms of violence happened before, during and after a signed agreement that 'ended' one element of the Colombian armed conflict.

But Maria's case represents more a pattern than an idiosyncratic experience. As we explore in greater detail in later chapters, research on the experience of women in and through periods of war suggests that they face multiple levels and types of violence (Fisas 2008; Meintjes et al. 2001; Nordstrom 1999). Nordstrom (1999), for example, has documented that during periods of war women-in-arms play a more equal role with men while they simultaneously face a much higher level of sexual threat. However, in the period following the signing of peace accords they experience a sharp decline in participation and equality, and an even sharper rise in violations, rape and domestic abuse (Fisas 2008). The notion that they enjoy a post-violence, post-conflict or peaceful period simply does not bear out in their lived experience.

Violence in both its open direct form and in its less visible structural expression does not simply disappear with the signing of an agreement by high-level, high-profile leaders. What does appear, however, is the use of the linguistic marker, *post-conflict*, metaphorically suggestive of a sequential, phased understanding of change. For many at the community level the destructive patterns, armed manipulation and threats reappear in old and new forms long after the papers have been enshrined as the culmination of negotiations.

Likewise, though not always noted explicitly, healing and reconciliation do not suddenly become possible and programmatically purposeful only when a peace agreement is signed and a particular phase initiated. We must remind ourselves that the academic or political language used to describe a particular moment so as to fit an understanding of social dynamics remains, in the end, a conceptual construct, a category into which certain patterns and dynamics are supposed to fit. These analytic concepts build around a metaphoric structure that by its very nature describes and hides lived realities (Lakoff & Johnson 1980). For example, the choice of the word 'post' follows the metaphor PEACE IS SEQUENTIAL, offering the image that something is over, finished and done. We have arrived, in essence, on the other side of whatever phenomenon the qualifier 'post' describes. The word 'post' may in fact better serve those with analytical, programmatic and political goals than those who must live in the dynamic swirl of day-to-day life in war zones.

Lived community experience captured in part through the opening stories is a dynamic context in which people simultaneously live and face elements of both conflict and peace; a context in which reconciliation and healing are embedded. This suggests that healing and reconciliation may be better captured through images that are less like linear progression and more akin to phenomena that contain yin/yang-like characteristics and relationships. For example, healing and reconciliation may be more like a *seed* inasmuch as this image contains simultaneously fruit and generative potential. Yoder suggests this in reference to trauma healing when she writes of the unique 'ability of the human spirit to begin healing processes and act in ways beyond basic survival needs, even when complete physical safety is not assured' (2005, p. 50). Even in periods of open escalation, people most affected by violence display an uncanny capacity to survive. Survival itself emerges from a creative act of resiliency and resistance. In spite of their life-threatening hardships, and while still living in the presence of their enemies, people as individuals and local collectives must find ways to bounce back, and foster life-giving and flourishing spaces and relationships even if in small doses, often expressed as a form of solidarity. Jake planted a coconut tree. Maria sought out and faced the commander, and later with friends got a small loan to raise chickens. Three cross-clan Somali elders decided to walk out and find their counterparts while the fighting was still raging. The women in Liberia sat and lined the streets. Survival in settings of harsh conditions always involves an act of creativity and innovation.

Lived experience suggests that this seed-like quality of reconciliation and social healing functions in ways that draw simultaneously on qualities and capacities for *survival*, *resiliency* and *flourishing*, albeit in varying doses, depending on the circumstances. These qualities represent responses that rarely are filtered through the lens and assessment of sequential phases. Particularly at the local level, people display temporal modalities that give rise to innovation before, during and in the period designated post-conflict which, as described above, is itself more accurately depicted as displaying characteristics of both the aftermath of war and the rebirth of new forms of violence.

Local communities face the ongoing challenge of how to nurture spaces for healing and reconciliation not as 'post' violence products but, as seen from their experience, permanently available and challenging innovations that must give birth and be reborn in the midst of less than ideal conditions. These conditions are rarely conducive for the very thing they most hope to forge – a safe, flourishing and meaningful life. In other words, survival links resistance, resiliency and flourishing as simultaneously available and circular phenomena – whether during or after spikes of open violence – precisely because direct and structural violence are not experienced at community levels as linear and sequential, even though they may officially be presented as such.

For local communities, national processes create a gap between raised expectations for change and the experience of increased exclusion, distance and intensification of local conflict in the period following formal agreements. This perception and the experiential gap account for a number of significant metaphors expressed by people in local communities who experience political transitions. These experiences are often articulated through linguistic expressions and provide insight into a metaphor shift in relation to social healing. To explore this shift we must first return to a discussion of the significant ways metaphor organises meaning.

Metaphors reveal and hide

Earlier we noted that key conceptual metaphors found in both the literature and more extensively in the programmatic conceptualisation of agency create a view that CONFLICT IS LINEAR and PEACE IS SEQUENTIAL. These descriptions represent what Lakoff and Johnson call orientational metaphors. In their words:

> But there is another kind of metaphorical concept, one that does not structure one concept in terms of another but instead organizes a whole system of concepts with respect to one another. We call these orientational metaphors, since most of them have to

do with spatial orientation: up–down, in–out, front–back, on–off, deep–shallow, central–peripheral (Lakoff & Johnson 1980, p. 14).

They note that 'most of our fundamental concepts are organized in terms of one or more spatialization metaphors' (Lakoff & Johnson 1980, p. 17).

In the field of peacebuilding linearity and sequentiality have provided important and useful ways to organise theory, thinking about the nature of change and, most importantly, agency, found in the construct of projects through which peacebuilding funding is allocated. At the same time this metaphoric organisation creates a dominant view that does not attend adequately to other simultaneous realities that may be equally important for how we understand and approach challenges like reconciliation and trauma healing in the midst and aftermath of violence. Lakoff and Johnson (1980) note that dominant organising metaphors both reveal and hide aspects of a complex reality. The notion that a metaphor hides aspects of complexity is particularly important. They write:

> The very systematicity that allows us to comprehend one aspect of a concept in terms of another...will necessarily hide other aspects of the concept. In allowing us to focus on one aspect of a concept...a metaphorical concept can keep us from focusing on other aspects of the concept that are inconsistent with that metaphor (Lakoff & Johnson 1980, p. 10).

As we noted, in the wider literature a number of authors acknowledge that reconciliation and healing are not linear processes, but for analytical purposes have found it useful to develop frames of reference built on notions of change happening in phases, stages or sequential progression. We repeat that, for analytical purposes and the development of organising theory, this is a legitimate endeavour and it corresponds to aspects of lived reality, often helpful in providing a sense of the big picture. Atkinson (2002) noted this when she referred to *Dadirri* as an Indigenous approach based on repeated and deep forms of relational mutuality happening through listening circles. At the same time she correlated aspects of this 'circular' metaphor of deepening to Herman's (1992) notion of phased changes in the progression of trauma healing (Atkinson 2002, pp. 243–4). When surveyed across many cases and over time, healing and reconciliation processes have important patterns usefully described in phases and linear progression. However, we do suggest that when the linear construct becomes dominant as an organising metaphor it hides other important elements of the complex lived reality. For us, 'dominant' means that a particular lens has been widely accepted as the *primary lens* through which change is understood and organised, and programmatic agency developed, envisioned and measured. At a minimum, this dominance moves quickly past and may in more extreme cases diminish and hide other aspects of lived realities. We could even say that these other aspects are contradictory, involving as they do sphere-like images of simultaneity, circularity and repetitive patterns, ritual and depth. In the larger picture these remain aspects less explored and, in the case of agency, at times disregarded because they do not easily fit the ways that governments and non-governmental programs organise their funding, structures of action and lenses of evaluation. These hidden aspects are then easily perceived as peripheral and at times counterproductive, especially from the standpoint of program development.

If we observe carefully we can see that the power of the linear orientation's metaphoric structure in defining how we believe things work and what matters is located in our common linguistic formations that suggest change happens in sequential progression. For example:

Shifting metaphors 57

Forward movement is progress.
Progress is good.
Indicators mark forward movement.
Movement through defined stages is progress.
Backward movement is a setback.
Setbacks are bad.
Going in circles and repetition is either being stuck or moving backwards.
Being stuck is going nowhere and unproductive.
Early phases hold unhealthy patterns that will be overcome in later stages.
Positive health is located in later stages.
Growth and maturity indicate achieved forward movement.

In sum, linearity and sequentiality as metaphor provide an analytical construct useful for observing broad and longitudinal views of conflict and change. The weakness of this construct as a dominant metaphor lies in the degree to which, once accepted, it hides, does not account for, legitimate, or explore competing and equally important aspects of the complex lived reality.

Community metaphors in the midst and aftermath

[handwritten: moving to the grassroots experience]

To compare metaphoric structures and illustrate hidden aspects of a complex reality we need to move from the language of analysts and politicians to the impulse and language rising from the community experience of people who are affected by violence and who are the recipients of peace processes and programs. In places like Colombia and West Africa we find a variety of different metaphors embedded and emergent in people's everyday language as they attempt to explain their experience, needs and hopes in the midst and aftermath of violence. Rather consistently, language organises around survival and facing the realities of daily life. The experience of these people often boils down to three framing challenges which are found over and again, expressed as daily realities in local communities in protracted conflicts: displacement, insecurity and voicelessness. To recast these in a positive light, their search seeks to answer these questions: How do we locate a sense of place? How and where can we feel safe? How will we find a voice in the affairs that affect our lives? As metaphor, these concepts – place, safety and voice – provide insight into both the deep reality of violence and the nature of resiliency. They also illustrate the components and significance of a metaphor shift. Each is worth deeper exploration into its corresponding metaphoric structure.

Place: locating oneself in the world

Literally and figuratively violence displaces people. Consider Colombia. Statistics show that in the 20-year period from 1985 to 2005 just short of 4 million people have been displaced due to armed conflict. In the decade from the mid-nineties there were more than 1500 documented massacres (UNDP 2007, p. 3). When discussed in the shorthand of international jargon and statistics Colombia is a country with millions of people labelled as *IDPs – internally displaced people*. The acronym 'IDP' is bantered about and mostly taken for granted as an organising category to account for people forced from their homes and communities, but the linguistic structure of the acronym carries meaning at more than one level, particularly if we penetrate the hidden caves of lived experience.

For those delivering resources, IDP is an organising category to classify people who are victims. For those in need of resources the designation of being IDPs includes them and calls attention to their plight. However, for those who find themselves in the category of internally displaced people the term suggests much more than simply a way to count numbers. It functions as an archetypal metaphor with numerous and simultaneous levels of meaning reflective of the experience faced by those affected by violence. Consider at least three levels of meaning as expressed by people in everyday living in settings of protracted conflict.

First, 'displaced' connotes the *literal loss of place*, the physical experience of being forced out of their homes and off their land. As they say in Colombia, conflict creates forced human mobility. People flee. They walk. They run. They try to find a 'place' to settle, often at considerable distance from their homes of origin.

At a second level, often beyond words to adequately express it, *displaced* connotes the lived experience of *feeling lost*. It is a paradoxical experience. To not have a place means that a person and often an entire community feel 'lost', although they still live in a place, as in a 'country', that is familiar but no longer known. In other words, 'displaced' means a person does not know where they are or what their place is, and they have lost any sense of belonging. The word often used in Colombia with reference to moving off land and local farms, *desarraigado*, literally builds from 'being uprooted'. By its very nature, to be displaced forces a journey of discovery. People must find their way. They must locate themselves and their bearings in a land to which they belong but in a geography that is unknown and without maps. When Maria and friends use the term *desplazados* to identify themselves they use a known category, but at a deeper level this category touches a metaphoric structure about locating themselves. This locating represents both a process that requires them to find a place to 'land and live' and to 'discover and find' who they are in this new landscape. *Place* represents the much deeper journey of relocating and recovering a sense of belonging.

Judy Atkinson in her extraordinary ethnography of healing among Aboriginal Australians, *Trauma trails*, notes the significance of place and location. She writes that when British colonisers first arrived they referred to the land as 'terra nullius (land of no peoples)'

(Atkinson 2002, p. 25). But for Aboriginal people this so-called terra nullius was a 'story place. Land holds the stories of human survival across many generations. Land shapes people just as people shape their countries' (2002, p. 27). Place provides a sense of location, belonging and connection. When reading through her stories and examples focused on generational trauma one finds over and again that people struggle to locate themselves, to find their place, both within their immediate settings and families and far more widely in reference to who they are as individuals and as an Aboriginal collective in their wider lived history. Atkinson's *Trauma trails* has the subtitle *Recreating song lines*. This throws into relief the key Aboriginal idea of songlines as mechanisms that create a map. Literally, over the generations, as people walked they sang, using the sound and lyrics as modalities to triangulate their location (Chatwin 1987). Atkinson uses this notion of songlines as metaphor to identify the journey of healing that links place with finding oneself in terms of geographic connection and transgenerational location. Metaphorically, place simultaneously is geographic location and time/space location; with it one finds oneself and re-creates meaning and a sense of belonging.

At yet another level, seeking place and belonging creates a search to locate a *sense of purpose*. 'Finding a place' symbolises the journey to locate bearings or coordinates that permit people to 'land on' and attach meaning to their lives. In this sense, displaced people search for significance, often in pursuit of finding direction in what is essentially a quest for identity: 'Who are we in this unknown social landscape?' 'Where' we are, then, is always intimately tied up with working out 'who' we are.

Take Maria's journey as an example. In Don Quixote-like fashion she set out to have the bones in the box officially named. This was a deeply confusing journey of identity with competing realities of displacement. She needed to prove her story in order to find her way home. She needed to have someone officially acknowledge her experience, to give a name to her husband's bones in order to attain victimhood so that she could receive reparations. At the same time she sensed that naming herself *victim* tied her to people and systems that produced her violation in the first place.

Inevitably, health and well*being*, are intimately tied up with the idea of place in both the literal and figurative senses of the word. For any of us, and much more for those with significant loss, when we have our bearings we know where we are and have a sense of who we are. Finding place in this deeper sense represents the lifelong journey towards health as belonging, having a place and sensing a purpose.

From a different lens let us take the word 'internal' from the category 'IDP' and explore its lived significance. On the surface and in its most common political usage, 'internal' means that people are physically displaced *within* their own country. This category emerges because international agencies and governments need to count people for the purposes of providing assistance, developing adequate responses and programs, and tracking the patterns of mobility. People who are forcibly displaced and cross a national border to arrive in another country are placed in the category of *refugees*. People forced from their homes but who do not leave their country of origin are not refugees; they are *internally displaced*. At this first most literal level *internal* simply creates a category to account for forced movement of people within a nation-state.

At a second level a metaphor shift plays out in the phrase in which the concept *internal* captures the lived experience of displacement as feeling lost *within* oneself: I no longer know who 'I am', in large part because 'I cannot locate myself' in this experience. Physically, psychologically and spiritually the inner and outer journeys through uncharted geographies are reflective mirrors. In the poem cited at the start of this chapter Yeats captures the deep and eternal struggle to find one's true self.[1] 'Mirror after mirror' he wrote, is not about 'vanity'. Rather it is about looking to find 'the face I had before the world was made'. I am on a search to find and locate myself. This speaks directly to the experience of people forced from their homes due to armed conflict.

On the outer journey the displaced must locate a physical place to live. At the same time this search reflects the inner, deeply spiritual search for finding meaning and place. This internal journey to find oneself – *place as metaphor* – represents the archetypal journey of health: when people find their place, when they touch, in and out, a sense of location, purpose and meaning, they experience a sense of health. When we look carefully at the opening stories we find time and again that perhaps the most significant aspect of people's journeys was those moments, spread throughout the experience, when they found spaces of meaningful location, belonging and purpose.

Place creates a metaphor of health very different from the orientation metaphor *linearity* with its sequential phases and stages. Based on our discussion we could suggest several shifts in association. For example, take the metaphoric structure that healing relates to finding place and experiencing a sense of belonging. This provides an image of spatial terms that reframes healing away from the notion of linearity and towards images of depth, rootedness, and even cyclical, season-like processes tied to location and land. Belonging associated with rootedness, for example, does not envision place as a phase or an event. It is constructed around physical and figurative locations; the nurturing of a land, digging deep into a sense of something that holds purpose and provides sustenance.

For many displaced in Colombia, given their rural and campesino origins, the constant question about a *plan for return* to their *fincas* or land represents both sides of the metaphor *place*: a longing for physical return to their land and the spiritual return to a sense of meaning and purpose in their lives. The small steps they take, some backwards and some forwards, are part of this digging and deepening. This journey parallels a second major metaphor – seeking safety as a way to feel at home.

Safety: feeling at home

People who live in contexts of open violence are permanently alert to their personal and collective security. They search for ways to feel and be safe, to find protection. Violence produces enormous insecurity and requires hyper-vigilance. As metaphor the search for *safety* and *security* creates more than one level of significance.

On the surface, in settings of violence the most immediate meaning of security emerges around physical safety vis-a-vis the presence of violent threat. People look for physical spaces and mechanisms that provide them with protection.

At another level insecurity creates the permanency of feeling uncertain. Uncertainty goes hand in hand with the experience of unpredictability. To survive in settings of violence people see everything around them differently. They suspend trust in what is happening around them. Nothing is what it seems to be. Life is no longer normal. Violence also produces internal uncertainty. To feel insecure means a person no longer has a clear sense of self and often responds to immediate events from internal uncertainty. At the level of metaphor, insecurity poses a challenge of how to recover a basic sense of trust in the outer social landscape and the inner personal journey.

Violence destroys what was understood and known. What was assumed, taken for granted as 'normal' on a daily basis, has disappeared and people suspend, or outright lose the capacity to feel *at home*. Home often serves as a relational metaphor of feeling *surrounded* by love, a sense of wellbeing, shelter and unconditional acceptance. Violence destroys this feeling and the capacity to be oneself without mistrust or pretension; it destroys a sense of at-homeness.

Notable in the geographies of violence and war, we often find the word 'disappeared' used as both verb and noun. In Maria's story for example, her husband and neighbours were considered disappeared. People *disappear*, they are on one hand not to be found, no longer around. They are gone. In settings of armed conflict this means they have either been kidnapped or perhaps killed. They were *disappeared* suggests they were killed but nobody knows when, where or how, creating a surreal suspension: presumed dead without conclusion. A category captures this state of animation: *the disappeared*. In these contexts, 'at-homeness' – a sense of being surrounded by trust like a warm blanket that once held a person, family or community – evaporates like a fog burnt off suddenly. In the blink of an eye, local communities find themselves exposed, visibly naked without protection or shelter. Rather than feeling surrounded by love and acceptance they are enveloped by threat, fear and animosity, and worse, the constant presence of complete unpredictability in the living of daily life.

This archetypal search and hope for security points to a key aspect of health: safety is not only finding a way to assure physical security but also expresses the search to find a way to feel at home in the world, to feel once again a sense of being surrounded by love and acceptance, such that it is possible to trust oneself, one's immediate family, others and the wider social landscape.

Here again we find an interesting shift of metaphor. Security as feeling at home suggests spatial metaphors of feeling comfortably surrounded, having a container in which one feels a sense of belonging and trust. SAFETY IS CONTAINER suggests the idea of feeling surrounded by acceptance and protection, a space where it is possible to be oneself, devoid of threat and to get on with living life without fear. These spatial metaphors point towards a notion of being encircled in the sense of being held, pointing towards notions of container as community and family. These spatial images lead to a third idea, the need for the proximity of meaningful conversation.

Voice: close enough to be heard

In settings of protracted conflict people in local communities often express a common view about the national peace process through a simple observation: 'Nobody listens to us. We do not have a *voice*.' As metaphor, voice, and its negative, voicelessness, function simultaneously at different levels of meaning.

At the first level, many victims of violence experience a profound sense of powerlessness, an overwhelming and deeply rooted feeling that they do not have a voice in the processes of response and the decisions that affect their lives or in the events happening around them, though officially these processes are portrayed as being conducted *on their behalf*. Their primary point of reference rises from the feeling of *being left out*, creating the experience that solidifies a profound sense of distance and exclusion. They are *talked about* but not *talked with* and, when they are talked with, they often express a sense that the talk was not meaningful because it did not lead to expected change, particularly in political processes purported to deliver peace to a conflicted country and to their local communities. Voice as metaphor has association with terms like inclusion, power and meaningfulness.

At the second level, voice as metaphor evolves in both a *spatial* and *sonic context*. Voice implies an image related to the proxemics of space and relationship. Voice signals that people are within hearing range, the shared space of a conversation. A conversation requires a spatial distance wherein the words – sound externalised – are accessible and interactive. As such, to have a voice suggests that people, and significant processes affecting their lives, are proximate: they are physically close enough that the vibrations of sounds touch each other, create an echo that bounces, reverberate and resonate between them. Note the degree to which these kinds of words are found in the everyday language that describes meaningful conversation and dialogue.

Metaphorically then, the sensation of voicelessness always means finding oneself in a space too expansive, distant and remote to *feel* or *be touched by* the vibration of sound. In such a space conversation is not possible and is meaningless. From the community level, the people hear and feel the words descending from the national political level but these are experienced as happening 'out there' and are so distant that the sounds they try to form in response, hoping for a bounce back and reverberation, fall into an abyss, never reaching the other side or returning with any sense of meaningful connection. Voice requires a localness of context and space within which people can feel the connection to the vibration of sound. When a person says, 'We do not have a voice' or 'We want a voice', the guiding metaphor suggests they seek spaces of inclusion and power that take the shape of acknowledgement, respectful exchange, meaningful conversation, and which affect actual decisions that affect their lives.

At the deepest, perhaps most complex level, voicelessness means losing touch with a sense of personhood. As metaphor, when a person no longer has a sense of voice they experience a loss of humanity. Voicelessness at this level suggests a falling out of touch with meaning and the disappearance of significance. Voicelessness creates the experience of being numb, without a capacity to feel, to touch or to be in touch. This is in fact the impact of violence. It deadens, numbs and silences life. Those who experience it close at hand experience a loss that reaches below and beyond words. Here we enter the terrain of the *unspeakable*, the search for finding ways to name experiences and events that are beyond words and comprehension. The search in such an uncharted geography represents a groping journey to touch and feel again, to find ways to feel the meaning of experiences that defy – and are never adequately expressed by – rational explanation. As Harrison wrote on the impact of violence:

People who cross the threshold between the known world and that place where the impossible does happen discover the problem of how to convey their experience. Some of us don't talk about murders or intergenerational sex within our families. We find words inadequate, or we lose them entirely. Those of us who insist on speaking what's often called unspeakable discover there's no tone reserved for unnatural disasters, and so we don't use any. We're flat affect; we report just the facts; this alienates our audience (Harrison 2008).

In these levels of meaning, voice as metaphor suggests other key aspects of health, found primarily in the need to feel *close enough* to processes that affect daily personal and collective life, such that a sense of meaningful conversation is actually possible. Again we find a spatial metaphor significantly different from linearity. Sonically, voice is based on vibration. People feel reciprocity, acknowledgement and meaningful exchange. Voice necessarily requires a context of community, a localness of spatial distance where participation and dialogue create direct experiences of connection, exchange and responsiveness.

Voice organises around an aural, sound-based metaphor. Sound, interestingly, is multidimensional and multidirectional. It surrounds and can create a sensation of being held. It is based on touch and vibration. When people speak of voice as having connection to change at the community level they use the language of echo: the sensation of feeling sound rise from within and take the form of words that enter a shared space and are received by and touch others. In return, a response comes back and touches the one who spoke. In this process people participate in creating resonance and experience meaningful conversation. Levi (2004) confirms this in her doctoral dissertation where she carefully documented the experience of collective resonance. In her empirical study many participants reported feeling a vibration as the group experienced what people reported as a feeling or moments of resonance in the group process (Levi 2004, p. 25).

As safety and voice are combined, healing begins to form and deepen. Interestingly, many of the key texts on trauma healing suggest two primal foundations: the building of a *safe space* as the container for *sharing story* (Atkinson 2002; Hart 2008; Herman 1992; Yoder 2005). Story is identified as 'acknowledgement' (Yoder 2005). Atkinson called it 'finding and exploring individual and collective stories'. In describing this in her concluding chapter Atkinson used the words 'deep' or 'depth' metaphorically and used them more than any other single word for what transpired when safety and voice interact in proximate space (Atkinson 2002, pp. 245–9). What perhaps has not been fully explored is the degree to which these primal metaphors have significant aspects that are sound based, unfolding in a context suggesting that HEALING IS AURAL.

Resiliency as metaphor

As a way to integrate these key metaphors it is useful to explore the concept of resiliency. Though rarely explored in the primary literature on political reconciliation, the field of trauma healing has lifted this concept to a central location (Hart 2008; Yoder 2005). As a scientific term, resiliency comes to us from the language of biology, physics and metallurgy. In the latter, resiliency applies to a particular group of metals that, when placed under extreme heat, will lose shape, soften and meld, but when cooled have an amazing capacity to find their way back to their original forms. In the study of plants, the capacity for resiliency has also been noted, particularly in crops or grasses which, when beaten down by winds or the weight of trampling feet, find the way back to their original form.

Resiliency describes the quality needed to survive extreme conditions yet retain the capacity to *find a way back* to expressing the defining quality of *being* and the essence of *purpose*.

In the social sciences resiliency has primarily been studied as a phenomenon in developmental psychology and social work (Bernard 2004; Harvey & Tummala-Narra 2007; Reivich & Shatté 2002). Here, researchers have been interested in the study of children who, while living in vulnerable and high-risk situations – parents with mental disorders, conditions of poverty, or violence – still found their way towards expressively healthy childhoods and eventually balanced, responsible adulthoods. In discussing the characteristics of these children and the environments that nurture this journey, authors describe resiliency with terms such as adaptability, resourcefulness, and a capacity to face and creatively negotiate risky situations.

When applied to the community level, particularly those local collectives who have experienced life-damaging events or contexts – natural disasters, human-generated traumas such as war, or social, economic or political structures that produce poverty and exclusion – resiliency describes the capacity to forge solidarity, to sustain hope and purpose, and to adapt and negotiate creatively with the challenges presented (Bridgers 2005; Greene 2002; Kehayan & Napoli 2005). A significant number of authors identify this capacity of response as a mechanism by which communities hard hit by violence find an innovative way to survive (Garcia 1996; Hernández Delgado 2004; Hernández Delgado & Salazar Posada 1999; Lederach 2005). In sum, the local collective becomes proactively engaged in purposeful ways that help them recover a sense of place, at-homeness and a voice. Their life journeys represent a quality of positive deviance that defines the very essence of resiliency: against the odds these people and communities flourish. In identifying what contributes to this transcendent quality, researchers chose the word resilient because it described this capacity to bounce back.

Resiliency as metaphor returns to our earlier notion of a journey that is both internal and outward bound and that rises from a

quality of character and spirit. To place the term in a life journey, resiliency suggests that no matter the difficulty of the terrains faced by the traveller, they stay in touch with a core defining essence of being and purpose, and display a tenacity to find a way back as a way forward that artistically stays true to their very being.

We could say the defining quality of resiliency is the capacity to stay in touch.

To return to the words of the poet, Yeats refers to this as 'looking for the face I had before the world was made'. In this sense, resiliency, as applied to the challenge of the life journey requires finding a way back to humanity, the sense of personhood and community that creates authenticity and purpose. Health, as viewed from the standpoint of resiliency, suggests the character of personhood and quality of community that faces, moves through, and bounces back from difficulty, damage or destructive experience, with a spirit that pursues and stays in touch with purposeful life and meaningful relationships.

Resiliency suggests insights that are useful to the exploration and inquiry into a metaphor shift. Community health in settings of protracted conflict can be used as a referent point. Perhaps most significant is the basic notion that community health may not exclusively nor primarily be found in the developmental measures used for comparative purposes (for example, economic status, education, levels of open violence) but rather correlates with the less tangible dynamics of how people and communities locate creative and proactive capacities for responding to the challenges they face. Resiliency requires an innovative capacity of response whether in the midst or aftermath of open violence. The metaphoric structure again points towards a spatial understanding of staying in touch with a sense of personhood, identity and purpose, so that innovating for survival while in the midst of violence or bouncing back following its destructive impact is within reach and can be mobilised. The organising structure of a resiliency metaphor builds around the images of social healing rising from deepening a sense of place, building containers of safety and touching voice both in and out. Resiliency in this view offers a number of metaphoric markers related to our earlier discussion.

In the face of violence, resiliency suggests an inner and outer journey that fosters the capacity to locate place and purpose as mechanisms to nurture and solidify a sense of belonging and purpose. The inverse is the sustained experience of displacement, which ultimately creates a sense of being lost while living in your home country.

Resiliency frames security as ultimately fostering and rebuilding trust in self, others and the lived social landscape, creating a feeling of community as at-homeness. The single biggest challenge in the midst and aftermath of armed conflict is how to do this while living in the presence of real and perceived enemies and continuing resurgent forms of violence. The inverse is the experience of being disappeared, the quality of profound insignificance to the point of not existing, being lost and unconnected, living in a constant state of vigilance, driven and governed by isolation, mistrust and fear.

Resiliency suggests container-like social spaces that encourage and sustain a quality of dialogue-based interaction wherein people feel they can touch, shape and be shaped by accessible and meaningful conversation. In such spaces, people feel a sense of voice that reverberates and creates resonance with events and processes that affect their lives. The inverse fosters spaces of voicelessness defined by distance and exclusion which translate into isolation and a pervading experience of powerlessness.

Resiliency underscores the importance of purposeful hope over the dependency of wait-and-see grievance, requiring a proactive capacity for proposal, engagement and sustained relationships in the midst of external challenges and local polarisation. In many regards, the primary quality of resiliency mobilises the imagination of the community as a healthy but highly diverse whole, while encouraging the journey towards finding authenticity and purpose for diverse individuals through place, trust and voice.

Conclusion

This discussion has created the platform for exploring aspects of a complex reality that are easily hidden by the dominant metaphors that CONFLICT IS LINEAR and PEACE IS SEQUENTIAL. By unpacking the impulse of communities living through and surviving violence we have noted the significance of metaphoric structures rising from their experience that shift the meaning towards organising concepts not primarily associated with linear sequence. We noted a primary notion that several of these metaphors create an organising concept – SOCIAL HEALING IS RESILIENT – that seems particularly important to and for communities living in contexts with sustained patterns of direct and structural violence. Three common and key metaphors suggested were the search for place, safety and voice. Spatial in nature, these metaphors organise an understanding of health around images of deepening, finding place, forging a sense of feeling at-home; containers that surround and hold a touchable space. Voice emerges in an aural context, sonic in nature that includes vibration and echo, which create a sense of meaningful conversation and a capacity to stay in touch. As a starting point this survey provides us with a basis for exploring the metaphor shift underpinning social healing in more adventurous ways.

SECTION II

THE SONICS OF HEALING

For twenty-five centuries, Western knowledge has tried to look upon the world. It has failed to understand that the world is not for the beholding. It is for the hearing. It is not legible, but audible.
Jacques Attali

CHAPTER 6

Sonic survival

PERSONAL STORIES

There are no easy ways to re-create the intensity of the lived experience when you find yourself facing life and death situations. Compared to many people I work with in settings of high violence, I have experienced relatively few such situations. What I have found remarkable in the times when I have faced life-threatening challenges has been the presence of music, more specifically a song, which unexpectedly provided grace and healing that somehow lifted me towards survival. I have often pondered on what seems to be unanswerable: why did a certain piece of music appear at a most unexpected moment? I don't have an answer to that question, except to share personal stories and invite the reader to join the inquiry. Two stories I share in this chapter, and a third is found in Chapter 8 where I explore the music of Van Morrison. The stories are spread across two decades. The first takes us to Central America and back to the eighties.

Story 1: the day I heard the voice of Harry Emerson Fosdick

I start this story with a description of a bookshelf I keep in my office. I reconstruct it each time I move to a new office. At the time of this writing it is found overlooking my desk on the third floor of the Kroc Institute in the Hesburgh Center on the campus of the University of Notre Dame, Indiana.

Books are like old photos. Photos often sit for ages in a drawer unattended to, then when you are looking for something else they come back into view. Time stops. The old photos speak, of life, people and experiences. Books have the same effect for me. Beyond their content they tell stories. When I pick up a certain book I think about where I bought it, when it came into my life, and the impact it had on my thinking and work. I imagine the authors. I think about who they were, how they approached life and writing, what they struggled with, and what they learned. In one of these drifting-through-book-moments I decided to pick only a few and stand them on a shelf so that each day as I entered my office I could not help but notice them and they would look down at me as I worked. I don't actually read them each day. I just see the titles, the names of the authors, and they remind me of who I am, who has gone before me, and the path I feel called to walk.

It is not a large collection. At one end it starts with a pocket-sized King James version of the New Testament given to me by my grandparents, Willis and Mary Lederach, at Christmas, 1976. I carried this tiny Bible in my back pocket for a period of time and over those years it somehow filled up with items. There is a list of groceries I needed to buy in a market in Barcelona. There is a letter that I wrote as a kid to my dad in the middle of one of his sermons. There are some coupons for granola bars. When I look through this book I discover that in 1976 I had underlined only four words from Ephesians 4:15 – 'Speak truth in love'. The dedication reads: 'For

John Paul with love and concern. Your Grandparents'. I imagine at the time their concern was likely the length of my hair.

Next to the New Testament are two small hardback copies of Leo Tolstoy's writings. I bought them in London on my first Mennonite Central Committee assignment in 1975. On the shelf one of them is turned open to the title page that reads, 'A confession: the Gospel in brief and what I believe'.

Next to Tolstoy is the face of Mahatma Gandhi looking down at me from his autobiography that carries the subtitle: *My experiments with truth*. That book I bought in Spain and had it shipped from India. It looks and feels like the first 1927 edition published by the Navijivan Publishing House. On the back cover it quotes Gandhi, 'I have nothing new to teach the world. Truth and nonviolence are as old as the hills.'

Next is a blank spot where John Howard Yoder's *Politics of Jesus* once stood. It has now been given what I hope is a temporary home by one of my wayfaring students. By my count it is probably the seventh or eighth copy that I have had to replace. Some time back I decided that if there was one book that I should give away it would be that one. Now it is just a blank space on the shelf, sort of metaphoric I thought when I looked for it this week. I need to buy a new one.

The final book is a 1945 hardback edition titled: *A great time to be alive: sermons on Christianity in wartime* by Harry Emerson Fosdick. I received it from my father some years back. I have it propped open to the title page so that from anywhere in the room I can see the words *A great time to be alive*.

My story involves Harry Emerson Fosdick. Fosdick was a theologian, a preacher and an author. This collection of sermons was written between the World Wars (Fosdick 1945). Here was a person who had the nerve to say: this is 'a great time to be alive' in the midst of the coming of World War II. At the end of the first essay he wrote '...our problem is not to see how little we can believe but what great things we can see in the Christian message and make real to the world that desperately needs them. This is a great time for great convictions' (Fosdick 1945, p. 3).

Fosdick also penned the occasional words to hymns. One of those hymns has entered my life and found a way to weave its rhythm and words through my experience of faith and God. At age 52 Fosdick wrote the words to the hymn 'God of grace and God of glory' first sung at the Riverside Church in New York on 8 February 1931. I remember singing this song as a child on Sunday mornings, though it was not until I was older that the words leapt out and grabbed my attention. In our congregational life we sing in four parts, harmony rising from the a cappella merging of voices. While we may disagree on many things, Mennonites share a love for singing together. My appreciation for this song is partly due to the influence of my dad and uncle, John Lederach and Ron Kennel, who shared the hobby of collecting the writings and books of Harry Emerson Fosdick. I remember them saying (and I paraphrase), 'This may be the greatest song in our hymnal'. The words make simple rhymes:

> God of grace and God of glory
> On thy people pour thy power;
> Crown thine ancient church's story
> Bring her bud to glorious flower;
>
> Lo, the hosts of evil round us
> Scorn thy Christ, assail His ways
> From the fears that long have bound us,
> Free our hearts to faith and praise.
>
> Cure thy children's warring madness
> Bend our pride to thy control

Shame our wanton selfish gladness
Rich in things but poor in soul.

Save us from weak resignation
To the evils we deplore
Let the search for thy salvation
Be our glory evermore.

Fosdick, 1969

The chorus brings forward the phrase, 'Grant us wisdom, grant us courage, for the facing of this hour and the living of these days.' I always imagined Fosdick writing these words with World War I behind him but with the prospect of World War II about to start. But I had no idea how deeply the song had been ingrained in my own psyche until I was walking the mucky soils of war and violence in Central America.

This is not an easy story to tell because our family lived through a complex, ambiguous and very difficult set of events. It was the first time we found ourselves facing serious levels of violent threat, were forcibly *displaced* from our home, and experienced various levels of trauma. A short version starts in 1984 with my involvement in a Mennonite Central Committee assignment to provide resources for peacebuilding in the region. As part of that assignment I became deeply involved in supporting the negotiations in Nicaragua taking place between the east coast Indigenous resistance (under the umbrella name of Yatama) and the Sandinista government. On the surface, these talks were aimed at ending the war, establishing agreements on social, political and cultural issues, and creating space for reconciliation. The same negotiation process was also a forerunner to what would eventually become the format for negotiations between the Nicaraguan resistance – known as the Contras – and the Sandinistas.

When our efforts to create negotiations first started we met fierce opposition from both Contra leaders and representatives of the United States government. At the time, the formal US policy was aimed at getting the Indian leaders of Yatama to join a single opposition front when dealing with the Sandinista government. The proponents of the same policy also believed wholeheartedly that the Sandinistas were communist ideologues with whom it was not possible to negotiate. Thus any effort that presented negotiation as a viable alternative to war was seen as a threat to the official US view. As a consequence, those of us involved in this mediation effort, most of whom were religious leaders from Nicaragua, found that as we worked on establishing negotiations we also made enemies and came under considerable pressure to stop our work. At times the pressure took the form of simple cynicism about whether the effort would succeed. At other times the pressure was much greater and included threats to our safety, some conveyed by messengers, some in writing. Few if any were ever traceable to a responsible source. They usually just said, 'Stop what you are doing, or else'. It was never easy to know how seriously to take the threats, but in this time of war and fierce enemies, anything was possible.

At the time, our family was living in San José, Costa Rica. I was the one member of the conciliation team who had a passport that permitted me to travel at a moment's notice between Indian leaders located in Costa Rica and the Sandinista government in Managua. For a brief period of time in the process I became the key shuttle. We would hold regular meetings of the Indian leaders in our home in San José and following those I would travel up to Managua to carry their messages and bring back the government's response. As might be expected, I came under pressure because I was seen as an important link in the fledgling efforts to create agreement to open and direct negotiations.

The first real sign of this pressure came when we were advised of a plan to kidnap our daughter Angie. The plan was put in motion by a series of characters involved in the Nicaraguan opposition who were connected with what we would subsequently discover were the illegal Iran–Contra operations. On being told that we had narrowly escaped a botched attempt to take Angie we moved out of Costa Rica and I continued to work on the negotiation process, travelling back and forth but without a home base.

The second wave of pressure came shortly after when I was informed that a contract on my life had been arranged. It was a little disconcerting to know that I was not worth more than a couple of hundred dollars, although when we first heard it we thought the whole thing sounded preposterous. Threats had come and gone so we kept working, even though I began to take more precautions, checking every day for devices under my car and going by different routes to meetings. Then the threats became real. On my return early one morning from a meeting in Nicaragua, Costa Rican immigration officials arrested me at the airport. I was forced into an unmarked car and taken to an unknown location for interrogation. That day, far away, President Oscar Arias was in Norway receiving his Nobel Peace prize for setting in motion the Central American peace accords and half of his government was with him. The progressive half. The other half, or at least elements connected to and paid by the CIA, were pursuing an agenda not espoused by their president. Let me say that this was not one of my more pleasant days. Mug shots were taken of me, I was accused of drug trafficking, there were hours of good cop/bad cop interrogations and I was charged with falsifying official documents. My interrogators seemed to have more information on me than I had about myself. They were quite insistent that I was Colombian and connected to a 500-kilogram cocaine shipment. I watched as they shuttled copies of my documents to a black-windowed limousine outside their office. Late at night, at the end of a long day, I was finally deposited at a local hotel, after a dizzying ride in the unmarked vehicle through the back streets of San José.

Early the next morning, several members of the conciliation team who had just arrived from Nicaragua joined me in my hotel room. We were discussing our next steps when I was called out of that meeting and went with one of my Nicaraguan colleagues to the lobby of the hotel. Two men involved in the east coast resistance met us at the front desk. They informed us that the assassination was on. I was targeted for sure. They were visibly nervous and shaken. My colleague from the east coast spoke to them several times in Miskito to verify the information. The two men insisted there was a contract on my head. They had specific details. The person who had put out the contract was well known in circles of the southern Contra front, an operative who went by the name of Felipe Vidal, or Max, or sometimes Cuban Max. He was from Miami, on the CIA payroll, undercover; his father had died in the Bay of Pigs debacle under the Kennedy administration. Cuban Max had apparently contracted a young man who, according to our two informants, was not mentally stable and in desperate need of money. They told us that both Cuban Max and the young man were in our hotel that very morning trying to establish a way that I could be identified so that the contract could be carried out. Agitated, they argued forcefully that I should leave the hotel and the country as soon as possible.

It was on leaving that hotel an hour later that I was visited in an extraordinary way by the 'God of grace'. I must confess that I was so frightened by this time that I was sweating straight out of my palms. It is amazing what fear and paranoia do to your mind. Fear creates different lenses. It makes you look at everything in a new light. My eyes darted everywhere, every face might be that of the assassin. I could not make my heart rate slow down. My mouth was dry. My stomach felt like a raw pit raging up into my throat. I was scared beyond words.

Faraon Dometz and I left the hotel to retrieve some personal belongings and documents from another office. Faraon was a Moravian pastor from Bluefields and a key member of our mediation team. We had been dropped off by a taxi and were finding our way towards the office when Faraon broke the silence and said, 'I am very afraid for you and your family.' We walked a bit more in silence. I remember my head being too full to even think. Thoughts ran in every direction and banged into each other. I felt confused, jumping from one idea to another about what to do, where to go.

Then out of the blue Faraon started to whistle. The single notes lifted into the air were the melody line of 'God of grace and God of glory' by Harry Emerson Fosdick. We had never talked about the song. He had no idea that I even knew the song. He whistled for the remainder of the two-block walk to the office. It was as if the air that came through his pursed lips was the very breath of God blowing on my face. I felt my heartbeat slow. For a moment I closed my eyes. The whistle carried me back. I could almost feel myself standing in a pew in my home congregation, surrounded by my people, holding an old red hymnal, turned to hymn number 434. I could hear the four parts in the chorus. And I could hear the voice of Fosdick: 'Save us from weak resignation to the evils we deplore'.

We survived. Some months later a delegation of ten east coast Miskito, Sumo, Rama and Creole leaders met face-to-face to negotiate with the highest-level Sandinista representatives. It was a negotiation that would carve a new path to end the wars in Nicaragua.

Story 2: How I met Bob Dylan at the Pearly Gates

In the mid-nineties I joined a small team made up of Juan Gutierrez (then director of Gernika Gogoratuz, a peace research institute in the Basque Country) and Christopher Mitchell (then Professor at the Institute for Conflict Analysis and Resolution at George Mason University, Virginia) to explore ways to address the impasse that had frozen the negotiations in the Basque Country. For a number of years we met periodically with key political leaders of all persuasions, various Spanish government ministries and representatives of the more radical Basque independence movement. Ideas began to emerge. A few unexpected meetings took place. Some progress seemed possible, though the efforts remained off the record and for the most part totally out of the news. As part of the initiative we asked to have contact, by whatever means possible, with people who had more direct capacity to represent the views of ETA (Euskadi Ta Askatasuna), the underground, the folks from the 'other side' who had kept alive an armed struggle since the years when Franco was still in power. Somewhat surprisingly, we were given a procedure for the contact.

In November 1997 we opted to conduct another round of discussions in Spain and the Basque Country. It started in Madrid with the Minister of the Interior and with the head of national security. From Madrid we left by car to drive to the Basque Country, hoping to arrive at a designated meeting spot late that night for a first connection with the new contacts. We were joined that day by Irune Ondarza. Somewhere in central Castilla it began to rain. By the time we reached Pamplona the rain had turned heavy.

As we approached the intersection where the superhighway crosses the roads leading into Pamplona we suddenly saw through the thick rain and partial fog the red lights of traffic stopped ahead of us. An accident had just happened mid-way up the exit ramp. Cars and trucks were piling into each other and were stacked back onto the highway for kilometres. We were travelling at about 160 kilometres an hour when Juan slammed on the brakes. It was a few seconds of complete powerlessness I will never forget. As the wheels locked it seemed for a moment as if the car lifted off the ground and picked up speed. I remember hearing the squeal of the brakes, the intake of breath from four people in the car, a shout and the horrid crushing of metal.

As our vehicle connected with the back end of a stopped truck I felt myself thrown forward against the seat belt with a force that shook my body. For a moment it felt as if my head might not stay connected with my neck. Then with an almost equal force I was thrust back the opposite way onto the seat. Everything went silent. Juan's head lay on the steering wheel. Chris in the front seat was hunched forward. Beside me Irune was crumpled around broken legs and hips, unconscious. And then I felt an overwhelming urge to release the belt and get out of the car, coupled with a panic that set in and stayed: *I could not breathe*. I remember releasing the seat belt, opening the door, taking a couple of steps and falling on my back in the wet grass of the ditch. My body would no longer respond. My lungs had spit out whatever air they had and around them crushed ribs were collapsing, shutting down the in-and-out of my breath. I felt myself moaning, twisting, then stopping as pain riveted my upper cavity, and I felt a panic of a kind I had never experienced. 'I cannot breathe', I was screaming inside my head though nothing but choking sobs emerged from my mouth. 'I have to get air.' The harder I tried the less air I got and the more I panicked.

Then from who knows where I heard the raspy voice of Bob Dylan. He was singing a line from his song 'Tomorrow is a long time': 'If today was not an endless highway'.

'This may not be a good sign', I remember thinking, 'Bob Dylan at the Pearly Gates?'

I kept hearing an alternating couple of lines:

If today was not an endless highway
If tonight was not a crooked trail
…
Yes, and if only my own true love was waitin'
Yes, and if I could hear her heart a-softly poundin'

Only if she was lyin' by me
Then I'd lie in my bed once again.

My panic calmed. I don't know why. I stopped trying to breathe through my mouth and focused only on one nostril: just a tiny bit of air each time, just a short rhythm. It took what felt like hours for the emergency personnel to get there. Chris came around to see me. He was alive and was being taken to hospital. I lay in the ditch for probably 30 or 40 minutes with rain misting down on my face, a few lyrics and Bob Dylan's voice rolling in my head and breathed short, small scraps of air through my nose.

The night seemed to go on forever. By morning, I was in intensive care largely paralysed with extreme pain, but conscious enough to hear the doctor say that I had broken almost every rib on my left side where the shoulder strap had caught me and more than half of the ribs on my right side where the waist strap had lifted. 'Twelve, thirteen ribs crushed,' he said, 'not sure how you are alive. About half of them are criss-crossed like a crucifix.' He showed me with an 'x' of his two index fingers.

It took another night before I was able to make a phone call home. My wife Wendy had already made plans to come over with her sister Janie. They would arrive the following day. My last request on that phone call: 'Can you find our CD of *Bob Dylan's Greatest Hits Volume 2*?'

'What?' she asked completely perplexed.

'If you can just bring *Bob Dylan Volume 2* with you,' I repeated.

At the time I did not know it but I was experiencing what Oliver Sacks (2007, p. 42) identifies as an 'earworm' – a musical phrase or portion of melody that repeats itself incessantly in the mind. Only my earworm was for the good. I could not get Dylan's melody out of my head. Bedridden, incapable of any movement that would not produce pain, I spent hours and hours awake only in my head.

I tried to reconstruct the whole song, a small challenge that kept me alive, though at times it also drove me crazy. I could hear my repeated lines. Sometimes I could hear a snatch of a new one like 'beauty in the silver singin' river' but I could not make all of the song come back. When Wendy arrived I thought I was seeing an angel. I was. She had the Dylan CD and my CD player. Late that night, four nights after the accident, I put earphones on and played it over and again. I was overcome with emotion. I could hardly believe my ears and the words.

Tomorrow Is a Long Time
If today was not an endless highway,
If tonight was not a crooked trail,
If tomorrow wasn't such a long time,
Then lonesome would mean nothing to you at all.
Yes, and only if my own true love was waitin',
Yes, and if I could hear her heart a-softly poundin',
Only if she was lyin' by me,
Then I'd lie in my bed once again.

I can't see my reflection in the waters,
I can't speak the sounds that show no pain,
I can't hear the echo of my footsteps,
Or remember the sound of my own name.
Yes, and only if my own true love was waitin',
Yes, and if I could hear her heart a-softly poundin',
Only if she was lyin' by me,
Then I'd lie in my bed once again.

There's beauty in the silver, singin' river,
There's beauty in the sunrise in the sky,
But none of these and nothing else can touch the beauty

That I remember in my true love's eyes.
Yes, and only if my own true love was waitin',
Yes, and if I could hear her heart a-softly poundin',
Only if she was lyin' by me,
Then I'd lie in my bed once again.

Dylan, 1971

I think I did hear Bob Dylan at the Pearly Gates that night in the ditch. Something Divine, beyond my comprehension, kept me alive. Sonic survival.

CHAPTER 7

The Tibetan singing bowl

MUSINGS ON SOCIAL HEALING, SOUND AND THE NATURAL FREQUENCY

In Chapter 5 we identified a key metaphor structure under the frame of HEALING IS AURAL. As metaphor it suggests healing and reconciliation may be approached and understood as having parallel associations that touch or build on elements of sound. We noted in particular the common appeal to 'voice' as a primary concept invoked by people struggling to survive and respond resiliently to violence. Voice had significance as the process by which people could find, feel and touch a deeper sense of identity and self, and also as the way in which local communities begin to express and deal with their challenges. Voice correlated with the search for authentic conversation. We suggested this required a container or space within which people felt safe but also close enough to hear and receive the echo of each other's voices; in which, literally, it is possible to feel the vibration of echo. As such, voice represents acknowledgement, recognition and participation in meaningful and accessible ways. Voice suggests that the proximity of context makes conversation meaningful, rooting it into place and creating a sense of connection and belonging.

The violation of human life and relationships creates a deep sense of irreplaceable loss. Violence destroys voice, belonging and place. In essence, the search for voice seeks to restore connection, meaning and purpose; foundational elements for authentic conversation in the social sphere. That authenticity is most relevant and perceived as real in the spaces in which people can actually feel the sounds of their voice moving multidirectionally, reaching within, out and back again, providing the foundation and potential for effecting change. This exploration into metaphor shifts poses the intriguing question of whether examples of aural phenomena can be found that deepen our understanding of how sound works and how sonic phenomena might be applied to contexts of social change. In other words, how and in what ways does sound as metaphor provide insight into social healing? We may find a useful starting point in the Tibetan singing bowl.

The Tibetan singing bowl

The Tibetan singing bowl has a long history that traces back primarily to Buddhist ceremonies, calls to meditation and even to healing. As vendors and practitioners explained when our first bowls were purchased in Nepal, the healing relates to the various tones, pitches and qualities the bowl's vibrations produce. One practitioner explained: 'When people are sick we place the bowl on the stomach or close to affected areas and call forth its song. A lower note tone helps the stomach. A higher pitch is good for the head or sinuses. It is the vibrations that heal'.

While there are quite a variety of machine-made bowls to be found these days, the older Tibetan bowls, often worn and dirty from years of use, look like thin-walled brass containers that could be mistaken for spittoons if left in the corner. The bowls vary from the size of a cup to a size that would cover a good portion of a kitchen table. The original bowls were most commonly constructed of a composite of seven metals and were always hand shaped and a bit irregular. Those who use the bowls regularly pay careful attention to the quality of sound. The most desired are master bowls that have clarity of pitch and can hold vibration and sound for a long period of time.

While the bowl can be struck on its side or top with a wood or felt-tipped timpani-style drumstick the singing bowl performs best when its sound is called forth by circling the rim with a leather- or felt-covered wooden stick. The user holds the bowl flat on the palm of one hand while a stick in the second hand is placed firmly against the rim of the bowl and begins to circle it, over and again in the same direction. As the stick circles the rim, though initially not perceived, vibrations are produced that rise into an extraordinary tone which can resonate for minutes. For readers who have never seen, touched or heard a Tibetan singing bowl, it functions on the same principle as a high-quality glass partially filled with water when a finger is circled on its rim. Sometimes, depending on the bowl and the skill of the player, a two-toned pitch will create a harmony. More common, however, is the rise of a single, clear note that emerges from the bowl and fills the room. In Buddhist practice the sound is used to call a person to meditation; to stop and follow the sound. Adept practitioners in Tibet, India and Nepal use the bowls as a direct form of healing for physical ailments. The use of the sound and the vibrations seem to have a parallel in the contemporary use of sonic and ultrasound treatments produced by machines. However, our interest here is less on explaining the physical healing and more on the intriguing aspects of how the sound emerges from the bowl and fills the surroundings, as a way to develop insight into the notion of a sonic understanding of change and social healing.

A first step takes us to the physics of sound rising from the bowl. We asked our colleague, Wendell Jones, a physicist and ombudsman who mediates on knowledge disputes at the Sandia Institute about the physics of the bowl and its ability to produce the sound. For those of us challenged by the complexities of hard science-speak his answer was amazingly simple and deeply metaphoric. He suggested that the easiest way to understand this was a simple diagram of the theory of natural frequency (see Figure 2).

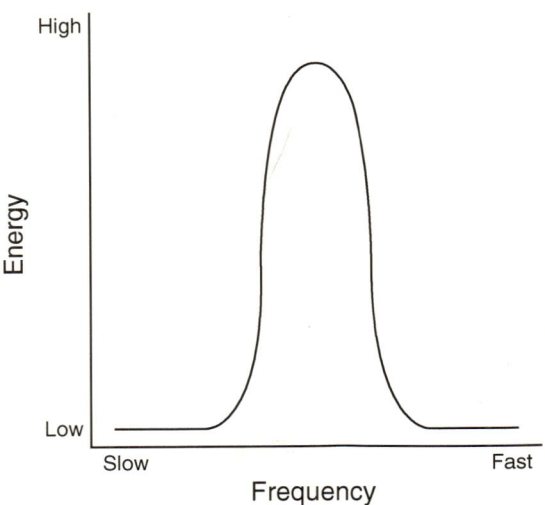

Figure 2. The natural frequency.

When plotted on two axes, natural frequency provides an interesting image by linking the rise of energy with the frequency of vibration. In simple terms, the stick rubbing against the bowl's rim creates friction. Though initially in microcosmic and undetectable ways, the stick is bouncing thousands of times, creating vibrations. If the circling is too slow nothing perceptible to the human ear emerges and very little is felt. No sound rises. If the circling proceeds at too rapid a pace the same is true: no sound rises. But at a particular moment, the moment called the natural frequency, the vibrations interact in a way that gives way to a sharp rise of energy like a spike, not a bell curve, on a graph.

When you first experience the bowl's capacity to produce sound it catches you by surprise. Seemingly nothing is happening in the first circlings, then a vibration emerges, almost imperceptible at first. As the vibrations interact and connect sound begins to rise in the form of a tone and, depending on the bowl, it may match a single note on the piano. The sound moves quickly from its initial faint quiver to a volume that can easily fill a room and surround the listeners. With the stick removed and the circling stopped the bowl sustains the sound, sometimes for minutes.

When the vibrations attain natural frequency a power emerges. In the Tibetan bowl the power arises as sound, but in other instances, for example engineers building bridges, the natural frequency can create a nightmare. When winds, people walking or cars travelling across the bridge create vibrations that converge into the right rhythms and patterns, the natural frequency produces a powerful combination with a capacity to 'explode' the structure in a few minutes. This was seen in the collapse of the Tacoma Narrows Bridge in the United States in 1940, which was captured on film.[1] Bridge builders and skyscraper architects now take into account the power of interacting quivers emerging from wind in particular and build in ways that control and deaden the vibration.

The Tibetan bowl, the image of the natural frequency and the nature of sound provide a number of key ideas useful for and parallel to our inquiry into social healing and voice. Several aspects of the Tibetan bowl and natural frequency hold particular relevance to our interest in exploring a metaphor shift.

Directionality

The Tibetan bowl and sound share the distinctive characteristic of multidirectionality. The sound rising from the bowl initiates with circling, literally going round and round. While the bowl is held it feels as if the circling, the bouncing of the stick on the rim, descends to the depth of the bowl and then in the moment of the natural frequency finds a voice that rises up and out. We find in this description three important types of direction relevant to our wider inquiry into sound as metaphor providing insight into social healing and to the more particular aspect of finding and touching voice.

First, and most obvious, is the movement of going around and around. Going in circles and repeating them over and again is not, however, seen as a movement of going nowhere. Rather, this movement of touching the edges continuously feels like a mini-ritual to call forth the sound. Patricia Burdette's (2003) research among the Lakota Indians, who place a very high value on ceremony and circle, suggested that restoration of health, physical, spiritual and communal, requires a process they referred to as 'calling the spirit back'. The stick moving around the rim of the bowl feels like the spirit is being called out of the bowl. Circling, then, can very much have a ritualistic quality in which the movement around has the purpose of creating a certain kind of space and moment.

A second movement pertains to the very image of the bowl. The Tibetan bowl is a container. It has a seamless circle on the rim with a vertical drop into the centre and bottom. As container, the bowl creates the space or location from which the sound is coaxed and held, but in terms of movement the sensation is one of going deep, made possible by the circling. Deepening becomes a directional focus of the container. The sound rises from the depths of the bowl. Tibetan bowls are used in ceremonies and the notion of ritual and ceremony provides a shift in metaphor structure that reframes the meaning of circling and deepening.

Lisa Schirch (2004) has provided our field with a unique and clear contribution with her exploration of the importance of ritual and ceremony as key features of transformational processes in protracted conflict. She suggests that ritual creates 'unique space set aside' that fosters human connection and a deepening of meaningful experience not always possible in direct, word-based negotiations (2004, p. 17). Ritual, however, often involves significant elements of repetition, of repeating ceremony over and again. While repetitiousness may be seen from a political or programmatic view of linearity and productivity as a weakness – defective and unproductive (in other words going in circles but not getting anywhere) – when seen in terms of the directional metaphors of ritual and ceremony, recalling, reiteration and repeating provide spaces that permit people to be present; to touch a deeper sense of self and reality, to find, nurture or build a deeper sense of voice, place and meaning.

A third movement pertains more to the rise of sound. Sound not only seems to rise from the bowl, it expands, moves out, touches and surrounds the space within its reach. Sound moves in all directions. The Tibetan bowl can be played in the middle of a room, yet people located anywhere in the room will be touched by the vibrations and will feel surrounded. Unlike the beam from a flashlight, sound is multidirectional and non-linear in its movement. Of particular note are the feelings of being touched and being held that are often experienced through sound and which we will explore in greater depth in subsequent chapters.

We should add here a word about the varied expressions by which sound holds a centrality of significance in human experience. Jacques Attali, cited at the beginning of this section, suggests in his study of the political economy of music that 'life is full of noise and death alone is silent'. He goes on to assert that 'nothing essential happens in the absence of noise' (Attali 2006, p. 3). Numerous religious traditions believe that the birth of the universe was based in sound, including the

Buddhist, the Hindu and the Mayan. 'In the beginning was the Word', proclaimed St John in his Gospel. Showalter (2005, p. 175) recounts the story of ethnomusicologist Monsieur Yapo taking a single string bow and saying 'this is how the world started' as he played.

We pass too quickly over our own everyday words, taking no notice of their origins or how some scientific theories develop from this sonic impulse. For example, in both Latin and Greek the origin of the word 'person' comes from theatre, more specifically from a reference to the mask through which the actor speaks. In modern Spanish the word *son* means sound. Vicent Guzman, Valencian etymologist and philosopher traces the origin of the Spanish *persona* to the Latin verb *sonare* which means, as he put it 'to resonate with intensity' (Guzman 2009). Thus the word 'person', in which the prefix 'per' (meaning 'through' or 'for') is connected with the word *sonare* that traces to sound, suggests that being through or for sound is an essential component of being human. Psychiatrists and neurologists have noted an interesting parallel. Lewis, Amini and Lannon suggest that 'emotions possess the evanescence of a musical note' and believe this helps explain why we say our 'heartstrings were plucked' or 'that struck a chord with me' (2001, p. 44). These authors, as do some neurologists, argue that our capacity to be in tune with others happens at the level of the brain, in what they refer to as the limbic resonance (2001, p. 44).

Quantum physics, in its endless search for the smallest particle that underpins all of life, has moved beyond the atom to arrive at what is called 'string theory' (Polchinski 1998; Zwiebach 2004). While physicists explain this as the unification of quantum mechanics and general relativity, the phenomenologist cannot help but ask, 'Why choose the word "string" to describe a theory of everything that underpins life itself?' The answer lies in the metaphor. Scientists exploring the invisible aspects of spacetime underlying gravity developed what they called string theory to describe the way subatomic particles are linked and how they vibrate. In explaining this for the uninitiated and physics-challenged (for example, we two authors) the introductory texts and websites that describe these ideas for the general public explain string theory as having a parallel with a guitar string which, depending on its tension, will emit different notes and tones. Oddly, physicists seem to believe that what is emitted may best be described as flavours, as if vibration has a taste, very similar to the understandings of Australian Aboriginal people who claim to 'recognize a song by its taste' (Chatwin 1987, p. 58). In essence, at the subatomic level there appears to be something like a string that vibrates and emits into connections and formations that construct life itself. We could perhaps argue that what we seek is the parallel in social settings where the invisible vibrations underpinning sound create the unnoticed mechanisms from which healing and reconciliation eventually emerge.

The Tibetan bowl and sound suggest several components in our metaphor shift, particularly those related to directionality. The container holds a space. Circling creates moments where different places within that space are touched through a thousand points of interacting friction. The finding and coaxing of the sound, like voice, moves from circling towards inner space and has a quality characterised as deepening. Sound, again like voice, rises from touching something deeper. In rising, sound moves expansively in all directions. It touches, penetrates, surrounds and interacts with a much wider space than the original container. In sum, if sound and the bowl have parallels to voice in social healing, the underpinning metaphors have little to do with linearity. The key directional movements and spatial metaphors include these: Circling. Inward deepening. Rising expansion. Surrounding. Repetition.

Vibration and resonance

Friction, vibration and the convergence into resonance provide yet another parallel and point of inquiry. The person holding the bowl and working the stick around the rim to bring forth the sound finds rather quickly that they initially pay attention to feeling the vibration before they hear the sound. The source of the sound emerges from the friction and vibration. Broken into micro-moments the circling stick moves from one bump to the next. The travelling round and round produces thousands of stops and starts, micro-vibrations, mostly imperceptible, tiny and insignificant. Yet as they interact over and again, they give rise to sound. Sound touches. Sound is felt.

Alan Watts, one of the early practitioners who brought Buddhist thought and practice to the west experimented a good bit with different ways of approaching both the ways we know and the ways we convey our knowledge. In his book *Cloud-hidden* (1968, p. ix) he starts his discussion by indicating that he finds merit in repetition, in circling around and over a topic in order to come closer to understanding. In part this was to respond to critics who called his essays repetitious. 'My thinking spirals,' he wrote, 'it does not follow a straight line...besides what I mean by understanding is not simple verbal comprehension – it is feeling it in your bones' (Watts 1968, p. ix). The notion that spiralling may in fact be congruent with the way social change happens we find described by Beck and Cowan (2006). They characterise multidirectional movement as something akin to a rising circular staircase: it goes round yet permits one to move back and forth between potential levels. We find something quite close to this in individuals and communities who are seeking to penetrate the unspeakable. They circle over and again through the questions that have no answer, up and down as if on a staircase that rises from lived experience without words, yet requires one to continuously navigate the lived moment. People experience and feel things that have no name or sound. Yet they feel it in their bones. In the words of sacred text and those chosen by Maria's brother-in-law when he first discovered the bones in the coffee field, the 'blood calls out'. This image of friction, of vibration, touches and captures

The Tibetan singing bowl 99

the impulse of voice in social healing: the long, circling journey to feel again, to feel it in your bones and to name what rises from the vibration.

On another level it is interesting to note that on this circling journey there is not one special bump or vibration that on its own produces the rise of sound and resonance. In other words, efforts to rationally locate a particular moment, bump or micro-vibration as *the* leverage point, *the* technique, *the* key or *the* explanatory insight appear not only futile but perhaps wrong-headed. The metaphor of the circling and sound requires us to see the system as a whole, rather than to focus on the analytical particularity that somehow holds the key. Resonance rises from the sum total interactions of the stops and starts, the bumps and micro-vibrations as space-held moment.

This notion may seem peculiar when related to peacebuilding or reconciliation, in which the effort to build knowledge has a propensity to seek technique and leverage points. Social change, when considered more systemically, may in fact approximate the metaphoric structure of the singing bowl. After years of research Andrew Mack (2005) in the *Human security report* suggested something of a parallel. His research, based on the composite data gathered from the most comprehensive peace research centres over several decades, indicated that a more peaceful coexistence was emerging, though it was not always perceived as such in a world that tends to focus on crises and to sensationalise conflicts. In two short sentences the report suggested: 'Not one of the peacebuilding and conflict prevention programs on its own had much of an impact on global security in this period. Taken together, however, their effect has been profound' (Mack 2005, p. 9).

While sound can be produced with a single tap on the side of the bowl, this sound does not have the same effect as the resonance rising from the natural frequency of the circling stick. There appears to be no easy shortcut to *feel* the sound rising from circling the bowl's rim. Paradoxically, once it emerges, the sound does not sustain itself beyond that particular iteration. It is as if resonance requires attention, circling and a repetitious nurturing. The sound rising represents a spacemoment rather than a result or even a process. This may well parallel our discussion on ritual, ceremony and spiritual inquiry. These endeavours, among the most significant in the human search for meaning, are lifelong, continuously coaxed and re-coaxed, spaces and places sought over and again. Indigenous people, like the Lakota and Navajo, drum in circles. Muslims pray five times a day, and fast for an extended period that is repeated each year. Christians gather for prayer and worship each Sunday morning, singing over and again familiar tunes. Jewish faithful physically rock back and forth as they repeat sacred texts. Buddhists follow the sound of a bell or a bowl towards and into mindfulness. While each practice may vary in form, the metaphoric structure suggests positive growth rising from repetitiousness as iterative acts that must feel, deepen and repeat. But is this not true for many of our most treasured endeavours? From spiritual growth to healing, from citizenship to democracy, from negotiation to peace and reconciliation, while we have tended to conceptualise these as linear processes leading to end products for analytical purposes, they are in fact circular and repetitive. Towards the end of her lengthy study of the Guatemalan peace process, Susanne Jonas concludes that beyond negotiation 'long-range peace processes are largely about constructing citizenship' (Jonas 2000, p. 234). In the same conclusion she quotes a comment by a prominent Guatemalan reflecting on the nature of their events: 'The peace process,' he said, 'will have to be invented over and over again' (Jonas 2000, p. 244).

Container

As described briefly, the image of the bowl provides a context, a 'container' within which the vibrations and resonance emerge. This guiding metaphor shifts our attention towards a space that provides context and that surrounds or holds the interaction of the vibration. We mentioned earlier that this image creates several of the directional insights, among them the context for the circling – the movement in and towards a deepening of connection, which then rises and expands. We also noted that the sonic impulse cannot rise from a single vibration, frictional bump or iteration. It requires an interactive space that holds the frictional bumps in continuous relationship to make the resonance possible. Herein a particularly salient aspect of the metaphor *container* raises an intriguing question in reference to our suggestion that HEALING IS AURAL. Specifically, social healing as resonance does not rise from the individual. It emerges from the interaction of many vibrations, individual and collective, held within a community context. In other words, social healing and reconciliation emerge in and around the container that holds collective processes, inclusive of but significantly more than the individual's particular journey.

This idea of container has a parallel to the approach of the 'third side' described in William Ury's book of the same title (Ury 2004). In his description, the third side represents the people, networks and groups in a setting of deep conflict who refuse to be pulled into choosing one side over the other in the polarising dynamics of conflict. Rather, the third side represents the collective of people who create a third element that simultaneously is present in the conflictive context and which surrounds the conflict in order not to let it escalate into uncontrolled division and violence. The metaphor he chose to describe the combination of presence and surrounding was a container that holds the conflict. If we are to follow a sonic metaphor linked to the idea of a container holding the space within which the vibrations interact, our attention is necessarily brought back to the challenge of proximity. The container makes interaction possible to the degree that the vibrations are in a proximity that

permits interaction and the rise of touchable sound. Social healing requires containers large enough to create spaces of interaction yet close enough to be felt and heard. Block (2008, pp. 93–5) in his wonderful and practical book, *Community: the structure of belonging*, suggests that the 'small group is the unit of transformation'. He posits that belonging requires a meaningful proximity of conversation. We return to the notion that lived community experience, which permits forms of continuous and direct interaction, provides organic and real contexts for social healing.

Finally, it is worth noting that in a parallel vein Senge, Scharmer, Jaworski and Flowers (2004) chose the word *Presence* as the title of their book, a spatial metaphor to facilitate their exploration of the 'human purpose'. The book follows a series of experiential endeavours they undertook as authors to better understand how ideas, creativity and engagement of the future happen in the human community. Their wide-ranging discussions arrive at what they call the theory of the 'U' which they literally drew as a large bowl-like figure (2004, p. 225).

In broad strokes the U shape represents the movement of insight, innovation and action. The down slope moves from thinking to presencing, here used as a verb, which is touched at the deepest part of the U. The up slope, the rise, often rapid and explosive, is the movement from presencing to doing, or what they call innovation, 'familiar to entrepreneurs in all domains' (2004, p. 224). While this certainly can follow the notion of moving from head to heart described by some in the work of reconciliation (Kraybill 1995) the metaphor Senge and colleagues chose has a striking parallel to our discussion of the Tibetan bowl as a container: the touching of vibrations and the rise of sound in the natural frequency.

Let us turn for a moment from the Tibetan bowl to real world events, in particular to the story of the Boroma conference in Somalia to empirically explore a few of these suggested metaphor shifts.

A short story: the Boroma conference

In the opening section we recounted a number of stories, among them a brief depiction of the Somali peace initiative that eventually led to the Boroma conference. The initiative of the elders who set out to visit their counterparts across Somaliland provides a context for and sheds some light on our discussion. From a descriptive standpoint four characteristics stand out.

Itinerate and iterate: the walking circle of talk

The elders' process was not really a process in the western sense of conflict resolution. It was a circle. The circle was built on two key components: itineration and iteration. First, a small group of elders, which they referred to as an *ergada*, itinerated. Literally they travelled to visit other people. And second, they went back time and again. If, as was the case when fighting erupted or difficulties emerged, the travelling group was unsuccessful, then a group of women would initiate renewed contact. This happened in the case of a failed meeting of the Haber Yonis and Dhulbahante subclans (Farah 1993). The *ergada* would travel around and around again. This is the essence of circles. You go around and you do it more than once. In addition this process of travel to the local communities and subclans created a proxemics of process that brought peace within touching range. People could hear, speak and see the process. It was not distant but close to home.

Interaction

A second facet, the mode of engagement, required sustained interaction and exchange. Talk. People met, talked and talked some more. To outside eyes, the talk seemed directionless. At times it relied on oral poetry, lengthy discussion without an end or even a sense of destination. The interaction went in several directions. It seemed, ironically, to propose more talk, such as by bringing people to a larger meeting. At the same time the interaction required contextualised micro-talk that penetrated into far more specific grievances and issues related to particular localities and subclan conflicts. In other words, the talk was multidirectional and multidimensional.

Past, present and future were flip-flopped on top of each other as if there was no real distinction between them. Rituals, eating, tea, chewing qu'at late into the night were vehicles, defying the notion of a 'meeting' and certainly defying the notion of 'effective use of time'. What seemed to matter was talk. Much of the interaction was public. Most meetings were open, under the tree in the village. The purpose of the talk seemed to be to open a space for participation, providing a voice to both individuals and smaller collectives. Eventually these many moments translated into a wider collective voice.

Evocation

Talk and interaction evoked things. It evoked emotions, at times anger and justifications. It evoked grievances. It evoked a sense of responsibility. At times the purpose and style of Somali discourse, while it appears to reflect a nomadic wandering, tends to be direct and even accusatory. The purpose of talk is to evoke. Somalis, who are never denied their word, are prone to evocation. A useful lesson was learned by a number of us helping to facilitate a large meeting of diaspora-based Somalis in Toronto. Many gathered from across clans and the event seemed to begin well, but as conversation progressed accusations and demands grew. The meeting suddenly got very heated. All hell seemed to break loose because the exchange was so direct, so accusatory and inflammatory that the agenda proposed for the day could hardly be pursued. Several of us internationals tried to intervene as good facilitators but a Somali colleague pulled us aside. 'There is a proverb we have,' he said, '"Before we understand each other my spear must enter you." This means, we have to test the emotions, provoke the justification before we talk.

Don't stop us. When we are loud, direct, even angry, we are engaged. But if we go silent and separate, then violence is near.' Circling talk engages. It evokes.

Container

Of particular interest to our inquiry were the remarks of the elders in the *ergada* just setting out on their journey who felt that little that was useful was required from outsiders. Their primary message was this: watch, accompany, interpret to others, but do not interfere. Respect us. Give us time. Let the circle go on. The emphasis of interpretation was rooted in their understanding that their endeavour would take a long time and that outside intervention too often comes wrapped in agendas and time frames that offer help but which demand outcomes related to foreign understandings of purpose and results.

This poses two additional understandings about a metaphor of container. First, there is a need to respect the local communities as the context that holds the space. Second, the natural frequency, as in finding the pace at which vibrations begin to mix, rises from this context and cannot be forced by external standards or demands. What would our metaphor shift offer as a different way to understand reconciliation when applied to these processes? Interestingly, we could pose this question about two initiatives aimed at reconciliation in Somalia in the early nineties. In Addis Ababa, the international community, mostly under the auspices of the United Nations convened a series of national peace conferences. At the same time the elders we spoke to in Hargeisa were beginning their travels.

The multiple initiatives that led eventually to the Boroma conference took more than three years. The conference itself lasted more than six months, with continuous conversation. The overall cost to the international community of the three-year process that led to the six-month discussions and the great peace conference in Boroma was less than half a million US dollars. As well as the declaration of a new independent republic the conference outcomes included the formation of a parliament, a reduction in violence of remarkable proportions compared to the south, and a number of local peace initiatives between the subclans that most needed them. Though not recognised internationally, the declaration of Somaliland has endured, and while significant conflicts and issues still face the north, the people there have shown a resiliency in both building peace and controlling the levels of violence.

In roughly the same time period in neighbouring Ethiopia the peace conferences hosted by the international community, attended mostly by key militia leaders (often referred to as warlords) and their entourages lasted about two weeks each with a cost in the multiple millions of US dollars per week. The costs included hotel accommodation for both Somali nationals and internationals, flights to Addis Ababa, car convoys including Mercedes Benz vehicles to transport Somali leaders, and the logistics necessary for conducting and running an event in the halls of what was then the Organization of African Unity (OAU). In the end declarations of ceasefires were proposed and offers to form a national government emerged though neither of these came to fruition. These were, from the view of international conferences, properly facilitated meetings, run with clear agendas and with time frames for action.

These basic figures concerning time and money raise not only a question of investment but more importantly the question of what would a comparison of containers that holds these different processes suggest for our inquiry?

The series of peace conferences facilitated by the international community and held in Addis Ababa created a *container* that focused initially on militia and political leaders. This container held a 'national' process, at times called a national peace conference or a national reconciliation conference. Because of logistics organisers had to limit who could participate. How many people can fit into a single meeting inside the halls of OAU? Across the events and meetings participation did expand to include a large number and wide variety of people, though the focus clearly favoured high-level militia and political leaders. From a *sonic* understanding the container holding the reconciliation process was cast so wide and deep, with so little immediate context that the friction produced – and there was a good deal of friction – never interacted in ways that formed a rising resonance or natural frequency. Words and conversation fell into an abyss without a reverberating echo.

On the other hand, in the Boroma process the containers were far more local. Containers in plural because these were spaces created and engaged over and over again through the movement of the *ergada* travelling to talk with local communities, building local conversation. Initiated and held by known and recognised local elders and women, the containers created direct, accessible and contextualised spaces. Little by little, going round and round, the local containers gave way to a larger one that, while still focused regionally, was able to hold thousands of participants. The space was close enough for the frictional vibrations to interact in ways that produced a rising natural frequency and resonance, culminating in the declaration of the Republic of Somaliland. At the same time the rising natural frequency and resonance had the capacity to circle back into smaller containers that addressed local cross-clan issues and conflicts. The containers were built around a number of key components. These all had significant connection to spatial and circular metaphors: itinerate, iterate, interact and evoke. The process required walking to local communities and talking, and both happened over and over again. At first glance this may appear highly idiosyncratic of a nomadic culture.

Ten years later the international community followed the intriguing developments of the Truth and Reconciliation Commission (TRC) in South Africa. A country with a much higher profile and international stake, the events far more documented, filmed and published. Many who study truth commissions place particular emphasis on the inventiveness of the South African TRC in creating an exchange of amnesty for truth as a means of engaging perpetrators in a public process. A different aspect of the process stands out from the aural metaphors. It was as if, on an opposite side of the continent, an *ergada* of another sort had been constructed. Important recognised elders began to itinerate. Conversation as had never before been heard emerged into the public arena. The circle began. It moved towards more local accessibility. It evoked. People touched it. They felt the vibrations. The process came close to their homes, close enough for the people to listen and have a voice. Perhaps the most significant differences between Somaliland and the South African TRC were issues of time and budget. In South Africa the process was not given time or a budget for multiple iterations; there was only one visit per location. And there seemed to be a lot more international presence, interest and support.

Conclusion

In this chapter we proposed the challenge of exploring at greater depth an example of a metaphor shift not dependent on linear modalities of framing social healing. We approached this by taking the image and function of a Tibetan singing bowl and paying careful attention to ways in which sound and container provide insight into social processes. Our bridge to real-life processes returned to the story of the Boroma conference in the early nineties and the early initiatives of women and elders who created a series of community-based conversations. We suggested it is possible to follow a sonic explanation, in terms of vibration, resonance, echo and containers that create alternative ways of seeking to understand both the nature and quality of social healing. Several key points emerge from this discussion.

When approached using a sonic-based metaphor, social change

and healing rise in a context of interactive moments that create vibration from which sound emerges. Metaphoric use of voice relates to the internal notion of 'finding one's voice' and to the externalised voice as meaningful conversation whereby communities affected by violence feel they are listened to and understood.

The Tibetan bowl offers images of how this works with reference to sound. A circling stick creates thousands of moments of friction that produce vibrations. Circling here can be understood as providing space and moments of interaction continuously, a necessary aspect of giving rise to sound, and it can be contrasted with the notion that going in circles is not going anywhere or that it is done exclusively for sequential purposes.

Interactive vibrations give rise to a spacemoment of natural frequency when they resonate in a sharp rise of sound. Vibrations evoke the sonic experience of being touched by and feeling sound, not just hearing it and they parallel the phenomenon of the unspeakable in which something is experienced and felt but cannot easily be expressed in words.

The Tibetan bowl helps us visualise the sonic nature of sound that moves simultaneously in more than one direction. The key directions include the movement to deepen, to expand and to surround. Each of these provides a directional metaphor relevant to processes of healing and reconciliation but which contrasts significantly with linear and sequential modalities.

Finally, the bowl provided the metaphoric image of a container that holds the space of interactive vibration and from which an expansive sound emerges that rings and echoes well beyond the originating spacemoment. A container that has sonic capacity suggests a space that permits vibrations to interact in ways that the natural frequency can emerge. As metaphor this suggested a proximity of interactive vibrations characterised by accessibility in local contexts and significant relevant conversation.

Following the lead of the sonic-based metaphor and bowl we applied this to processes that led to the Boroma conference. We noted that the women and elders who helped create and then held the spaces needed for the conference had significant parallels with the singing bowl. The key characteristics included itineration, iteration, public interactive space and evoking conversation. They travelled to local communities. They returned over and again. They created and evoked conversation. Circularity fostered a deepening conversation that eventually led to moments of resonance.

This discussion suggests the metaphor shift from a line to sound creates different ways to think about the nature of social healing. The sonic-based metaphor suggests social healing is about deepening and expanding space rather than a process of phases and sequential steps leading to an end product. It emphasises a dynamic that pursues the touching of voice and the interplay of voices and echo, or what we might describe as seeking how resonance rises and recedes, rises and recedes. It poses an intriguing dilemma of finding the *containers* that might best hold the interplay of friction, vibration and sound in a given locality.

In many regards healing ultimately is about restoration of voice, both for individuals and communities. Social healing requires that the voices interact, interplay and, in the ideal of ideals, give rise to moments of resonance, then repeat again. From this view and metaphorically speaking, social healing is made up of spacemoments of resonance, voices touching voices in a common space. The natural frequency we noted is not something that, once produced, sustains itself indefinitely. It must be nurtured and coaxed, over and again. Social healing not only has a pace that must reflect the people and contexts in which it emerges – the natural frequency cannot be forced by outside notions of frequency – but it must also be attended to over time.

CHAPTER 8

Following the healing muse

VAN MORRISON AND THE INARTICULATE SPEECH OF THE HEART

Introduction

We opened this book with the words of the poet Pinsky who addressed the paradox of our attempts to find words for experiences that defy them. Hayner's (2002) title *Unspeakable truths* shows a similar concern. It has a distinct parallel with the work of many authors who struggle with the unavoidable fact that no words or programs will adequately express or redress the experience of violence. As Minow (1998, p. 24) suggested, collective violence produces the 'imperative for people to render as truthful an account as documents and testimonials will allow, *without giving in to the temptations of closure* [our italics], because that would avoid what remains inevitably indeterminate, elusive, and inexplicable about collective horrors'. She goes on to note the important antidote – making every effort to 'introduce individual memories and individual voices in a field dominated by political decisions and administrative decrees'.

The admission alluded to here in 'political decisions and administrative decrees' is simply the overwhelming challenge that words are inadequate to address those ineffable aspects of experience. Collective violence foists upon us lived experience never fully understood, much less captured in the spoken word. The primal howl – *Why?* – remains permanently a cry. Unanswered. As singer-songwriter Van Morrison titled his album, we find ourselves in the terrain of the *inarticulate speech of the heart*.

In this chapter we face a similar paradox: through the limitations of the written word, the medium of these pages, we will enter the experience of music and, in particular, one musician's effort to explore spaces of healing. Based on sound, vibration and rhythm, song and music provide a very different kind of medium and metaphor by which to explore healing. They are not reliant on linear modalities of making sense of things. We first feel music and only subsequently attach rational explication to the feeling. Music touches the human experience. It resides in an emotional memory that interacts sometimes in unexpected ways with the cognitive memory. Neuroscientists tell us that the brain holds music and sound in locations that deal with memory, perception and meaning in ways that are quite different to other modalities of human interaction and speech (Edelman 1989; Levitin 2006; Sacks 2007; Storr 1992). To investigate this, medical scientists, for example, have conducted studies of what people remember while under anaesthesia. While anaesthesia holds most of our faculties and senses temporarily in check, Gaynor cites Linda Rodgers's research that the 'auditory pathway, unlike all other sensory systems, has an extra relay. Auditory fibers are not affected by anesthetics, so they continue to transmit sound. Simply stated: We never stop hearing' (Gaynor 1999, p. 85). He further notes that sound and vibration interact in a holistic manner with the body. 'If we accept that sound is vibration, and we know that vibration touches every part of our physical being, then we understand that sound is "heard" not only through our ears but through every cell in our body' (Gaynor 1999, p. 17). When we approach music and sound, we are dealing with a phenomenon that penetrates the human experience, sonically and physically, in ways that go beyond mere words.

The exploration in this chapter poses a series of challenges. While music is universal, tastes and familiarity with music and songs vary tremendously across individuals and cultural groups. Needless to say, my exploration of Van Morrison's music will not likely speak to everyone in the same way I experienced his work. Our purpose is to seek reference points within the work of this artist to help us open up and understand the broader metaphoric themes of this book: healing as processes of locating oneself, finding home and touching voice.

This exploration has a personal touchstone. My most intense experience with Morrison's music came in the year following the car accident described in Chapter 6. While physically I had to wait for my ribs and breathing to find their natural location and rhythms, little by little I recognised that spiritually a similar healing process was underway. In a sabbatical year following the accident our family relocated to the mountains of Colorado, a move that revealed unexpected gifts in both forms of healing. I thought I would pursue a major new academic book. I even had an outline and title. I never came close. Instead, I spent time lost in thought in the woods, and most of my writing time under the tutelage of a poet and penning a novel about a disaffected mediator drawn reluctantly back into an international crisis in Central America who struggled with whether most of his life work had been for naught. Walks in the forest to rebuild lungs and legs brought the rawness of high mountain life and beauty into sight and touch. However, a decade later, my most intense memories of that time have sonic connections, particularly to the music of Van Morrison, whose life work I collected in the course of that year. I can still feel the sun pouring down while I sat on a wooden porch, my heart soaring to 'Whenever God shines His light'. I remember listening to the lines of 'Moondance' while watching the stars in October night skies, stars that appeared so close you could touch them. I remember coming back from a walk into the mountains and listening to lines from 'Alan Watts blues' and its search for the space to recuperate where the singer finds himself high among the clouds and beyond the reach of the world. In the intervening decade questions have kept rolling in my head: Why did I experience a sense of healing through Morrison's music? What exactly happens in and through his music that creates this impact? Is it possible that interaction with this music will suggest metaphors that underpin the journey towards healing?

Van Morrison was born in Belfast in 1945 and grew up in a working-class Protestant neighbourhood. He attributes his musical interests to an unusually wide-ranging set of 45s and LPs his father collected of American blues, gospel and country music, coupled with the mix of traditional Irish, skiffle and what was soon to become the early years of the Irish rock and roll scene. From Mahalia Jackson to Ray Charles, Hank Williams and Woody Guthrie to Debussy, Morrison's tastes and appreciation were far more eclectic than those of many of his contemporaries and they affected his interests and writing over the years. Numerous biographers mention this variety and influence in Morrison's early exposure and in particular highlight the impact of blues greats Leadbelly and Jelly Roll Morton (Heylin 2003; Hinton 2000; Turner 1993). His first instruments were saxophone and guitar and by his early teen years he was in and out of several local bands in Belfast. This experience led to paying jobs by his mid-teenage years. He first started songwriting in those years and has continued to do so throughout his career. At the time of this writing he had released more than 35 albums with hundreds of songs.

As a singer-songwriter Van Morrison has displayed remarkable staying power across five decades of contemporary music. He has a love–hate relationship with the business world of music and does not write songs with the intention that they become top 40 hits, though some have become just that. He is best known for an adventuresome eclectic style that crosses blues, jazz, rock, country and folk music. Turner (1993, p. 177) noted as far back as the early nineties that his position as an '...influential singer-songwriter is assured. He has created one of the most critically acclaimed albums [*Astral weeks*] of the rock era, has inspired another generation of musicians (Bono of U2, Elvis Costello, Bruce Springsteen, to name but three)...' To explore the vast richness and sheer volume of music Morrison has produced would go well beyond the scope of our inquiry. We will focus specifically on his continual effort to link spirituality and music, to link the inner and the outer journey, and on the understandings we may glean from one artist's lifelong struggle to reach into those difficult spaces of healing in the human experience.

In writing this chapter I face the daunting challenge of how to engage both the initiated and those totally unfamiliar with Van Morrison in my exploration. It feels like navigating a narrow pathway with rather threatening ditches on each side. One ditch is inhabited by rock and roll geniuses, and critics and fans of Van Morrison who will take issue with every observation I make, arguing that I should go deeper and have a better understanding of the music and its meaning. I have no particular expertise in music, be it folk, rock and roll, or jazz. I am not a musicologist and am not accustomed to writing in a style squared and set for the music scene. In the other ditch live those who know little of Van's music but are keenly interested in the themes this book explores and who will beg for fewer references to his music and more concrete applications to the real-life processes of healing and reconciliation. The narrow pathway then arrives at a cliff edge with the potential for a fall into thin air: a conversation with a non-existent partner, Van Morrison himself.

In pursuit of the Muse

At the time of writing there exist seven major biographies of Van Morrison.[1] They all cover the same chronologies of Morrison's bands, his phases and his discography, though each biographer has their own nuances and their own opinions. Some of these biographies are an exposé of Van's personal weaknesses; others are a glorification of his gifts. Morrison has always held biographers at arm's length. His response to their requests for explanations of his songs is, literally, 'Let the music speak'. In interviews he repeatedly says that he is not capable of putting into words what his music means, where it comes from exactly, or what significance it may have with reference to themes like healing. 'Music is what I'm saying,' Morrison says in an interview with Hinton, who quotes Morrison on the whole point of what he is trying to do through music: 'to make people listen to *themselves*' (Hinton 2000, p. 232) [italics original]. For Morrison music is the medium, the message and the messenger. So I propose to take him at his word, because the most I can do in an endeavour as unusual as this – searching through the experience of music for metaphors about the nature of healing and reconciliation – is to pursue and engage the Muse, the creative impulse and the imaginative spirit that calls to the artist and inhabits the art.

The Muse. This is precisely the term used by Wole Soyinka (1999) in his short set of essays on memory, forgiveness and reconciliation. He ends the book by recounting a story of the mystical power of the aged African balafon (a type of xylophone) that ended a war. As Soyinka wanders through the story about the visit of the Muse he speculates on forgiveness, mercy and generosity, which have always been the great gift of Africa, above all other continents and peoples. But how does one create a dialogue with a Muse? Van says frankly that writing music comes from beyond and within. He simply must make music and follow the inspiration, the Muse. In Greek mythology the Muse is one of the nine daughters of Zeus and Mnemosyne, the goddess who calls forth the capacity to remember and inspires people to creativity. The Muse is the goddess of *memory and the creative arts*. My proposal does not pursue a direct dialogue with Van Morrison the person, but rather with Van the Muse, the spirit that inhabits the music, and in so doing explores why his music touches people in ways they experience as conducive to healing. Such an exploration requires that we visit the music and explore what it appeals to, the lands it inhabits in our human experience, the metaphors it suggests.

The meditative songs

From Morrison's vast music production our purpose is best served by exploring what I call his 'meditative' songs. In an effort to understand healing and the spiritual quality of his own experiences Morrison produced a series of songs that have similarity of structure and purpose. During a period of his writing, he referred to these songs and even whole albums as intentionally oriented towards creating a space for meditation. He wrote and performed the song 'In the garden', for example, in a way that takes the listener 'through a definite meditation process' and similarly he approached 'Cyprus Avenue' to 'build it up to a point where we could go into meditation' (Hinton 2000, p. 255).

The songs that most fit the meditative description started with the album *Astral weeks* (produced in 1968), though perhaps more representative are those that appeared in the mid-eighties when he was making explicit efforts to explore a deeper spirituality and healing. At the time he was reading books like Cyril Scott's *Music: its secret influence throughout the ages* (1933) and he even co-sponsored an academic conference in London on the power of music to change social consciousness. Notable from the years 1983 to 1991 are four songs: 'Got to go back', 'In the garden', 'Take me back' and 'Hymns to the silence'.

The songs follow a common structure. They open quietly, with a slow rhythm, and usually one lead instrument stands clearly as a solo line mimicking a voice, like the guitar line in 'Take me back' or the mournful oboe that leads in 'Got to go back'. Morrison's voice is embedded in these musical preludes and settles into place with a moan, a murmur, a spoken but incomplete phrase. In 'Got to go back' he utters an 'Oh yeah'. In 'Hymns to the silence', as if signalling that singer and listener are approaching a threshold, that a borderland rife with uncertainty and risk is about to be breached, the murmur of 'get the feelin', oh yeah' rises.

The simplicity of the prelude leads from these quiet beginnings into crescendos, sometimes multiple crescendos where the lyrics loop incessantly around a precious few words, scat-like repetitious iterations, sometimes numbingly repeated. 'Take me back', a nine-minute song, contains significant middle portions where over and over again the key words are repeated alone or in phrases. Reflecting the title, the repetitions sound as if both singer and listener are literally trying to travel back, reaching back through the utterances as if it were possible by way of the chant to arrive at and be in a place and time where the singer did not have difficulty making sense of the world and had a greater capacity to simply understand what he found around him. Beyond nostalgia the iterations search for a pathway to recover innocence and wonder, the locating of a long-lost sacred place.

Near the three-quarter point the songs begin to cascade from the crescendos down into slower, deeper pools that circle yet again around the key repetitions until they reach a silence. In the case of several songs, in particular 'Hymns to the silence', the song arrives at a complete silence that foreshadows not the end of the song, but an intentional space that holds the active presence of being *in the silence*. Morrison consistently suggests through his music that he is able to physically feel the space silence creates, a depth that appeals to human experience beyond words or listening. His meditative songs bathe the listener in the experience of feeling surrounded by the silence. In some songs and spoken pieces he asks, over and again, whether the listener can also feel this silent space.

The song 'Alan Watts blues' has an intriguing background related to this feeling. Morrison reads widely and eclectically. This is particularly true of his interests in religion, spirituality, healing and music. At times in his songs he will reference what has influenced him through books and reading. Alice Bailey's (1950) ideas in *Glamour – a world problem* appear in 'Dweller on the threshold', Jack Kerouac and Mezz Mezzrow show up 'On Hyndford Street', and as a strong counteraction to the control mechanisms of Scientology he coined the title of his album *No guru, no method, no teacher.*

Alan Watts was a teacher, philosopher and a student of comparative religions. He is widely considered a key author in interpreting Buddhism in the context of the west. One of his books, *Cloud-hidden, whereabouts unknown: a mountain journal* (1968), includes journal writings from extended periods he spent in the mountains of California. He begins the book citing a few lines from the *Chia tao* titled 'Searching for the hermit in vain' – a short poem that describes a searcher asking for the whereabouts of the Master, who it turns out is exactly as the title of Watts's book: cloud-hidden, whereabouts unknown.

In 'Alan Watts blues' Morrison sings of a similar need. He is tired of the dog-eat-dog world of commercial music and the endless effort to build empires and control. In the song he travels to the mountains, a retreat where, in solitude and lost in thick fog, he can find himself and a sense of purpose and meaning.

In the preface of Watts's 1968 book we find an explanation of his approach to the writing which he did when he was living at a cottage in the foothills of Mt Tamalpais just outside San Francisco and it has a significant parallel to Morrison's music. As noted earlier in his opening pages Watts (1968, p. ix) says he thinks 'in spirals.' He goes on to say about his teaching that 'most students do not understand one's ideas unless they are repeated – under differing analogies or in varying forms and words, as a musician constructs variations on a theme. Besides, what I mean by understanding is not simply verbal comprehension: *It is feeling it in your bones*' [our italics]. This feeling in the bones, a vibration-based sense of sound and repetition seems to be precisely what Morrison meant by feeling the silence.

Through these songs the listener experiences the music almost as lullaby, as a sense of being surrounded and held. Boyce-Tillman (2000) has noted this capacity of music to function 'like a container'. 'Music,' she writes, 'is a way of holding.' A lullaby, for example, holds a person though it 'can be sung without physically touching the person'... yet the 'song is a vehicle of transmission of love' (2000, p. 54). Music, sound and vibration, as so well described by Gaynor, touch every cell in the body. In essence, music permits feeling things not always easily conveyed through the spoken word, the touching of a level of experience not conveyed by explanation or conversation. Sound penetrates to a deeper level and can create the sensation of feeling held and surrounded.

In many regards Morrison's songwriting tries to reach this level beyond words. He once noted that he drew inspiration from a piece by George Bernard Shaw in which he talks about 'the idea of communicating with as little articulation as possible, at the same time being emotionally articulate'. His effort led to the album titled *The inarticulate speech of the heart* (Heylin 2003, p. 377). As with the impact of Gregorian chants, the repeated hums of single-syllable Buddhist and Sanskrit mantras, or the appeal of West African *jembes* and Native American drum chants, the singer and listener feel the vibration and sound with a magnet-like quality of being drawn in deeper. Morrison's spoken and sung iterations, reminiscent of John Coltrane and Miles Davis on their respective saxophone and trumpet, circle over and again, each with a touchstone melody, yet infinite.

A number of biographers draw attention to the fact that Morrison's first instrument and love was always the saxophone, which appears in one form or another on most of his albums. DeWitt (1983, p. 58) notes that 'Van's unique voice is similar to a saxophone and he has a way of interpreting songs that no other artist possesses'. His voice, intonations and phrasing imitate the instrument, as if he is hearing and following the unspoken yet perhaps deeper resonance of the music. On the rare occasion when Morrison uses the word meditation in the title of a song – 'Evening meditation' – only a hum and occasional moans follow the melody line of the instruments.

Turner (1993, pp. 111–12) suggests the exploration into the inarticulate speech of the heart dates to early albums, most notably to the multiple recordings of 'Listen to the lion'. The song 'Lion' was first recorded on the album *St Dominic's preview*. Turner writes: 'Van continued his experimentation with vocal sounds that began as words but then splintered into grunts, moans and yelps as he sought after a language beyond words. He pictured a lion, deep in his soul, that had to be heard, and his singing was his way of turning into the primal roar.' The various recordings of the song, in studio and live, provide an intriguing insight into the difficulty of penetrating the deeper aspects where healing may be lodged. Considered lengthy for rock songs that are played on air, recordings of 'Listen to the lion' last between 8 and 11 minutes. The song is built around simple mantra-like lyrics based on six lines that speak of the lion inside, the search for soul and the source of love. The words are not particularly noteworthy on their own, but when phrased and repeated in jazz-like mode, the listener is again drawn towards the deeper source. Turner (1993, p. 178) suggests that 'as a singer Van's natural talent is in the expressive quality of his voice – the unexpected blackness of the sound that emanates from this small Ulsterman – and also his phrasing. The poetry he creates is not to do with order of the words on the page but arises from his skill in exploring resonances.'

Three phenomena merit attention in the meditative songs as points of reference for our study: the place of repetition in healing; the centrality of sound, nature and beauty in locating a sense of humanity and self; and a sonic approach to the omnipresent challenge of time in processes of healing.

Repetition: finding the space of wonder
Morrison's penchant for lyrical repetition started in his youth and early experiences with trance-like moments. Biographers note how Van, like several other contemporaries including Bob Dylan, had intense moments of transcendental wonder when growing up. For Morrison these started at an early age, had nothing to do with hallucinogenic drugs and inspired his search through music to understand experiences he had great difficulty explaining.

Turner (1993, p. 102) writes in his interview with Van about the song 'And it stoned me', '... it has often been regarded as an example of nature mysticism, but as Van explained to me in 1985, it was written about an experience he had as a child. "I suppose I was about twelve years old," he said. "We used to go to a place called Ballystockert to fish. We stopped in the village on the way up to the place and I went in to this little stone house, and there was an old man there with a dark weather-beaten skin, and we asked him if had any water.

'"He gave us some water which he said he'd got from the stream. We drank and everything seemed to stop for me. Time stood still. For five minutes everything was really quiet and I was in this other dimension. That's what the song is about."' Later Morrison discovered his experiences and lyrics brought him to poets like Blake, Wordsworth and Yeats, who in varying degrees had similar experiences throughout their lives (Hinton 2000, p. 24).

To approach and open this space of childhood wonder Morrison employs a scat-like repetitious phrasing. Lester Bangs (Hinton 2000, p. 100) referred to his style as incantation, citing the song 'Madame George' in which Morrison basically sings three rhyming words 'twenty times in twirling melodic arc so beautiful it steals your breath'. We find the repetition in numerous songs, particularly those that aim to go back and find their way to a more sacred space, a time when Morrison recovered his sense of being like a child again. In the song 'Take me back' for example, he repeats some combination of the phrase 'take me back' dozens and dozens of times in a hybrid form between spoken-chant and melody. 'Van is obsessed with how much musical or verbal information he can compress into a small space', writes Hinton (2000, p. 100), 'and, almost conversely, how far he can spread one note, word, sound or picture. Here is an album [*Astral weeks*] about people stunned by life, completely overwhelmed, stalled in their skins, granted one moment of vision and a whole lifetime with which to deal with it.'

This poses an intriguing question for our inquiry: How do we explain the apparent connection to healing between circling and repetition that appears not only in music like Van Morrison's but also in therapeutic processes generally?

The most dominant view of repetition related to therapeutic healing, of getting people to recall and retell experiences, focuses on returning to important though often subconsciously submerged events in the past that damaged and violated life. These events occupy a place of prestige and power in the landscape of a person's and/or a group's narrative that provides markers which form and sustain identity and meaning. If conscious and more explicitly embedded in personal and collective memory these function as the markers of chosen trauma or, conversely, of chosen glories (Volkan 1977). For many people, however, significant events of the past submerge into a subconscious memory. The memories then play out symptomatically through indirect and at times dysfunctional and self-destructive expressions. In large part the therapeutic process orients itself towards the process of identifying these key landmarkers and events. The retrospective telling and retelling of the event or events, a creative act that simultaneously links perception, memory and inventiveness – for none of us can re-create past events without some dose of storytelling creativity – provides opportunity to reframe, that is, to rename the experience. By so doing we create new or at least nuanced variations of meaning that no longer have the power to unilaterally and negatively define our existence, significance and life.

From this perspective, therapeutic repetition suggests that in the retelling the experienced traumatic event becomes more commonplace in a person's life story. Repetition, if you will, flattens the significance of a particular event, removing the sharpness of the trauma as *the* defining event and lens that gives meaning to or, as may be the case takes constructive lifegiving meaning away from, one's life story – past, present and future. In so doing repetition creates the platform from which a new kind of power emerges to help a person rediscover, redefine and rename their life story.

Boyce-Tillman explains this as a natural aspect of music. 'The process of re-forming the person,' she writes, 'the acceptance of the more hidden aspects of the personality, leads to a "re-membering" of the personality. The newly accessed areas are now reintegrated to form new patterns, more reflective of the re-formed person... music has certain characteristics that enable it to play a real part in the processes of integration and de-integration' (Boyce-Tillman 2000, p. 50).

Therapeutic explanations, more based on spoken word, seem to place emphasis on the process of lifting out the event, talking about it, and then setting it aside. We must take note that within this view 'repetition' focuses on the past primarily as a landscape filled with beasts to be named and released. 'Letting go of the past in order to move in a healthier fashion into the future', though perhaps not expressed explicitly, represents the purpose sine qua non of repetition in therapy and captures its metaphoric purpose: repeat to release in order to attain growth and wellbeing.

This linear explanation of repetition may, however, miss the deeper metaphor of what happens in the process as seen from the heart of the artistic process. Seen as art, repetition creates an inner sense of being an 'author', a 'poet', a 'composer'. It may represent the process of touching the 'being' human again – re-creating life and location by naming things. The notion that repetition facilitates the entry into a space pregnant with the potential to rename more closely approximates the possibility that the key transformation underway is one that permits people who carry trauma to transcend the weight of being an object at the mercy of events, and permits them to enter the *essential space* of becoming artists. To use Van Morrison's words: 'Poetic champions compose.'

The direction and understanding of repetition that emerges in Van Morrison's music – more akin to Gregorian chants, mantras and native drumming, to mention a few – creates a much different metaphor that opens the space to recover childhood curiosity. To be child-like captures a quality of seeing everything as new, unknown, in need of exploration and names. In the meditative songs this return to the child-like innocence provides Morrison with a doorway to find 'places' in which it is possible to recover a sense of wonder and understanding. His return to childhood locations, from Cyprus Avenue in Belfast, to a schoolroom in Orangefield, or the early experiences of a garden after a summer rain, create a sense of transcendence, a return to the moment of innocence and potential. In the song 'Got to go back' he returns to classroom daydreaming and makes reference to the music of Ray Charles, an early influence on his music, concluding that this was a time when he believed in his soul. This sense of feeling safe, in touch with the soul, carried over into recognising, as he states it, that he could get in touch with his internal capacity for love, and in this act experience a sense of renewal and sustenance. Recuperating the innocence of childhood not only *locates* the singer into a time and place with capacity to infuse a restored sense of self, but provides the door that opens into a space for healing. Intriguingly, from the classroom the singer moves to the title of the song, imploring the listener that we have 'got to go back' with the paradox that the past holds both healing and the capacity to recuperate the dream. We find here the way in which sound provides a moment and space that simultaneously holds the past and future.

Notably in these songs we find the extensive use of incantation-like lyrics and repetition, circling over and again a few phrases, as if the singer seeks something deeper, beyond the words. In essence, repetition, not the content of the words, is what seems to re-create the opening to experience wonder. Atkinson (2002, p. 250) found this in her work with Australian Aboriginal transgenerational trauma; she referred to this as a 'primary humanness'. She wrote, 'healing was shown to be transformational as people entered an evolutionary process of reclaiming the natural creativity of childhood' (Atkinson 2002, p. 250). Repetition embraces the feeling that something sacred exists in the innocence and trust that was at one point experienced, and which must be found again, to be brought back into a present so overwhelmed with cynicism and fear. Morrison never attempts to put the past behind him, rather he seeks to enter it as a way to recuperate the soulful good. The incantations serve as a gateway opening to a meditative space to touch something positive, once experienced but lost and now again desired. Over and over again Morrison understands this as a sacred space touched in and through the music and repetitive nature of his lyrical incantations that ultimately leads the singer to be in and feel the presence of the transcendental, the Divine. Circling and repetition provide a way into healing because they touch and rise from a deeper place within the soul, a comfort and acceptance of oneself, a feeling rooted, of being located and feeling close to home.

Simply, repetition opens us to the experience of feeling surrounded by unconditional love.

Comparatively with other understandings, circling and repetition do not *flatten* the trauma in order to control it, rather they create a gateway permitting one to touch a deeper sense of self, voice and the recovery of the sacred nature of life so damaged in the violations experienced. As Boyce-Tillman (2000, p. 51) suggests, music by its very nature 'allows for juxtaposition and simultaneous combination; it therefore can accommodate difference and differing degrees of unity. It allows for things to stay separate or to be recombined into new ideas. It allows for the existence of chaos in certain sections and more ordered sections at other times. As such it provides a mirror of a mature person happy with order and acknowledging the presence of chaos.'

Applied to our topics, the exploration of Morrison's music and Boyce-Tillman's description of music suggest the analogy that reconciliation and healing hold significant qualities we can only describe as circular in nature. They require repetitious and ongoing iterations, and simultaneously require people to seek order while still living with the presence of chaos. Rather than using a directional metaphor that healing follows unidirectional sequential time that leads to an end product, the journey of healing more closely approximates life itself with its thousands of experiential moments that are ongoing, simultaneously multilayered and multidirectional, moving fluidly and holding past and future.

In the programmatically oriented world of peacebuilding and development projects we have grown accustomed to metaphoric language that 'produces' things, 'takes us somewhere', and which can be conceptualised as having a 'beginning and an end' in which we 'intervene' and see our 'impacts'. These modalities of organising activity are heavily influenced by, and dependent on, metaphors of linearity, stage-based movement and control. Sound and music create the metaphoric shift wherein circularity, repetition and simultaneity become phenomena worth pursuing in their own right, precisely because of their inbuilt capacities to *deepen* and *touch* aspects of human experience that require constant nurture and exploration.

The directional metaphors of repetition, circularity and deepening have precedent in other aspects of our experience, though we tend not to connect these to the challenges of social healing and reconciliation. The Holy Sacrament or Communion within Christianity; the place of ceremony and prayers, with chant and movement in Judaism; the daily prayers and annual fasting within Islam; mantras, sound and meditation as practised daily by Buddhist seekers, all point to deepening through repetition and circling behaviours. Never understood as one-time events that propose a finality of outcome, these activities require the creation and re-creation of spacemoments that touch the deeper journey of human experience, provide meaningful location and the presence of the transcendent, qualities that capture the experience of Morrison's meditative songs.

The sonics of healing: place, beauty and nature

The meditative songs also explore the importance of place, the memory and revisiting of locations, vividly available, of the once known, and the seamless moving between the past and the present. As numerous biographers note, many of Morrison's songs return to childhood, his early memories, his longing for a sense of belonging while living far away from the land of his birth, *displaced* from Ireland in America. His themes of returning home, back to the street where he grew up, the places of childhood – these times and locations are places where he had a capacity to make sense of the world.

Several features of place merit attention. Morrison's lyrics do not create an abstract nostalgia but rather a specificity of location. His songs identify concrete remembered places: Orangefield, Cyprus Avenue, Hyndford Street, Cherry Valley, Beechie River, St Donard's Church, moth catchers in the evening, ice cream at Fuscos, playing around Mrs Kelly's lamp, and the list goes on.

Mixed with the specificity of place we find a preciseness of *sonic* references that were a part of Morrison's early years: Radio Luxembourg and Debussy, high-heeled shoes clicking on the sidewalks of Cyprus Avenue, early Sunday morning church bells, whispers of voice that reach across the river, the songs of Mahalia Jackson or Ray Charles on the shortwave. Central rather than peripheral, music creates the *soundscape* of memory. For Van Morrison, sound provides the mechanism of triangulation, the instrument by which he locates himself in space and time. Sound and song become tools that locate a person, provide a compass that makes sense of things and creates meaning.

His transcendental poetry provides a third element for location. Morrison came so naturally to his lyrics that he only later tried to figure out what his writing style and substance meant and where it came from. His songs carry a *ubiquitous presence of nature* that locates his experience, and they have a haiku-like transcendental quality. References to nature appear over and again throughout his songwriting: gardens and fields soaked by rain in the summer, afternoons sparkling in gold from the sun, enjoying the river's song or taking in a field of flowers. Referring to this, Turner (1993, p. 170) quotes Morrison reflecting on this 'mysticism in poetry. Other people call it nature poetry. Why was I writing this kind of poetry when my contemporaries weren't?

'I wanted to find out where I stood and what tradition I came from. Well, eventually, I found that the tradition I belong to is actually my own tradition. It was like getting hit over the head with a baseball bat.' He was, of course, referring to locating himself in the tradition of mystic poets such as Blake, Wordsworth and Yeats.

As an example of these features of seeking place, consider at greater length the song 'Take me back'. The songwriter begins with a walk by a river, though he is deeply perplexed and saddened by the state of the world and things – particularly suffering – that he cannot explain. This feeling of having no rational explanation for suffering leads to him cry out six times for help. The repetitions seem to go on for minutes, then suddenly he appeals to the listener's own shared memory of when, in the past (especially in childhood), the world seemed to make more sense.

These repetitions, chant-like, walking down by the river, lead into a slower and softer part of the song where his voice drops to a whisper, wavering between spoken word and singing, begging the listener to accompany him on the journey back, to find once again a sense of wonder and beauty. The journey back locates itself almost exclusively in two ways.

First, the lyrics contain nearly a dozen references to nature, day and night, and summer. These references are lifted primarily from his childhood memories around the outskirts of Belfast and the city waterfront. Second, the lyrics provoke memory within the experience of nature through sounds, particularly the songs that arrive over the radio waves, or the quiet late night gazing on the bay with the lapping of the water. By the end of 'Take me back', following the many repetitions, he settles into a space, slowing to a soft-spoken incantation that evokes a sense of eternity, zen-like, in which a single moment holds the whole of time. This moment has a divine feature for Morrison, and he capitalises the word 'Light' to indicate how the moment and the feeling provide a sensation of acceptance, love and wellbeing, in which he uses the religious language of grace and blessing.

In both the sonic and lyrical experience of this song the singer tries to locate himself, to feel again, to understand and to re-experience a sense of wonder and beauty. The location of this place through the sonic experience and repetition – to be in the presence of the *eternal now* – functions like a dose of healing to reconnect the artist with his capacity to feel and, therefore, to be more fully human.

The idea that song creates a sense of meaningful location and place is not entirely new, though is perhaps not fully explored in terms of what takes place through the phenomenology of healing. In his classic work *The songlines*, Chatwin (1987) attempts to follow and understand the Australian Aboriginal notion that meaningful location in their harsh desert environment happened through song. Wanderers, they knew the landscape, tracks and locations by singing them as they walked, creating a sonic pathway called a *songline*.

The songline creates a map, but not one that is visual like those that we see in an atlas. For Aboriginals, physical geography emerges through song, location known and experienced through the entoned vibration of sound; finding oneself sonically linked to elements around. This has a similarity to the way migrating birds use sound to locate their place and find direction or the way dolphins bounce sound off features in their underwater world to know their place. 'Aboriginal Creation myths tell of the legendary totemic beings,' Chatwin wrote, 'who had wandered over the continent in the Dreamtime, singing out the name of everything that crossed their path – birds, animals, plants, rocks, waterholes – and so singing the world into existence' (Chatwin 1987, p. 2).

In one exchange Chatwin (1987, p. 108) records a conversation he had with his colleague Arkady:

'So a musical phrase,' I said, 'is a map reference?'
'Music,' said Arkady, 'is a memory bank for finding one's way about the world.'

Through song Aboriginals locate themselves in the world and by way of music find their meaningful place. Songlines literally create a map for travel and provide a sense of location.

In our wider inquiry, this begs the basic question of whether the real impact of violence, of being *displaced* at multiple levels both physical and psychological, creates a similar challenge. Violence destroys our ability to feel human. We are lost in a landscape that has no vibration, no way to locate ourselves. At its deepest level healing functions like a metaphoric journey to find ourselves, a search to find a location with meaning in a barren landscape. This journey may in an extraordinary, though mostly unspeakable way, represent the sonic odyssey to re-touch vibrations that create bearings and make sense of our place in the world. People are trying to *feel* again. This is why we so often hear from those living through violent conflict or in its aftermath that they are trying to 'feel' like a person. To be human is to feel the basic vibration of life.

Consider yet another parallel. The song, 'Take me back', has an intriguing analogy with the description philosopher and psychologist Viktor Frankl provides in the portrayal of his own experience at the end of World War II. A Holocaust survivor, Frankl vividly recounts the experience of his long and extraordinary journey through the Nazi camps. His story speaks to many aspects of our inquiry into surviving violence and pursuing healing. Of particular relevance here are his reflections about the first days following the long-awaited but unexpectedly abrupt moment of his liberation.

Confused at first, as guards and commanders fled, Frankl and a few of his fellow detainees who had been held back to attend to patients dying from typhus suddenly found the gates of the camp thrown open and the outside world available to them without restriction. In the first hours and days, uncertain about what was happening or how to ensure their security they ventured cautiously onto a road outside the camp. It led them into a vast field of green grass and flowers but he reports, 'we had no feelings about them' (Frankl 2006, p. 88). It was as if they could see but could not attach significance to these things that represented the normality of life, of growth and beauty. The sheer ugliness of the years of inhumane violation did not permit them to feel the reality of the beauty. Some days later he recounts that he found himself alone, back in the field. It is the specificity of his story that parallels Morrison's song 'Take me back'. He recounts seeing the 'flowering meadows' and larks rising to the sky. He could hear their 'joyous song'. At one point, overwhelmed with seeing, hearing and feeling he fell to his knees and repeatedly prayed but a single sentence:

> 'I called to the Lord from my narrow prison and He answered me in the freedom of space.' How long I knelt there and repeated this sentence memory can no longer recall. But I know that on that day, in that hour, my new life started. Step for step I progressed until I became a human being (Frankl 2006, p. 89).

Frankl suggests that his journey to re-become a human being, remarkable in its profound simplicity, followed his touching a space through repetition of a simple phrase that permitted him to experience anew the nature and creation around him. Sustained violence had robbed him of the capacity to see and feel beauty. He felt in a deep sense that he had lost the capacity to be or feel human. We find here precisely the terms in which Morrison's music portrays and explores the space of recovering a sense of beauty, wonder and love.

The eternal now: temporal simultaneity

We have noted that Morrison's meditative songs focus on finding a way to reach and hold, even if only for a moment, the eternal now. The experience of living in the moment, what Morrison calls the 'eternal now', which his songs reach for, creates the soundscape he explores. It may help to explain both his search and our experience of music when we have moments in which a sound or song transports us to another place and time, when in a single moment we simultaneously experience two temporal realities. Music, and for each of us, particular songs or sounds, have this capacity: they transport us in time. Through a melody or song past emotions and feelings are re-experienced intensely in the present moment. Morrison refers to this as being 'caught', which in his case took him back to childhood memories of Belfast.

Morrison's biographers note how much his music plays with this aspect of human experience, in large part because the singer-songwriter constantly explores ways to understand his own intense childhood experiences of mysticism. Hinton (2000, p. 256), for example, writes that much of Morrison's effort to recover a sense of wonder takes him back in time: 'The present not the past is another country, and Van is in exile.' Heylin (2003, p. 188) takes the point much further, arguing that songs like 'Cyprus Avenue' create a composite of 'sketches' that are 'circular in that they begin and end in the temporal universe, with our singer still "conquered in a car seat"... rooted in the moment'. Morrison's songwriting, he suggests, moves seamlessly within the same song between the past and the present in ways that are barely noticeable to the listener. The song 'In the garden' Hinton (2000, p. 257) notes has this same quality, where 'Van recreates the trances of his youth, going into meditation in which he meets the Holy Trinity in a suburban garden, while sitting at ease with his own family'.

Sound evokes. It evokes sensations, memory and experiences

from the past as if they were present in the here and now and also, curiously, it evokes the capacity to see visions of what could be, a sensation of living forward in time. This quality to induce temporal sensations, particularly the past, is called anamnesis by those who study the impact of sound on the human experience. Augoyard and Torgue (2006, p. 21) define this term as 'an effect of reminiscence in which a past situation or atmosphere is brought back to the listener's consciousness, provoked by a particular signal or sonic context. Anamnesis, a semiotic effect, is the often involuntary revival of memory caused by listening and the evocative power of sounds.' Through song and sound we experience a sense of transportability, that is, we have moments when the past, present and future merge, when we are capable of holding at the same time a sensation of being in more than one spatial and temporal sphere.

The simultaneity of the eternal now has parallels with a variety of contemplative religious traditions.

Buddhist understanding of mindfulness entails a primary discipline of meditation that brings a person's awareness to focus fully on the present moment. Thich Nhat Hanh in his book *Being peace* (1987) connects several themes. He notes that sounds, the use of a bell in particular, signal a calling to mindfulness. He in fact refers to it as the 'bell of mindfulness' that functions like the voice 'calling us back to ourselves' (Nhat Hanh 1987, p. 145). The purpose of the sound, he suggests, requires us to 'stop' and through the stopping, to concentrate on the moment and notice what is there. Ironically, walking meditation, a practice he has developed, has the same goal. He describes this as 'walking not in order to arrive, just for the walking. The purpose is to be in the present moment and enjoy each step you make. Therefore you have to shake off all worries and anxieties, not thinking of the future, not thinking of the past, just enjoying the present moment.' He adds that taking the 'hand of a child' enhances this kind of walking. 'You walk, you make steps as if you are the happiest person on Earth' (1987, pp. 148–9).

In Christian contemplative movements the same concerns and disciplines pertain. 'Listen' is literally the first of the disciplines provided in St Benedict's guidelines for monks in which he suggests they learn to 'listen with the ear of the heart' (Szabo 2005, p. xv). In the preface to Thomas Merton's collection of poems, Kathleen Norris writes that 'the poet who is a monk lives in a way that intensifies this process, as a life pared down to its essentials encourages close attention to resonant tones of scripture and lighter notes of wind and birdsong' (Szabo 2005, p. xv). From a theological view one significant interpretation of Jesus's life was his capacity to live in the moment, to notice people and things around him that lifted the ordinary and everyday towards noticing that God was in those things, people and moments. His strongly worded critiques focused on the religious establishment who, with their insistence on proper religious expression and form, had lost the capacity to notice the presence of the Divine. His teaching, that God is found in those who are thirsty, hungry, naked or a prisoner; in other words, to notice God in those who are around you and to attend to them with love, represents an act of living in the present, the eternal now. This is precisely the primary idea conveyed in the book, *Compassion* by Nouwen, McNeill and Morrison (1983, pp. 120–1) who note that 'emptying himself' was the act by Jesus in which he 'did not cling to his divinity, but became as we are' leading to a capacity to 'be present to the suffering world here and now...'

In Morrison's music the simultaneity and seamless moving between temporal experiences provides an intriguing way to think about the challenges posed by time in reconciliation and healing. Both reconciliation and healing require a capacity to link and hold together the experience of the past which is still available in the present, while finding mechanisms to move in a healthy way towards a yet-to-be-lived future. Linear approaches to this challenge tend to see the *past* as holding the difficulties that must be laid to rest, the *present* as somehow needing to free itself from this grip of the past, and the future as something that calls to us and that we are to shape or, more narrowly, find ways to control. Time falls on a line.

But seeing time as a line emerges from an analytical construct. There are other ways time is experienced (Lederach 2005). Mbiti suggested an African understanding that moved towards 'the past that lies before us' (Mbiti 1969). Hannah Arendt (2000), for example, understood the temporal dilemma as a lived paradox. In her view humans live simultaneously in a multifaceted moment. In the aftermath of the Holocaust, struggling with the enormity of experience, she saw this as the human dilemma: we can remember the past but cannot change it; and we can imagine a future, but cannot control it. Morrison experienced this as mystery that held him for a short period of time, and to get back to that mystery was a journey only made possible though music. With reference to these time frames Morrison suggests something perhaps closer to lived experience inasmuch as all three – the past, present and future – coexist, are present and available to each other at the same time. In the song 'Got to go back' he weaves these seamlessly through a single set of phrases that form the repeated chorus. He starts with the memory of childhood then shifts to the present moment where in the repeated chorus the effort to go back holds the promise of healing and dreaming. The past and future are experienced in the moment of the present.

To use the terms we are exploring in this book, it is as if, simultaneously, survival, resiliency and flourishing are connected with memory, living and dreaming, experienced and drawn on by people in the best and worst of times, for each exists in different proportions in the lived moment. Graphically, simultaneity is not easy to convey. But Figure 3 is an example by which the present can be visualised as the space that holds the overlapping capacity to remember the past and imagine the future.

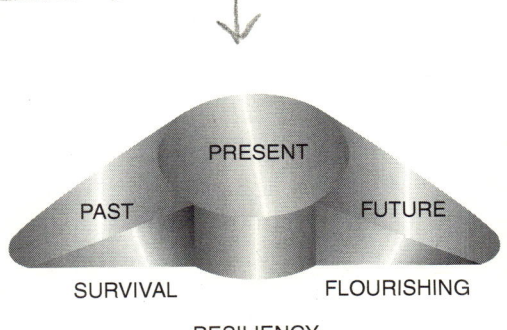

Figure 3. The simultaneity of temporal experience.

If we were to visualise temporal experience as having depth rather than sitting on a continuum, we would approximate what poet Kazim Ali (2008) in his essay 'The architecture of loneliness' described as the physical archeology of living history in cities that parallel the simultaneity of past, present and future. Writing in historic cities in Europe, he suggests we literally walk atop history and at times its ancient walls rise to surround us. The image he creates suggests time as depth and expansion, available in three lived dimensions.

Simultaneity of temporal experience approximates the theory of neural Darwinism as proposed by Nobel Laureate Gerald Edelman. In several of his recent books Edelman explains how studies of the brain describe the processes by which humans handle and make sense of time. In the provocatively titled *The remembered present* (1989) he provides an in-depth exploration of how the brain creates consciousness. To summarise – paraphrasing here in layman's terms – his basic theoretical argument is that the 'remembered present' is a fleeting moment that takes in immediate circumstances through a series of rapidly moving scenarios that are perceived, held momentarily, captured, sorted and interpreted. For animals, the remembered present is their exclusive temporal experience. In this moment a process of selective association happens in which an extraordinary number of variables about their immediate environment are perceived, sorted, associations created and meaning derived. This remembered present functions as a 'first nature' the near-instantaneous assessment of a moment.

In his next book, *Second nature*, Edelman (2006, p. 100) suggests that the capacity to be conscious of this first nature, that is, the ability to reflect on it, distinguishes the human brain from that of most animals: we are capable of simultaneously holding in the moment of lived experience a longer term memory that retains past experience, the capacity to plan into the future, and a concept of who we are in our context. In his words: 'an animal with primary consciousness lacks an explicit narrative concept of the past, cannot extensively plan a scenario for a distant future, and has no nameable social self' (Edelman 2006, p. 38). We notice again the human act of 'naming'; the artistic act of creativity suggested here is what defines consciousness and defines us as human beings.

Edelman argues that while most of us tend to have a Heraclitean view of time – we view and talk about time as a river-like movement from past to present to future – this is an illusion. He writes: 'in a physical sense, only the present exists. The integration of core states leading to conscious states takes a finite time of two hundred to five hundred milliseconds. This time period is the lower limit of the remembered present' (2006, p. 93). Higher order consciousness of the kind we experience as humans adds the capacity to notice, experience and reflect on the duration of time and to create meaning around that experience in far more expansive temporal frames of reference. This we construct as falling into past, present and future. However, curiously, the three temporal phenomena coexist literally in the present. As part of making sense of things we are constantly engaged in creativity by the very mechanisms through which we see patterns, make associations and attach meaning. In Edelman's words, 'every act of perception is to some degree an act of creation, and every act of memory is to some degree an act of imagination' (2006, p. 100). In other words, history requires a creative act and imagination a memory.

This can perhaps be illustrated through an extreme case offered by Oliver Sacks in his book *Musicophilia*. Sacks tells the story of Clive Wearing who, following a devastating brain infection, was left with a form of amnesia that permitted him a memory span of only a few seconds. In writing of the experience his wife Deborah noted that nearly every blink of his eye meant the loss of memory of what had just happened, leaving him 'deprived of consciousness and life itself' (Sacks 2007, p. 188). Clive notes in his journal that he has just woken up, a minute later he writes the same thing with no recollection of what he had only moments earlier written or experienced. He cannot create new memories – except in music. A musician all his life, even after the infection he retained an extraordinary ability to play music, and when he plays the piano he becomes fully present. Sacks writes:

> It may be that Clive, incapable of remembering or anticipating events because of his amnesia, is able to sing and play and conduct music because remembering music is not, in the usual sense, remembering at all. Remembering music, listening to it, or playing it, is entirely in the present (Sacks 2007, p. 212).

'He has,' Sacks concludes, 'dropped out of space and time altogether. He no longer has any inner narrative...yet one has only to see him at the keyboard or with Deborah to feel that, at such times, he is himself again and wholly alive' (2007, p. 213).

Sacks ends the story with a letter Deborah had recently written. 'Clive's at-homeness in music and his love for me are where he transcends amnesia and finds continuum – not the linear fusion of moment after moment, nor based on any framework of autobiographical information, but where Clive, and any of us, *are* finally, where we are who we are' (2007, p. 213).

Finding our way home, to feel 'at-homeness', this is the great journey of healing.

Conclusions

This discussion of sound, music and, in particular, one musician's life journey to use his artistic expression to better understand his mystical experiences provides us with a number of insights into the challenges of social healing and reconciliation. To explore music and sound as metaphor requires a shift of perspective that suggests and reinforces spatial and circular aspects of personal and social change, as opposed to those that envision these phenomena as primarily or exclusively falling along a linear process. In this exploration several key images rise from the music and from our probing into the aural nature of human experience that are suggestive of the metaphor shift and which provide diverse avenues for envisioning aspects of social healing.

- Sound evokes. It holistically penetrates the human experience, touching us and putting us in touch with aspects of our lived experience not easily expressed in words. Sound has evocative capacity, at times in reference to painful experience, and notably for the purpose of our wider exploration, as a mechanism to open and touch constructive dynamics that help us 'feel' the spiritual and healing elements of human experience. Sound evokes creative perception. It creates moments where we notice the seamlessness between spirituality and the everyday, this thin membrane that must be continuously recognised and traversed, penetrated if you will, as an integral part of feeling whole and nurturing healing. Music helps us notice this aspect of human experience and invites us over and again to move back and forth between the deeply spiritual and the daily activity.

- Sonic experiences locate us. Like songlines, sound and music and, at times, specific songs provide a form of triangulation, a mechanism that creates capacity to feel that we know where we are, who we are, and how we might find our way home. We have noted violence creates the overwhelming sensation of being lost, displaced, in both the inner and outer worlds. Healing seeks to find bearings again. Sound and music have this innate capacity to touch us in ways in which, not unlike the Australian Aboriginal notion of invisible but sonically perceived maps of our surroundings, we can perceive our lived social landscape in new ways and find our place. We strip the power from violence by breaking beyond the sensation of displacement with the courage to utter our names and to name things around us.

- Sound surrounds. Sound and music create a sensation of being held. The sonic experience, particularly in music and in specific songs, can serve as a container that stimulates insight and the potential for creativity. The sensation of being surrounded creates spaces of feeling the potential and perhaps the reality of being accepted, the presence of unconditional love, which can be described as being held, feeling safe, experiencing a sensation of 'at-homeness'. We feel the 'silence'. Music permits us to feel more fully *human* in our very *being*.

- Sound and music transport us. Music stimulates the experience of feeling transported to another dimension of time and space. Through music we notice the simultaneous availability of past and future narratives within our reach in the present. Music facilitates the experience and potential of the eternal now that transcends the linear, Heraclitean view of time. It suggests a view of temporal simultaneity that nurtures a continuous and creative engagement of this uniquely human capacity to live into our God-given paradoxes. Music embraces the past with its power of story and identity, while invoking the imagination of who we could be, both past and future held in the cauldron of the co-created now that we share with others.

- Repetition opens towards sacred connection. Rather than understanding phrasing and circling, which are so embedded in music and song, from the perspective of linearity's metaphor as 'not going anywhere', we can envision them as a doorway that opens onto meditative spaces. These spaces bring us simultaneously closer to our inner voice and to the Divine, and are moments and spaces so filled with a sense of connection that we recover a feeling of wonder and joy. Metaphorically repetition suggests we understand the circular nature of healing as something analogous to prayer, chants and communion, all repetitious and continuous spaces that reach for *depth* and *nurturing* rather than distance, goals or end product.
- Sonic experience touches and creates beauty. Song and music can invoke the human experience of feeling in touch with nature. We noted that an overlooked aspect of violence is its power to strip us of our capacity to notice and feel beauty. From this perspective, dehumanisation does not simply involve the act of being treated as less than human or like an animal. A significant impact arises from this violence: dehumanisation numbs our capacity to notice and feel the very spirit of lifegiving creation and creativity around us. Sonic experience can create the spaces to feel beauty within and around us, a feeling that in numerous cases we found referred to as 'feeling human again'. From this perspective, healing approximates to the journey to recover the capacity to *feel* nature, beauty and human.

Our life journeys as individuals and communities are filled with a myriad of experiences. Some of those experiences are more easily understood and explained; the painful ones are felt but not easily explained in words. We circle around ways to understand and touch the feeling. This is particularly true for those who have suffered and continue to face situations of violence. Their landscape has been damaged and will never be the same or an easy one to navigate, particularly as they often face wave after wave of violence. Healing in this landscape requires ways of locating oneself and the creative act of naming what has been experienced in a context in which words do not adequately touch the depth of the lived experience. These are the spaces that, as human beings, require *feeling* as much as, perhaps more than *explaining*. This is a mystery. A mystery we all face. Here we find the music and lyrics of Van Morrison suggest directional metaphors, not so much as a way forward but as a way round and round, down, up and beyond.

SECTION III

THE WOMB OF CHANGE

Listening to the silence in the stillness brought seeds of awareness and then a Deep Knowing – Spirit to Spirit. We Are Women.

With that knowledge came new life and movement and we women joined together and we rose up and danced a women's dance of birth and re-birth, of life healing, of re-generation, of re-creation.

My great-grannie gave me a gift – she taught me. We Are Women. We are not victims. Nor are we merely survivors. We Are Women. We have creation powers.

We are the Creators of the Future.
Judy Atkinson

CHAPTER 9

When mothers speak

Somewhere between the girls raped in war and prostituted in peace, I have lost the clear distinction dividing war and peace. I think this is a positive step, a useful ambiguity. It is a step that leads us into questions of who profits from war, from silence, and from the lives... of girls on a global scale.
Carolyn Nordstrom

Introduction

When the guns finally went silent in Liberia ex-combatants began to reappear, out from the cover of the bush. A generation of youth with a lost childhood – child soldiers, children mothers – carrying the heavy weight of an unspeakable past on their backs while groping for a future with no horizon in sight. Their feet took them towards the roads leading to the edge of villages and towns, the communities they once shared as family, the places from which far too many were stolen and kidnapped a decade earlier. Not uncommonly, they would stop at the edge of town, dwellers on a threshold between the simultaneous push and pull of blood: the pull of the ancestral flow born in the wombs of their mothers and the push of the pools of blood they had spilt in the madness of the war.

Outside one small village mothers watched as the young soldiers started to appear, gathering by day under the shade of a large kum tree at the entrance to the village. With no guns, little food, ragged clothes and a decade of matted hair down their backs, they had nowhere to go back to in the bush but did not know how to enter the village they had destroyed. The lies their commanders had told them and the shame of who they were carried them only as far as the tree. Day in and day out they lived under the tree. They named it the 'Tree of Frustration'.

The men and elders of the village kept their distance and skirted the path that ran by the tree. Every now and then a few women would leave some food and in time they began to talk with the boys at the tree. Little by little they built a relationship. Sometimes they sang. Sometimes they stayed and ate. Sometimes they talked about the ancestors and the community. Sometimes they prayed. Months passed. The women started asking why these youths did not come back into the community, until finally the boys agreed that maybe they could try it.

The women told the boys their bush appearance scared everybody in town. They needed to clean themselves up before they came back. Their wild unkempt hair had to go. In this village mothers were responsible for cutting hair, so together they agreed to have a 'cutting hair ritual' under the tree. And the women came – mother caretakers for those who were lost. As one of them put it, 'We cut hair like shit from morning to night.' Beyond words, cutting these boys' hair was an act of reintegration and of love. A weight far greater than hair fell from the boys' shoulders; the mothers' hands and scissors spoke: 'We forgive you. We want you to come back and be our sons.'

While a real and growing relationship was built between the ex-combatants and the women, the men, responsible for re-creating village order after the violence, wanted to deal with the boys without the women. They relegated the women to less important roles. The mothers who had the courage to speak under the tree found themselves once again voiceless and marginalised in the village negotiations. Strong-minded elders reverting to old practices put the women 'back in their place'. But the former child soldiers from the Tree of Frustration gathered by the side of the women, 'These are the mothers who have brought us back into the community. You must listen to them'. As one woman expressed it, 'If these boys had not stood up for us, we would not have gotten anywhere' (Gbowee 2006).

Sickly all the time

In 2007 Mariatu from the Kono district of Sierra Leone held her young sleeping child on her lap. She covered the newborn in a batik of bright greens and reds, colours that contrasted with the dark mud hut, as she began her story. 'I was captured together with my younger sister. They killed her because she refused to hold the gun. I was captured, and then they carried me away and I was given a gun. We would attack, we would surround the town and then we would fire. We would kill some and then we would get out everything there: food, clothing, everything and then we would carry it. The group that went to attack the village was called *Operation No Living Thing*. Operation No Living Thing killed my father, my uncle, and now I don't have parents' (Mariatu 2007).

Mariatu's story resonates with that of thousands of children across the small West African nation of Sierra Leone. As documentation now shows, much of the violence in the civil wars fought in Sierra Leone and Liberia was carried out at the hands of children, where 70 per cent of all combatants were under the age of 18 (Mack 2005). In Sierra Leone, both the Revolutionary United Front

(RUF) and the civilian army, the Civil Defense Force (CDF), systematically broke down children's past identities and rebuilt them as soldiers and rogue fighters, eventually creating a nearly unstoppable and terrifying war machine (Wessells 2006, p. 13). Commanders forced children to burn their own villages, and kill their family or clan members. They gave the children a new home in the bush, new names like 'Rambo' or 'Superman', and created a new family with the fighting factions (Bombande 2006; Wessells 2006).

In her own words, Mariatu expressed the enormous challenge facing her as the war ended. 'I am sickly all the time. I am not well. My heart is hot [me 'at be 'ot] due to the gun sound.[1] And I have stomach problems because of the gun, because I used to carry it.'

Sickly all the time comes as no surprise. Unspeakable violence, rampant in too many villages, is never fully understood or laid to rest. 'Your mind is the weapon,' Morris said, 'all you have in your mind is violence. It's embedded in you. And it is creative. You can do unimaginable things, terrible things with this creativity.' The images of children burning down villages, burying pregnant women alive, and placing decapitated heads on sticks spread fear throughout the country for more than a decade, and remain alive in the minds of those who witnessed the unimaginable. The memory lives too, for those children who can still see the blood on their hands, who still see the images of killing before them. Their hearts burn and stomachs ache at the memory of blood and death. Healing does not come easily for these child soldiers. How are communities restored to health when devastating violence was carried out at the hands of children who destroyed the very traditions that once held the communities together?

A mother's tears

On the night of Operation No Living Thing's invasion of Freetown, the scorching red and orange flames of fire startled Haja Kassim

(2007) out of her sleep. 'We looked north and saw fire, we looked west and we saw fire, the only place you couldn't see fire was south because that was down along the wharf.' Haja survived the fire, but not unharmed: a long scar stretching from her wrist to her neck reminds her daily of the terror of war. Only weeks after the RUF's invasion of Freetown, the Interreligious Council of Sierra Leone (IRCSL) issued a statement vehemently condemning the violence of the civil war and called for dialogue.[2] With nothing left to lose, Haja found her voice among other faithful religious leaders crying for peace. Together, they found strength as their unified voices cut through the chaos and violence that raged across the city.

Haja was soon asked to join the IRCSL in one of the first confidential meetings with the rebels based outside of Freetown. 'I was the only woman with the team at that time and I asked myself, should I take this risk to meet with the rebels? We were very afraid. But, when peace came you just had to *grab* it. I decided to go.'

The United Nations (UN) peacekeepers drove the group of religious leaders to the edge of Waterloo. From there, the team continued, unprotected, into the bush. And they waited. Young children began to emerge, with ragged fatigues, army helmets and AK47s strapped to their backs. They gathered around the interreligious team. The men began talking to the young rebels, attempting to build their trust. But a palpable tension filled the air.

One young man refused to sit – he circled the group, gun ready in his hands. The contrast was stark: the religious leaders had no arms. The UN peacekeepers waited in their vehicles miles outside the bush. The leaders were completely vulnerable and no one knew what might happen next.

Then Haja's voice rang out across the group. 'My children,' she began, 'my children, I am old enough to be your mother. And we the mothers are not happy to see you in this condition. We the mothers are not happy to see you so far from home. We the mothers want you to return home. We are *crying* for you. The *mothers* are crying for you.'

The tension disappeared as the young rebels left their weapons and gathered around Haja, this time as children, not as soldiers. The young man who had previously circled the group lowered his weapon. He walked over to Haja, placed his helmet on the ground and offered her a seat. Others came to sit next to Haja and they began talking. They spoke of their mothers. They spoke of their homes. They asked to pray with her. 'They were wonderful prayers,' she later reflected, 'it's hard to understand how people with such godly hearts and such a religious knowledge could decide to go to the bush and arm themselves.' Haja listened. She prayed. And she spoke once again, 'Leave the bush. Come out. Come home and let us have peace in Sierra Leone.' Her voice cracked and the tears began to run down her face. The rebels surrounding her were the same rebels who had burnt down her house. She could not stop the tears. She cried for the suffering of war, for the violence that raged across her country and for the children who fought a war they had not begun.

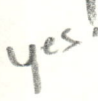

The rebels were touched. Her tears and the voice of a mother brought them back, rekindled their memories of home. They saw their mothers in the face of Haja. Her tears were the tears of all mothers. They promised to work with the interreligious council. They promised to begin dialogues. They promised to try to bring peace. They begged Haja to take messages for their families, their mothers and broadcast them over the radio.

When Haja and the others began to leave, one of the young men approached Haja and said, 'You look like my mother. You remind me of her. Let me give you this,' and he placed a piece of paper in her hands. Haja and the Interreligious Council began the long walk to the edge of the bush, where they found their vehicles waiting for them. As they were driving back to Freetown Haja looked down for the first time to see what the young man had given her. There, resting in the palm of her hand was a US $100 bill.

Back in Freetown Haja fulfilled her promises and played all of the messages across the radio. She was called traitor and rebel-supporter. She was stigmatised in the community because of her radio broadcasts. But she never stopped building the trust and confidence of the children she met in the bush. Eventually, the rebels agreed to join the peace talks and the long process towards a formal peace accord began. One piece of a complex puzzle, trust, started to emerge through the voice of a mother. Transformation trickled from her tears and vulnerability. The strength of a faithful Muslim woman who in the midst of the debris of war – severed limbs, painful scars and burnt houses – had dared to imagine a different world for her children.

Haja understood that one of the greatest challenges facing her nation was the healing and reintegration of children whose early formative years were not spent at home in families and schools, but were centred around traumatic experiences of kidnapping, violence, death and violation. Child soldiering dismantles common western notions of warfare that assume a separation of victim and perpetrator. In Liberia and Sierra Leone children experienced the seamlessness of being victim–perpetrators (Wessells 2006) that created and sustained a complex system of violation and destruction.

We note several important phenomena that appear time and again in the stories of child soldiers. These phenomena, which rise from the experience of extreme and sustained violence, provide insight into developing platforms conducive for social healing.

First, we consistently find the de- and reconstruction of identity and place. This commonly begins through forced kidnapping in which children directly experience the destruction of their homes and the death of their loved ones and find themselves 'captured', 'carried', 'taken to the bush'. As discussed earlier *displaced* represents a literal experience, a powerful forming metaphor, rather than a statistic of war, in which these young people must relocate themselves, their place and the meaning of life if they are to survive. They are renamed in the transformation of identity. Security and belonging are renegotiated around surrogate, parent-like figures. The act of destroying the old identity was for many bare-boned literal: children were sent to wipe out their own villages and family members as an act of breaking their former ties and reconstituting dependence and allegiance to their new identity (Beah 2007; Eichstaedt 2009; Honwana 2006; Singer 2006; Wessells 2006).

Second, and again consistently, construction of meaning requires mechanisms for negotiating a multiplicity of simultaneously held but highly polarising and contrasting social realities. Violence of this nature requires people to hold and move between identities and social spaces like victim–perpetrator, between rituals of violence and community, powerlessness and Rambo, separation and belonging, motherlessness and mother. These are not well characterised as linear, sequential realities but as fluid, surprising, explosive and latent all at once. Sharply contrasting, even incompatible identities are, given the extreme circumstances, simultaneously present and available in time.

Third, few if any of those who have experienced this kind of extreme displacement find words to speak the unspeakable. The realities experienced are felt in the bones but are not easily named or conveyed. In fact, perhaps the greatest loss, the greatest sense of displacement, is the complete lack of ability to find a voice to name what has happened or is happening in the confusing social realities that one is a part of – living, experiencing and simultaneously constructing.

We again find here key metaphoric themes and challenges to

which social healing must attend: displaced with loss of place and the search for home; speechless with loss of voice and the search to speak and name; and motherless, without a womb and the search to belong.

Gender and violence

A young woman like Mariatu exemplifies much of what we have discussed so far but adds the complexity of what faces young women in particular. As a girl soldier her constructed social roles and identities, none of them sought or desired by her, include kidnap victim, combatant, sex slave and mother. Gender-specific violence was pervasive during the war. 'When I was in the hands of the rebels,' Mariatu explained, 'several of them raped me and I became pregnant... When I was pregnant there was an argument between the rebels to open my stomach to guess what child it was – some said it was a baby girl, some said it was a baby boy' (2007). Pregnant women were buried alive, bets were placed on the gender of a fetus and wombs were cut open to win cigarettes. Sexual slavery of girls as young as seven was widely used and systematic gang rape of daughters, mothers and grandmothers became the favoured tool of war, devastating individuals and whole communities.

Rape not only shatters a woman's sense of self, power and belonging but also destroys the social fabric of families and communities. Today, the spread of HIV, rejection of rape victims and stigmatisation around 'rebel babies' – children who were conceived as a result of rape during the war – continues to pose challenges for women (Meintjes et al. 2001, p. 26). As Nordstrom (1999) suggests in the quote at the beginning of this chapter, for women there is no clear difference between war and peace. Blurring the false dichotomy of war and peace, war is a 'useful', if not necessary, 'ambiguity' (1999, p. 16).

The systematic use of rape as a weapon of war in places like

Angola, Bosnia, Liberia, Mozambique, Rwanda and Sierra Leone has garnered international attention. Many attribute these unthinkable acts of violence to the chaos of warfare. However, the systematic violence, which fuels mass exploitation of women during warfare cannot be minimised or dismissed so easily. The use of gender-based violence is an exacerbation of cultural and structural violence present before the war erupted – and present *after* a peace accord is signed, unless specific attention is given to women's particular experiences. In the United States, for example, one in four university women face the violation of sexual violence (Fisher et al. 2000). This statistic does not describe an individual experience of violation, but rather the prevalence of systematic violence on college campuses within the United States. The fluidity of borders in the 21st century requires that the global community begin addressing the structural and cultural violence that lies at the heart of sexual violence – violence that moves fluidly across places of war and peace.

In the aftermath of war, cultural and structural violence continues to impact women in devastating ways, particularly through economic and political inequity. With the loss of husbands and sons, many women must find ways to take up the role of breadwinner. To do so they must overcome the obstacles to employment in societies unwilling to change notions of gender roles. Eighty per cent of women refugees experience an increase in sexual violence during times of displacement (Nordstrom 1999, p. 15). Domestic violence increases in the 'aftermath' of war (Nordstrom 1999, p. 15; Rehn & Johnson Sirleaf 2002, p. 16). According to the *2008 Peace process yearbook* (Fisas 2008, p. 21), women represent only *four per cent* of participants in high-level negotiations in the past several years. Despite the demands of the *United Nations Security Council Resolution 1325: On women, peace, and security* (2000), which stipulates the intentional appointment and representation of women at all levels of peace processes, of the 57 people appointed by the Secretary

General to leadership posts in 2007, only three were women (Fisas 2008, p. 21). The war zones for women span the public and private domains – from the frontlines of war to the frontlines of the home, women experience violence in a way that dismantles the false dichotomies of war and peace, conflict and post-conflict, private and public.

The reality of women's lives in the midst and aftermath of war poses a challenge to the notion that reconciliation is a linear process. For women, violence does not end, nor does it decrease, after the signing of a peace accord. In the most disturbing of realities, *peacekeeping* operations have actually resulted in an increase in sexual exploitation and prostitution, as well as HIV/AIDS (Rehn & Johnson Sirleaf 2002, p. 70).[3] A symbol of peace for some has become a symbol of violence for women. Violence and peace cycle in and out of times of war and supposed times of peace. In the upheaval that war brings, women often find more leadership roles. This is true in two senses. First, as combatants, they often rise to significant leadership roles, and at home, when men are gone, fighting, hiding or dead, they are the de facto leaders. Ironically, as we have noted, a peace accord often entails the loss of voice and leadership for women as life returns to 'normalcy', translating too often to a return to patterns of male-dominated local and national leadership (Meintjes et al. 2001).

For girls like Mariatu, the deep violation of sexual violence and child soldiering is only exacerbated by reconciliation efforts that too often ignore the participation of girls in warfare. In Sierra Leone, girls constituted 30 per cent of the RUF's armed forces. However, during the first month of the disarmament efforts, girls composed only 15 of the 1,213 children released (Carlson & Mazurana 2004). Writes Carolyn Nordstrom (1999, p. 15), 'unseen is to unexist'. Girls like Mariatu are invisible, non-existent as they struggle daily to find healing. Unseen, too, are the contributions of women in the midst and aftermath of protracted violence. The unique and effective approaches women use to foster social healing too often remain unnoticed, an invisible reality, lost because of the systematic exclusion of women's voice and representation.

The leadership of women, as we have seen in the stories throughout this book, is absolutely necessary for cultivating a just peace. Women's leadership in reconciliation efforts offers an organic and intimate knowledge of women's particular needs to begin healing. Take, for example, the story of Haja Kassim. The men who attempted the initial talks with the RUF could not reach the rebels and the tension began mounting. Only when Haja's voice, the voice of a mother, rang out did the rebels begin to gather and listen. Her tears struck a chord with the child soldiers present. Important to note is the fact that these rebels had seen the tears of mothers all too often. After all, women were the primary targets during the war. The power of Haja's tears was different precisely because she was in a position of authority. Vulnerability displayed by someone in *control*, someone with *power* caught the rebels off guard. The child soldiers had come to talk tough. Bargain. Make demands. With people, they assumed, who would do the same. And here before them was a woman, a survivor and a leader, who had come to share, to cry, to embrace. Unexpected, given her simultaneous and seemingly contradicting roles as mother, victim, vulnerable person and leader, there was nothing the child soldiers could do *but* gather around Haja, her unconditional love calling them home. Haja's experience as a *mother* combined with her role as a *leader* gave rise to a natural frequency of its own. Within a short period of time, her voice and presence completely shifted the nature of the initial meeting with the RUF. Like the Tibetan singing bowl, the unexpected tone she brought as both a nurturer and a leader gave rise to a sharp spike of energy that rang out and touched those present.

In the stories at the beginning of this book we drew on multiple examples of the unique capacity women have to foster spaces of social healing when they are given voice and opportunity. When the formal disarmament processes in Sierra Leone and Liberia fizzled women began to mobilise. They organised around a rehumanising approach to disarmament, empowering their children through love, rather than the gun. Mothers sang their children home in a re-integration ritual. Haja's tears reawakened the memory of a different life for the rebels of Operation No Living Thing. The women at the Tree of Frustration disposed of the violent identities of their children as they cut their long matted hair, freeing them from the weight of war. Indeed, the innovative work of West African women to bring healing and peace to people like Mariatu, Morris and the ex-combatants under the tree provides an enormous resource for those grappling with the question of reconciliation in the midst of human suffering. Returning to several of our stories and in particular the Tree of Frustration, a number of key ideas and characteristics emerge.

Lessons from the Tree of Frustration

The capacity of the human spirit to re-imagine and re-create a world in the midst of violence remains a global phenomenon. Stories of healing and reconciliation abound in villages across Liberia and Sierra Leone. The Tree of Frustration story recounted at the beginning of this chapter is one of those riveting narratives that involves mothers who began to engage young combatant men who were not their direct children. There is profound wisdom and complexity – layers of learning – found in the actions that emerged from their intuition, not as a quantifiable technique, but rather as what we could call the surrounding power of love.

The Tree of Frustration suggests a number of key lessons for social healing that centre on the metaphor of mothering; one not easily characterised as linear and sequential, but rather one that rises from the wisdom of experience, from holding the other as a child.

This seems extraordinary given what had transpired in the village but simultaneously suggests that the experience of being a mother held a particular understanding of the deep harm of war; one which gave rise to the capacity for these women to mobilise their imagination and recognise their perpetrators as victims and part of them. Healing found under the branches of the tree was like the shade; the slow moving, reappearing dance of food, play and motherhood that gave way to voice and belonging. A few lessons from mothering emerge here.

Lesson 1: Surrounding gives way to voice

At the centre of the small Sierra Leonean village, Myama, sits a small, circular open-air hut. Visitors to Myama are quickly ushered into the hut as the villagers gather round. One by one different leaders and villagers welcome the visitors – a ritual explained by one of the leaders of Myama: 'Even though visitors bring the kola nut to break with the chief, it is not only the chief who has the power to welcome visitors. The villagers all must take part in the decisions. That is why we met in the palava hut.' In Sierra Leonean Krio, *palava* means conflict and palava huts provide a traditional space across West Africa in which villagers can meet to settle disputes, make decisions and talk about community affairs.

Palava huts play a central role in village life. Conflicts are settled in much the same way as our welcome from the villagers, through repetition and collective participation. The conversation circles around the hut – and begins again. As decisions become clearer, the repetition does not end, but it increases – each villager giving voice to the solution. In this way, each individual can take ownership of the decision. As the voices circle around the hut, the decision delves deep into the heart of the community and then rises into one unified voice, and the conversation envelops those present – sounding throughout the village. The traditional approach to conflict resolution found in the palava hut does not always require the physical space provided by the mud hut. Rather, the palava hut symbolises a cultural understanding of how to engage and transform conflict. Transformation stems from a collective responsibility to restore harmony – responsibility that expands in width and depth from repetition, sustained sharing and the collective ownership found in giving voice.

The mothers in Liberia also created a palava hut at the Tree of Frustration. Day in and day out they repeated their trip to sit with the young boys. They brought food. They told folk tales, laughed together and shared stories. Most importantly, they created a shared space in which to be together. For months they made the trip to the tree and their relationship with the youths became deeper with each subsequent return. There was no attempt to address the larger reasons why they ventured to the tree every day; there was no initial effort to talk about the war, the need for reintegration, the desire for reconciliation.

Simply, they surrounded the tree and the young men. Ironic, since in wartime, in the words of Mariatu, 'We would surround the town and then fire,' in Operation No Living Thing. Here, in contrast, the mothers chose to surround with something we can only describe as the courage of love, a courage beyond the capacity of the men in the town. They allowed relationships to emerge, strengthen and expand as their talk circled. Months of storytelling gave way unpredictably to a burst of energy, a question known by all but never spoken: 'We know you want to come back into the community, so why don't you? Why don't you come home?'

This sort of 'surround sound' tradition is found in the West African palava hut, which recognises the need for shared space, ownership in the journey towards restoring harmony in the community, a circling through repetition and collective participation. This tradition, however, is not limited to West Africa – nor is the healing gained from repetition and the power of circular storytelling limited by geographical and cultural boundaries. I have found palava huts and the need for circular storytelling in many places where hurt and deep violation have left individuals and communities severely broken – without a strong sense of voice or belonging.

I lived in a Catholic Worker community in South Bend, Indiana, with close to a dozen other women – women who have experienced rape, domestic violence and the shackles of poverty and homelessness. We found a palava hut of our own: the front porch. Every evening we gathered on the porch for several hours and talked. We talked about music, books, cigarette brands, motherhood and God – and as the days and months of sharing continued, the stories deepened. We talked about violation, about the deep trauma of sexual and domestic violence, about substance abuse, about prison. It was a ritual that circled and repeated, expanded and deepened. For those who have faced the devastation of homelessness, the seemingly insurmountable challenge of retrieving a sense of self and place is crucial – though the probability of that developing in a transitional housing situation remains unlikely. Yet the bond that formed in our evening porch-talk had the capacity to nurture the kind of sisterhood and community that locates self and place. The more voices present on the porch, the deeper the sharing. Like the Tibetan singing bowl, the individual frictions increased and gave rise to one song: it was a song of pain and destruction, but also one of hope that rang out from our front porch–palava hut, and was heard in the streets of South Bend and across the Atlantic to the small village of Myama, Sierra Leone.

Social healing is found in the palava huts throughout Ghana, Liberia and Sierra Leone where communities restore harmony through the power of storytelling; in the women at the St Peter Claver Catholic Worker House in South Bend, where sisterhood is built through their collective voices circling into one united song; and in the mothers at the Tree of Frustration, who understood the need to return daily. Take food. Talk. Tell stories to young combatants. Surround with care and love.

Lesson 2: The importance of ritual

'We cut hair like shit!' one mother joyfully exclaimed at the Tree of Frustration. Hair cutting was a remembering of the past – a reconnection to their children, their former lives and their ancestors. It was a symbolic act of love and forgiveness that went deeper than words, touching a memory of life and relationship that seamlessly linked the past and present. As Chief Kamanda (2007) of the Kono district in Sierra Leone insisted with regard to reintegration, 'You must try and bring them [child soldiers] back to where they came from, try to bring them back to their own memory.'

The cutting hair ritual at the Tree of Frustration stemmed from an old way of life, a life before war, where the cutting of hair was a mother's role. Though mundane, a haircut was a sign of intimacy and love, a space of touching and holding, of surrounding the child. As the hair of the ex-combatants fell, their identities as soldiers receded. The hair cutting created a new pathway seamlessly linking several realities. As they walked together back into town they simultaneously walked together back into the past, the long lost past of the ancestors that lay before them (Lederach 2005). In other words they walked forward into an earlier life, an earlier identity, as sons and daughters. The mothers at the Tree of Frustration reached deep into their traditional beliefs and practices and found a source of healing. A haircut offered a symbolic yet powerful act of reconciliation – eventually leading to successful reintegration. They brought their children back to where they came from, back to their own memory. They cut hair like shit – and there found trust and reconciliation as they remembered a past that held life, love and harmony.

Many rituals across West Africa reflect traditional practices performed at births in which women are dressed in white, children are cleansed with water and the rituals of naming performed (Bombande 2006). These rituals are the literal rebirthing of child soldiers into communities. In the village where mothers did in fact *walk* their sons and daughters from destruction and exclusion towards healing and acceptance new rituals were created: rituals of song (spirituals of lament and joy), rituals of journey (walking towards a past life, towards the ancestors, towards renewal into the village) and rituals of motherhood, the rebirthing of lost sons and daughters. In recognising the need for a reconnection and rebirth in the communities, women chose to join hands and literally sing their village into healing. Their songs brought everyone back to a memory of a life without violence, where harmony among villagers and with the ancestors existed.

Social healing is located in something we may again best describe as surround sound, the collective of voices raised in song. Indeed, there is profound hope in these broken voices *singing*. Singing provided location, security and acceptance. It is as if on a totally different continent the songlines of the Aboriginal Australians were present: our geography, our landscape, our place is known by the songs that give birth, name us and bring us home.

The women in Liberia and Sierra Leone have been effective in their efforts to sustain the reintegration of child soldiers because they recognise the need for traditional, spiritual rituals to lay the foundations for reconciliation. As an experienced peacebuilder in the region, Emmanuel Bombande (2006), reflected on his contrasting experiences with reconciliation across that region:

> The whole project of disarmament and reintegration had to take into account, not how disarmament took place, but how these young ex-combatants were re-rooted back into their communities...And we observed that in the communities [where] the old women were killed, reintegration became more difficult. But

in villages that were not touched by violence, old women were able to play a role in which rituals were performed to receive back young people. This points to the role of the woman that is so powerful, but has not been articulated enough.

These women, who have risen to meet the challenge of reconciliation in the midst and aftermath of war, have recognised the importance of identity, spirituality and collectivity. In the stories of Haja Kassim, the Tree of Frustration and the Women of Liberia Mass Action for Peace Campaign, the women found a way to call to their children, to remind them that a different life was possible. They rose up together to bring their daughters and sons back to their own memory, back to where they came from, back home.

Social healing, in this context, must reconnect communities to their ancestors, to their living history and to one another after a decade of devastating separation. Rituals that remember life before war help re-root communities and deepen reconciliation efforts. Time and again, the theme of 'collective responsibility' emerged in interviews and conversations with West Africans. 'No one in Liberia is totally innocent. We are all responsible for the destruction of Liberia,' Jake said as we wound around Buduburam Refugee Camp, 'and we are all responsible to begin rebuilding our communities.' For him, notions of family went beyond a specific bloodline, making the need for communal healing central to building any kind of sustainable peace.

In the context of West Africa, collective responsibility stems from a deeply rooted spiritual epistemology – one that recognises the flow of past, present and future in the contours of daily experience, where the ancestors continue to impact the life of a village. The spiritual components necessary for healing in many villages across West Africa are often ignored in western notions of effective reconciliation. Yet there is profound wisdom in a cyclical approach to reconciliation that recognises the interplay of the past in the present and of both past and present in what is to come.

Lesson 3: The need for play

The women at the Tree of Frustration sang and told old folk tales. In their conversation they reawakened a memory of a different life and a different world. They reminded the youth at the tree that peace and acceptance were possible. In their willingness to sit and listen they created a sense of security, they allowed the young combatants to feel their dignity again. These wounded healers found a connective power in song, prayer and laughter. In their mothering, they gave a glimpse into the future – a future where security could come from community, where families could be built again, and a future where power did not need to come from a gun. Rehumanisation seems to sit at the core of mothering precisely because it recognises the perpetrator as a child, as someone's son or daughter.

'Women at school often ask me how I deal with all of the challenges in my life, how I deal with being homeless, and still laugh every day. I tell them that sometimes you have to laugh just to keep from crying,' explained my housemate during our nightly porch-talk in Indiana. Laughter in the midst of suffering is not new or uncommon. In fact, the opposite is true; the need for comic relief, laughter and play is widespread. This need is most often talked about as a mask for pain and sorrow – laughter used as a way to hide tears. However, a different reality may simultaneously be at work: play and laughter remind us of our humanity, of connectedness, or as Van Morrison suggests, recovery of times when we experienced a sense of innocence and awe as children. From the streets of South Bend to the red dirt floors of war-ravaged homes in Sierra Leone, dance, laughter, play and ritual abound in places of suffering. The muse is a powerful reminder of what it means to be human.

Conclusion

In Ghana there is a proverb that says: 'If there is a stalemate, go consult the Old Lady.' This is not just a traditional saying, but a power found in the women in this region of the world. 'There is an element of being Woman,' a Ghanaian woman explained, '*Womanhood* for the African context. They are our mothers. They are the people who have given birth to us. We must give them that respect.' The West African woman is, indeed, at the forefront of fostering transformative processes in places where civil war has shredded the very fabric of society. Nowhere is this destruction more profound than in the systematic use of children and women as weapons of warfare. These women, whose bodies became the literal frontlines of violence, whose helplessness and victimisation became exaggerated at the hands of children, are now at the forefront of the reintegration process. Within their stories of profound loss, an equally deep understanding of healing emerges that tells the story of how women have led and sustained the rebuilding of lives and communities. They have much to teach us about social healing.

The mothers' success, however, lies less in their socially constructed roles as women – and more in the imaginative approaches they have used to cultivate healing in the midst and aftermath of war. They provide an unmatched resource of creativity for peacebuilders across the world, yet their approaches remain woefully underrepresented in the larger reconciliation literature (Turshen 2001). The false notion that peace work is inherently women's work eternalises women in a role that is not the reality on the ground – women play as many roles as men during wartime: from soldier to reconciler. As Nancy Scheper-Hughes (1998, p. 228) writes:

> In the end, it's simply not the case that men make wars and women make peace, or that mothering 'naturally' opposes militarism...motherhood is, of course, as social and as fluid a

category as fatherhood. Only by intentional design, rather than by a natural predisposition, do women devote the thinking and practices of motherhood to peacekeeping and world repair rather than to war making and world destruction.

Too much of the peacebuilding technical literature takes an essentialist perspective that scarcely accounts for or simply fails to give credit to women who have, by *intentional design*, imagined a way to work for the healing of their communities. Perhaps more importantly, an essentialist perspective ignores the enormous resource of women's particular approaches to reconciliation, which are translatable across the borders of gender, culture and nationality. Mothering as *metaphor* highlights the remarkable work of individual women on the ground, while also recognising that their particular methodologies are contributions adaptable to the wider field.

Mothering offers a different metaphor and a shift for social healing and reconciliation. The shift requires, much like the genius and daily grind of being a mother, a willingness to embrace the messy stubbornness of violence with persistent love. But it also requires seeing the originally birthed humanity, not the socially constructed categories created in the midst and aftermath of war.

We know that violence increases for women after the signing of a peace accord and this necessitates a resiliency of imaginative response. Mothering encompasses the messiness of grounded experience and the imagination that mobilises the spaces needed to surround and hold hurting children and communities, even while mothers themselves experience and are working with their pain. The very nature of motherhood involves a lifelong journey of accompaniment. As such, mothering mobilised with intention and purpose reaches for something beyond the demands of immediate justice, the techniques of problem solving or the stages of healing. It nurtures restoration, the gathering of dignity and people. Beyond neutrality, mothers foster authentic relationships. The women who rose to lead their communities found power in their connectedness, in their sisterhood and in their vulnerability. The metaphor of mothering offers a new, multidirectional paradigm for reconciliation, one in which the surrounding love of song and dance, sisterhood and collectivity and the presence of the ancestral world restores a sense of place, gives rise to voice and begins the journey towards social healing.

CHAPTER 10

The poetry of social healing

When I talk about language (words, sentences, etc.) I must speak the language of every day. Is this language somehow too coarse and material for what we want to say? Then how is another one to be constructed? And how strange that we should be able to do anything at all with the one we have!
Ludwig Wittgenstein

Introduction

Around a dimly lit room in the Freetown Cultural Center poets gathered from all corners of the city. Chairs shuffled. Conversations rose then fell silent as the first voice rang out:

> Spray formaldehyde.
> Spread the purple carpet.
> Lay the ritual book of mock condolence,
> Let the regal ghoul and masons of insurrection
> Behold the bitter harvest of their implement.
> Shroud the pawns.

> Line the coffins.
> Sound the knell.
> 'Let the dead bury the dead.'
> Dust to Dust.
>
> May the seeds and roots of this gory age remain forever damned!

The last words in Tom Cauuray's poem 'Epitaph of a nation' hung in the room. And once again the voices of the Falui Poets Society joined together as they had during the eleven-year war.

Resilient poets

The statistics from the Sierra Leonean war quickly become mind-numbing, numbers that lack faces, are too large to comprehend. From 1991 to 2002: 4,000 mutilated; 10,000 children abducted (Elagab 2004, pp. 249–73); 150,000 displaced people in the capital alone. Countless dead. Unspoken numbers raped (Lord 2000, p. 14). But poetry, like the title of the collective volume from the Society poets – *Songs that pour from the heart* – reverberates beyond the small spaces that the poets found to share words of this unspeakable history.

On a rainy night in July 2007, convened this time at the request of Portland poet Kirsten Rian who had heard the echo of their voices through a written BBC report (Boreham 2007), they gathered again. The Falui Poets Society had more than just survived the war. During the decade of horrors their individual voices had found each other and flourished in the anguish. The voices that night sent chills down the spine of those of us from outside who listened, transporting us into the memory of the unimaginable from the war-torn country, the collective birthplace of their nation surviving a war.

Despite – or perhaps in spite of – unimaginable violence, the

Falui Poets Society gathered to search for words in the midst of war. They met in darkened rooms and small corners across Freetown. Penned words and spoken phrases provided small doses of resilience, bouncing back and against a decade of apparent impotence. In collective voices they found healing. In bits and pieces they documented both violence and the small spaces of peace. Their lines sang pain, expressed sorrow and the loss of innocence, and groped for pathways home that no longer seemed to exist. Oumar Farouk Sesay's (2007, p. 17) 'Once Again', captured that yearning for home, for a mother's love:

> This wound in the Earth
> Is the grave of my heart
> I traverse a landscape
> Stripped of its own heart
> In Search of Hope
> A scar in the Earth
> Marks the grave of my soul
> I roam with a soulless
> Body searching for my soul
> In the womb of the earth, my life compass
> Drifting like driftwood
> In turbulent waters
> A site on the vast Earth
> Blurs my sight
> I grope in dens and graves
> Without a sight
> For Oumou Kultum Sesay
> Buried in the earth's womb
> And search for her likes
> To mother me once again.

The poem speaks of wandering, the lost womb of the earth as distant as the impossible retrieval of the birthplace, of the one who gave him life. Sesay feels empty, longs for nurture, to be surrounded again in love. As in the Gospel lament, Sesay is left a motherless child. The devastation of war robbed him of not only his mother, but also of any sense of place and belonging. His mother buried, he hunts for something of 'her likes' to mother him, the verb as infinitive, in order to feel human once again.

That night in July held hope as well, the rebirth from the barren ground, the potential of a new dawn. For many, the birthing began in the very act of giving voice to poetry, the capacity to sing unspeakable words. It seemed as if a release of pain emerged in the outpouring. Their words were never content to sit silent on a page. Over and over again they needed enunciation to have life. 'When my pen pours poetry', Sesay (2007, p. 37) cried:

> It spurs my pulse to pour
> The passion of my soul
> To make ink for my pen
> When my pen pours poetry
> It crushes the gates of my
> Heart and lets out my
> Pain for the
> Monsters that munch
> The mutton and leave
> The bones for the mongrels
> When my pen pours poetry
> It pours for a social change

His repetition of lines circle and move so that the listener feels the crushing of the gates, the outpouring of the soul and the beginning of change to come. Here Sesay approaches a healing that links the need to touch the soul to letting it pour pain, as if he were able to 'make ink for his pen', the instrument that finds its way to voice and place. Poetry, for Sesay, is a necessity to find healing, a releasing of the unimaginable pain suffered by war.

This notion of pouring, or the movement from the deeper spaces of the unspeakable experience towards those of the outward expression parallel the suggestions of poet Mark Nepo about the connections between poetry and peacebuilding. In the course of a workshop with that title Nepo spoke of the inner and outer worlds as separated by a 'thin membrane' that easily thickens. The challenge of poetry, like that of peacebuilding, is not the focus on the technical aspects of language. Rather, like 'an inlet opening to a powerful sea' poetry moves seamlessly in swells between the two worlds. 'It is not that you write a poem as if it were an entity external to you,' he suggested. 'The poem is already there. Poetry is discovery and retrieval. Let it out and then have the courage to notice it' (Nepo 2008).

Ted Kooser, poet laureate of the United States, described a similar phenomenon in his book *The poetry home repair manual* (2005). Drawing from a Jared Carter poem describing homeless men gathered around 55 gallon drums in the early morning, Kooser suggests the most important lines of Carter's poem rise from the poetic imagination: 'the next time you'll notice them on your way to work' (2005, p. 8). In the everyday poetry is in and around us, but becoming poetry requires noticing. This parallels something very fundamental that exists both in poetry and healing. People begin to take notice of things that have been there all along and then rise from the noticing towards something that takes shape. In the case of poetry, this expression might move into words that are sounded from the lips or written on the page. In the case of healing, gut-felt experiences that are noticed and touched over and again try to find their way into expressive form that in essence transforms the experience and the meaning, though they may not be adequately expressed in words.

Valencian philosopher and peace researcher Vicent Guzman (2008) refers to this as the fundamental significance of poetry in its Greek origin, *poïesis*. In its origins the word had meaning attached to the idea of work or the craft of producing something well. But this is not just any notion of work. It is not, for example, work as in the drudgery of a job. It is rather in the way one might refer to a *work of art*, that is, work as craft and beauty. He suggests, for example, that the phrase in the New Testament, 'blessed are the peacemakers', which in Spanish translates with what in English would be, 'blessed are those who work for peace', pulls the words 'work' and 'make' from the use of poïesis, meaning the art and craft of weaving peace. One could perhaps say blessed are those who poetically craft peace. Guzman (2008, p. 7) suggests in fact that peacebuilding requires this notion of producing a creative response to violence as a poetic act, a 'representation of life' with craft and art, not just technique.

These notions of the poetic capture the place of voice and response in settings of violence so well expressed in the craft of the Falui Poets Society. In the wars of West Africa the experience of the everyday exploded. It detonated and burnt the lands and people and, as the poets from the Falui Poets Society suggested, it numbed and deadened the inside world as well. Their poetry travels in both directions. They notice the sickened outer world of war with its devastation and they notice, little by little, the inner world numbed by the experience. *Songs that pour the heart* (Sesay & Kainwo 2004), as they coined it in the collective volume, allowed the swells of experience to move back and forth between the inlets. This movement, the swelling in and out follows the poetic ebbs and flows of resilient healing.

During that evening in early July, the repeated expression of pain and joy, created a palpable sense of healing in the room. A decade in the making, even their own ink flowed in swells, the voices gathered every few months throughout the war and gave birth over and over again to small doses of collective healing in the midst and aftermath of the violence; a resiliency of voice that, when spoken, will reverberate for generations. Poetry, when presented in the collective voice, resonates as an art form less concerned with correct grammatical expression and more rooted in the popular art of the spoken word. The meaning emerges when the words are spoken – in the listening and the voicing. It is in this collective sharing that poems touch the pulse and 'passion of our souls'. For the Falui Poets Society healing and hope came out from the shadows, rose above the sound of bullets and bombs during those long nights of poetry readings in the midst of war. And today, those prophetic voices continue to pour forth their hearts for a social change, a social healing.

The poetry of social change digs roots in hope as memory. After the ceasefires were signed Sesay (2007, pp. 14–15) was asked to write a poem of love, to which he answered:

> No I cannot write it here
> That poem that will clean
> Hate ridden hearts with a
> Love that has no
> Color, creed, and race.
> No I cannot write it,
> But I want you to read it
> In the childhood anthology
> It is there, the poetry of love
> That brought us here.
> I can see it in that child
> Feel it in her smiles
> Sense it in her chemistry
> Hear it in her breath.
> Yet I refuse to write it
> But I want you to read it

> Read the rhyme scheme
> In the rhythmic movement of
> Their feet in the playground.
> Read the similes in their
> Smiles, and the metaphor
> In their mood.
> Read it, it is there
> The poetry of love
> But I cannot write it.

Poetry of healing expresses a blunt honesty. It suffers no fools. It humours no falsehoods. Found in the rebirthing of life, in the midst and aftermath of violence, it does not cover the continuous swells of experiences as if they did not exist, but it keeps noticing – the 'similes in their smiles/Read it, it is there/the poetry of love/But I cannot write it'. This capacity to notice the poetry of life points to resiliency, a bouncing back towards staying in touch and staying true which, in unexpected ways, can allow people to flourish in the face of life's darkest moments.

Robert McDowell suggests 'poetry is the most honest verbal expression among any people, at any time, in any situation'. He cites Allen Grossman who called poetry 'the historical enemy of human forgetfulness' (McDowell 2008, p. 9). This was precisely the view of Carolyn Forché in her seminal anthology *Against forgetting* in which she argues that forgetfulness is not an option for the poet. Of the poetry drawn together in her volume she writes 'these poems will not permit us diseased complacency' (Forché 1993, p. 32). Recalling her subtitle, *Twentieth-century poetry of witness*, she continues that a poetry of witness often faces a false dichotomy among those who wish to classify it as either 'personal' or 'political'. Instead, Forché proposes that a new term, 'the social', more accurately locates the poetry of witness. 'The social,' Forché contends, 'is the sphere in which claims against the political order are made in the name of justice' (1993, p. 31). She continues:

> A poem is itself an event, a trauma that changes both a common language and an individual psyche... So, if a poem is an event and the trace of an event, it has, by definition to belong to a different order of being from the trauma that marked its language in the first place (Forché 1993, p. 33).

The Falui Poets Society represents an example of cyclical poetry of change, the creativity of the human spirit to rise above devastation, to transcend the 'trauma that marked [their] language in the first place'. From drama to dance to poetry, individuals and communities have found ways to resiliently heal and respond to the unspeakable. Through a re-imagining of language itself they have found ways to feel then name the unspeakable.

Women's poetry of truth-telling

> We need to pierce that which destroyed or constrained women's voices... it is important to highlight the abuse of women, to explore these issues openly, to lift the veil of silence. Only by speaking out have women begun the healing process (Graybill 2001).

In recent years acknowledgement of the particular challenges women face when giving voice to sexual violation has come to the forefront (DeLaet 2006; Graybill 2001; Hayner 2002; Meintjes et al. 2001; Porter 2007; Ross 2002). With the explosion of truth and reconciliation commissions in post-accord societies around the world an emphasis on the centrality of *truth-telling* in fostering reconciliation has garnered international attention and support (DeLaet 2006; Hayner

2002; Minow 1998; Thompson 2005). The need for truth – finding ways to share and express one's experience – is a crucial component of locating self and place. Yet women's voices remain strikingly absent. In her remarkable ethnography of the South African Truth and Reconciliation Commission, Fiona Ross discovered that of the 204 people who testified during the first five weeks of the Human Rights Violations Committee Hearings, only thirteen per cent of 'cases reported were directly concerned with violations perpetrated against women' (2001, p. 253). Surprisingly, women actually represented 58 per cent, a majority, of all of those who testified. But Ross soon realised that the majority of women who testified never spoke of their *own* experiences of violation, but overwhelmingly of the violations of *others*, and in particular of their sons, husbands and brothers (2001, p. 254). Truth-bearers they were, but with a more outward than inward reach.

Given the untold numbers of victims of rape and sexual violence, the lack of representation of these voices is staggering. The women at the hearings could not find the words to express their own devastating experiences, perhaps because, as Ross suggests, when violence is not knowable in everyday language, the experiences in turn become 'unrepresentable' (2001, p. 272).

The physical brokenness and utter loss of self that follows rape and sexual violence devastates beyond words. Battlefields move from physical land to bodily terrains. Women's bodies become the sites that both suffer then hold the violence. Numerous religious texts speak of the body as temple, the place inhabited by the Spirit that first gave life. Rape shatters everything known, sacred and trusted into small incoherent pieces, and among these pieces, as documented by Ross, is voice. Words may come to express the loss of and for another, but finding voice to express the profoundly intimate loss women experience as the result of rape requires a depth of expression that is not easily found.

For many women, the very real fear of rejection that follows a public testimony of violation also contributes to the silence. Stigmatisation as a result of rape and sexual violence is pervasive in the aftermath of war. A return home for women who bore so many conflicting identities – soldier, mother, daughter, sex slave, child and rebel – poses unprecedented challenges. Communities emerging from decades of violence do not have the capacity to understand the violation, much less the tools to begin deconstructing the gender inequality and discrimination that lie beneath the surface: exploitation during wartime in the form of rape and in peacetime in the form of rejection and increased domestic abuse. In the end, in too many places like West Africa, the Lake Region of Central Africa, or Colombia, entire generations of young girls, are left estranged, ignored and in the shadows.

To externalise the experience of violation may culturally reinforce the stigmatisation. The shackles of this fear remain tightly wound around the women's bodies. And the stories fester deep inside, the memory of rape gnawing at their souls as they desperately attempt to re-create their sense of self and place. Reverend Moses Khanu (2007), a human rights commissioner in Sierra Leone, said it well, 'It is very difficult for a woman to stand up and say "I was raped." *Traditionally, it is not possible.*' Traditionally, women do not have the space to share their deepest violations – nor the words to express their loss and brokenness.

Where then is voice found in the midst and aftermath of the unspeakable? When the language of the everyday becomes too flat, brittle or coarse, how are spaces to touch the bone-level of experience created? We turn again to stories.

Story 1: Speaking the unspeakable through poetry – Makeni, Sierra Leone

We bounced off the edges of potholes and trenches from the hard July rains to reach a small schoolhouse in the Makeni district of Sierra Leone, a former RUF stronghold, where a group of young girl mothers awaited our arrival. Inside, circled around desks and benches they sat, talking and laughing, young infants tied against their bodies, wrapped in brilliant batiks that gave life to the dull cement walls and dirt floor. With the sounds of a lively soccer match in the background, we began introductions. We had come to the schoolhouse with Catalyst for Peace to engage and support local efforts in reconciliation in Sierra Leone (Hoffman 2008). The schoolhouse was a venue for a poetry workshop led by Kirsten Rian (2009), an experienced practitioner who uses poetry as a tool for healing and storytelling within communities that have experienced the unspeakable loss that comes from devastating violence. With simple metaphors, everyday images, and small examples, Kirsten began to draw out the voices of the young women.

Pens went to paper. Chatter bounced off the walls in the telling that surrounded us, enveloping the room with voices.

'In my mind, I have no support.' Kadiatu Koroma spoke with a low stuttering murmur finding itself. 'In my mind, I have a child. The father of the child is dead. He died in the war'.

Retracing an experience never spoken to anyone Kadiatu stumbled with her words. I sat beside her as she spoke and wrote her words on recycled paper. The war had stolen her childhood and with it her education. She had never learned to read and write. But literacy is not a requirement for the art of poetry. The poems of life are embedded in the feeling, the noticing, the experience and the observation. Kadiatu slowed, it seemed as if she was reaching deep inside to find words beyond and below words, images and personal experiences of the unspeakable. Then her voice reverberated and echoed off the block walls.

> In my mind, I have no support
> In my mind, I have a child
> The father of the child is dead

He died in the war
My papa was killed
My mama was killed
by the rebels
And when they killed my mama
they captured me.
I was a young child
Now, I have no one to help me.
In my mind, I am sorry
In my mind, I see many many things
they tied us
they beat us
And they threatened to kill if I don't agree
In my mind, I see people killed
by the road –
dead people
And we would pass them
There was no food to eat
There was no medicine
And I felt sick
I felt sick when my mama died
when my papa died –
I felt sick
In the bush, the rebel died.
My body is in my heart.
I try to find food for my child
But now, I have no business
And this time,
I just cry.

In finding new ways to express the inexpressible through these lines, Kadiatu gave voice to the brokenness of her body and soul. The suffocation, the pain and absolute destruction voiced, then penned in a single line: *My body is in my heart*. When everyday language could no longer express the inexpressible she gave birth to a new language through metaphor. Kadiatu reached deep within herself and from that place truth trickled out. Those of us lucky enough to share that space with Kadiatu felt the resiliency of the human spirit. No longer helpless before the violation that ate at her soul, Kadiatu discovered a new way to release the suffering that lived inside, that she felt in her bones. And those bones spoke. Reaching deep, touching and claiming her voice, Kadiatu kindled hope and a rebirthing from within.

Harrison (2008) observes that we do not have a proper language and tone to speak the unspeakable and that this results in a flat affect when violation is recounted. Perhaps more devastating than silence is the 'matter-of-factness' with which so many girls violated during the war in Sierra Leone spoke of their rape and sexual violence. Rehn and Johnson Sirleaf (2002, p. 12) found this pattern in interviews they conducted with women in multiple settings of protracted conflict. Their inner world was so numbed that even the most severe violations no longer held significance. Violation had become the new norm. Hope had fled their lives long ago. They were left lifeless and mechanical, their inner world deadened both by severe violation and the loss of language with which to express the inexpressible. We found a striking difference between the space created when we engaged the young women like Kadiatu in our more formal research interviews and that created in the poetry workshop. When the women responded to our questions about their war experiences they spoke the stories in what Harrison calls the flat affect, a mechanical recounting. The interview format did not create a space with tools to express the inexpressible, only a *matter-of-fact* channel. But poetry inside the school provided something with greater depth and feeling as if it were *matter-of-bone*. The space opened and released the young women from the cages of their deadened world. A small flame ignited and something more lifegiving emerged. Formal court-like testimonies and prescribed interview processes do not provide the tools or create space for sharing below and beyond words. Questions are asked and rehearsed. Responses are given with little or no potential for non-traditional modes of speech. The formal provides little space for language that moves beyond words to touch voice.

Poetry, however, gifted a space that reached the inner world which then poured outwards, touching those present. The girls located a sense of self and place through a new creative power. They began to reclaim their stories that had once been deadened by traditional forms of examination and language.

To touch voice is to locate the power to reclaim ownership of self, body and expression. Here we find another metaphor: VOICE IS POWER. Voice is located in the imagination of girls like Kadiatu. The capacity to re-create expression gives rise to voice from within the sacred temple that was destroyed. The body that holds the violence now rumbles with the vibration and echo that touches deep within yet bounces out to join others.

Story 2: The loyal daughters – South Bend, Indiana

Drama, like poetry, has the power to connect listeners and participants. The stage creates a shared space where people can feel the voices moving and touching. In recent years, the creation of V-Day, a global movement to end violence against women and girls, has emerged in conjunction with the drama *The vagina monologues*. Compiled by Eve Ensler, the *Monologues* re-creates a set of real stories from women across the world, a mini-truth commission portrayed on stage; women giving voice to their experiences. The stories move from an individual voice to a collective one when heard on public stages. For many women the experience of the play is intensified in the walking home together that night or over a cup of coffee, where over and over again a single feeling emerges: 'It was like hearing my voice, my story acted on stage.' Sound is felt deep in the bones as the voices of women circle, reverberate and intertwine with the stories held by those listening. When voiced together on stage, the stories rise into a powerful chorus of women.

The first time I heard *The vagina monologues*, the stories left me breathless and wanting more. I remember how the voices in *The vagina monologues* reverberated in my head for days after, the stories literally sending chills throughout my entire body. I was working at Silliman University in the Philippines at the time and participated in *The vagina monologues*, personally giving voice to the stories of women. The experience was a powerful one; the monologues were slightly changed to fit the cultural context of the Philippines and new monologues were added to give voice to the Filipinas who had experienced the violation of sexual violence. *The vagina monologues* span across cultures and oceans: as noted ealier, one in four women studying at universities in the United States experiences sexual violence. Sometimes we lose the faces, the suffering, the *truth* of women's lives in these numbers. I have faces, I have stories, I have long nights of tears to account for the statistic, to make it *real*. In the last six months of my senior year at the University of Notre Dame, six friends of mine experienced the violation of rape. Six friends in six months suffered sexual violence. Philippe Bourgois aptly reflected in his ethnography, 'rape runs rampant around us in a terrifying conspiracy of silence. It becomes a public secret that enforces an important dimension of the oppression of women in everyday life' (2004, p. 344). Listening to *The vagina monologues* was the first time I felt the power to release the stories of my friends and co-workers that had been held for so long in bitter secrecy. In the hearing of the *Monologues*, I no longer felt the numbness of secrecy, I no longer felt alone as I walked alongside those violated. The stories, given on a public stage, broke the 'terrifying conspiracy of silence' that had begun to gnaw at the souls of those around me.

A fascinating consequence of the *Monologues* has been the creation of local monologues across the globe (Nordstrom 2006). In 2006, Emily Weisbecker produced and directed her own version of the *Monologues* at the University of Notre Dame, Indiana. *The loyal daughters* brought together the voices and stories of violation experienced by women students at Notre Dame. After the monologues were performed, a spontaneous sharing began between those acting and those listening. For the first time, women gave collective and public voice to the tragedy of their own violation. Through the shared narratives, on the space of a stage, authentic conversation emerged. It was as if the vibrations of a social echo could be felt as woman after woman stood to speak, lifting the veil of silence. And in that room for many of the women and men watching and participating, the long journey towards healing began.

Story 3: 'We passed through the war' – Sierra Leone

Worlds away from the performance of *The loyal daughters* young girl soldiers created their own drama. I met Miriam in Sierra Leone while working with Catalyst for Peace.[1] Her story echoes throughout the world, touching those who have lived through the unspeakable.

At the age of 11 the Revolutionary United Front (RUF) kidnapped Miriam. They raped her repeatedly, along with other girls that night, and dragged her into the bush where she began life as an RUF fighter. She bore a child from the first night of her induction. In the coming years she carried in and around her contradictory identities: rebel, daughter, mother, sex slave and wife. She fought. She looted. She set up camp for the RUF. With a baby strapped to her back, and an M16 cradled in her arms, she suffered, witnessed and participated in unspeakable violence.

When Miriam finally escaped the RUF she faced new challenges as she tried to find her way home to reunite with her family. Although she went through ritual cleansings, her village refused to allow her and her 'rebel baby' to return. They denied Miriam her birth-name. Her forced identity solidified in her naming by those around her: rebel. Miriam was left without place, name or voice: a motherless mother.

But the capacity of the human spirit to create and re-imagine a new world shines through in the most hopeless of situations. Refusing to be voiceless Miriam went to the chief. She offered to stage a drama with all of the child ex-combatants, a play about their experiences in the war. She wanted to create something with the other girl combatants, 'together, so that we could bring something about in our lives, to pass through the war'. The chief agreed.

Miriam began organising the former combatants to put on a drama about their lives before, during and after the bush. The fear of stigmatisation created strong barriers. The girls could not bring themselves to tell their stories of pain. Traditionally, it was not possible. But Miriam did not give up:

> So I told them now, look, you are not going to say what happened to you directly. You can put someone in your own place. You can use someone else's name. And whatever you saw in the war that you think is most difficult for you to say, don't say it yourself. Don't put yourself in that position. Put another person in that position.

And the girls agreed. The stage created enough distance, enough security for them to tell their stories without fear of rejection, without fear of public shame. And the stories poured out in swelling waves between the thin membrane of the inner and the outer world.

Before the entire community, with even the chief present, their collective voices rose. It was a night to remember, a night that still reverberates in the memories of those present. It was as if the sounds penetrated and surrounded those in the room. People wept. The chief cried uncontrollably. 'At that moment,' Miriam later recounted, 'we passed through so many difficult times.' They found their voice. They told their truths. They passed through past and future; memory and hope held together for a collective moment. The collecting of individual women's voices, wounded healers, created a poetry of honesty.

Drama and poetry in these settings represents the seed-like quality of simultaneously holding seed and mature fruit. As they find pathways to touch their voice and lift those voices together healing emerges beyond the individual – it touches and holds the community. In her poem we feel Kadiatu's vulnerability, her excruciating pain, her body curled tightly into her heart, her brokenness. We see Miriam on stage, reliving her memories of war as she *passes through* so many difficult times as if earlier she was a wanderer in some other playwright's drama. But now, from a new place, she becomes the playwright, the author weaving her story anew. We witness women who found the strength to stand up and speak the secrets of violation in the theatre at the University of Notre Dame.

Without the voices of girls like Kadiatu and Miriam, an entire population remains silenced, hidden, unseen. Their stories and experiences cease to exist. Yet, the poetry of truth locates their voices, allowing these women to traverse the lands of their ancestors and reclaim ownership of the bodies that once held the battlefield of war within. Reaching inwards, the poetry of healing pours outwards, surrounding and holding broken communities together.

Lessons from the poetry of change

There is much to learn from the narratives of the poetry of change. In each of these stories several themes emerge. First, poetry gives way to a new language, a new way of finding voice. Second, the power of poetry emerges in the speaking, rather than the writing. The echoes of voice must reverberate. Third, poetry is both at once deeply personal and deeply collective, constantly and simultaneously moving between the inner and outer worlds.

Birthing a new language

Traditionally, it is not possible to speak of violation, as Reverend Khanu noted. The poetry of change is *non-traditional*. In the stories above, people found ways to touch voice beyond *words*. Kadiatu found new expression in poetry. Oumar Farouk Sesay called us to find the poetry of love around us, in the everyday. Miriam created a new space, on stage, for the young girl combatants to give voice to their unspeakable stories. In listening to *The loyal daughters*, women who witnessed the echoes stood to give voice to the secrets that had gnawed for too long at their souls. When experiences become unrepresentable and conventional language insufficient, voice beyond words needs a new language. The discovery of voice through poetry, the act of speaking through drama, the power of witnessing to the echoes of violation personified on stage all move to touch what is below and beyond other forms of language. It is as if the bones themselves speak.

The spoken word

Poetry carries a collective component. The power of the words is found not merely in the writing but in the speaking. From beat poets, to hip hop artists, to spoken word artists, the beauty of the art lies in the voice. This is particularly true for the Falui Poets Society and the practice of poetry that Kirsten Rian used with the young girl combatants in Makeni, where the chorus of voices had the capacity to *empower* and *heal*. Poetry, as Mark Nepo suggested, is everywhere and available to everyone. Oumar Farouk Sesay (2007) said several times in conversation that poetry is an art form *for the people*, for the grassroots. Literacy is not a requirement. Poetry first and foremost emerges in sound and vibration, *spoken, heard, and felt*. Likewise, Miriam's stage created a unique space for voice where vulnerability was minimised as the stories of violation reverberated from deep within the anonymous actors, touching those who witnessed the healing. The fear of stigmatisation lifted. The stories poured forth. Truth-touching shapes and creates a container for truth-telling. To notice poetry in the everyday provides spaces for creative naming. The poetry of change fosters a dynamic space for the truth to emerge.

Intimately personal, deeply communal
For the Falui Poets Society, *The loyal daughters* and Miriam's play the individual stories and poems are deeply personal. The poetry of change reaches into the depths of individual experience towards the place where both violation has settled and voice has been silenced. At the same time when the vibration of authentic voice re-emerges, in these cases through the vehicle of spoken poetry, the aural waves are powerfully collective. The echoes of the individual voices link and rise like a choir singing. In their book, *A general theory of love*, psychiatrists Lewis, Amini and Lannon (2001, p. 63) suggest this kind of phenomenon represents an example of *limbic resonance*, the mechanism by which people attune to each other's deeper experiences. This rising and expansion towards a shared space of experience moves seamlessly from the depth of individual experience and finds its way up and out into the collective and back again into each individual. A new sense of community emerges in the collectivity of voice. Poetry weaves a fabric of memory and hope. Beyond and below the content of words, in the form of this invisible but tangible movement of shared experience, we find the *poetry of social healing*.

For Miriam and other girl combatants, collective sharing in a safe space like the stage led them home. Their brokenness reverberated across the community members who were present. The chief wept. The girls were no longer rebels, but children reborn with names: Fatuma, Mariatu, Miatta, Miriam, Rosaline. In the enactment of the drama, they passed through the war – reaching backwards towards a different life. They returned home that night.

For many of the women who witnessed the stories of *The loyal daughters* at Notre Dame the poetry came in the collective outpouring of stories. Each monologue joined together relaying a single message: I am. I am not alone. We are. Power is located in the hearing and re-hearing of stories. Rape is not an individual problem, but a systemic sickness. The voice emanating from feeling it in the bones of an individual woman vibrated into the collective and unexpectedly moved others to echo back in the shared story. The collective voicing created an impromptu container, a form of a local truth-telling commission. Burdens were shared. Support was palpable. Voice into voices came in waves.

The violence experienced in the midst and aftermath of war does not easily find adequate representation through everyday or more formal ways of speaking. For the conversation to become meaningful it must descend towards the bone-depths, be touched and rise again with a name. Poetry, with its origin in poïesis gives birth to a new language by locating voice and opening the space to name what is felt but not easily expressed. Drama, song, dance and poetry find ways to both feel and give voice to the unspeakable, spaces wherein individuals and communities pass through the brokenness of violence and give birth over and over again to the wholeness. This is the poetry of social healing.

Epitaph for a poet

There will be no postmortem,
The cause of death is genocide:
Yea! Tens of thousands slaughtered in ten bloody years
By the savages of the savage corporal,
Who came to rule with matchets, bombs and bullets.

Tom Cauuray

In the midst of writing about the resiliency of the Falui Poets we learned of the tragic death of Tom Cauuray, one of their early members. The news came by email from Oumar Farouk Sesay. Tom's body had been found partially decomposed days after his death in a hotel room, cause of death unknown. We wept.

Though details of his last minutes will remain without clarity, we understand the cause of death. Tom suffered too greatly from his losses in the war, living an almost unbearable burden. Lines from his 'Epitaph of a nation' kept running through our heads: *There will be no more postmortem. The cause of death is genocide.*

The war and memory of the war took Tom's life. When the fighting in his native Sierra Leone began, Tom was studying in the US. As news of increased violence reached Tom he could no longer bear the separation from his family. He dropped his studies and returned. On arrival he learned that not one person from his immediate family had survived the brutality of the war. Racked with guilt and shock Tom grieved the irreplaceable loss. Not one surviving relative. In the days to come, he himself came face to face with the violence. Captured by the rebels, Tom was forced to strip naked and walk the main streets of Freetown and, only by chance, he narrowly escaped his own death. Though, in the end, the memory of the war and the loss of his family eventually took the will to live. *The cause of death is genocide.*

In the days following Tom's death, the Falui Poets decided that, *as poets*, they should arrange his funeral, they should re-member Tom's life and his contributions to this world. They had, indeed, become Tom's family, just as poetry had been his source of life. Farouk Sesay reminded us that Tom once said, 'the spirit of art transcends artificial boundaries'. Tom found solace in poetry and family in those who shared the spirit of his art. Farouk wrote: 'our concern and love for Tom is a manifestation of that spirit. We are indeed one big family. His is a voice that must not be silenced by death.'

The uncomfortable truth of Tom's words must live on – the spirit of his art must continue to transcend the boundaries of the living and the dead. The deep and haunting quality of his voice still rings and will remain forever etched, felt in the bones of those who heard Tom speak his poetic lines. And here Tom lives on. The spirit of his art transcends the boundaries of time, a voice that will never be silenced by genocide or death.

SECTION IV

THEORY, IMPLICATIONS AND CONCLUSIONS

'Our people,' Flynn said, 'say they recognize a song by its "taste" or "smell"... by which, of course, they mean the tune. The tune always stays the same, from the opening bars to the finale.'

'Words may change,' Arkady interrupted again, 'but the melody lingers on.'
Bruce Chatwin

CHAPTER 11

The resonating echo of social healing

MUSINGS ON AN AURAL THEORY OF CHANGE

This set of essays proposed a challenging task: is it possible to develop metaphor shifts, based both on lived experience and illustrative but improbable parallel phenomena? Necessarily, such an effort must experiment boldly while at the same time returning to hard questions of practice and theory. From the first lines of the book we noted that any inquiry into the themes of healing and reconciliation for communities facing the unpredictability of the messy midst and aftermath of violence enters a terrain filled with paradoxes. How do we find words to address the unspeakable? How are pathways towards a purposeful life carved in an ephemeral present that holds repetitive lived patterns of the past and the oft-dashed though still alive memories of a hoped-for future? In settings of collective violence what links individual healing with large-scale reconciliation?

In building the platform for our experimental inquiry we suggested that while the complexities of reconciliation and healing are fully recognised and acknowledged in the literature, the demands of political expediencies and programmatic projects create and tend to reinforce a dominant metaphor. Most prominent are linear understandings of change found, for example, in the temporal and directional language of 'post-conflict' or the notions of reconciliation and healing as following progressive stages. That metaphoric structure, though developed for analytical purposes, tends to reinforce a dominant understanding that reconciliation and healing happen in a phase after armed conflict, follow patterns understood as sequential phases, and are programmatically developed and evaluated accordingly.

Our metaphor shifts suggest alternative images that, at a minimum, lead in several theoretical directions. In the preceding chapters we gave ourselves permission to examine aspects of healing and reconciliation guided by metaphors that do not correspond to linear and sequential modalities of envisioning the nature of change. Notably, from the perspective of communities facing deep-rooted violence, the challenge of healing lies not in waiting for a proper phase but rather in nurturing resiliency of response that happens before, during and after repeated spikes of violence. Using spatial and directional metaphors we explored themes like sound, music, mothering and poetry of change as ways in which this resiliency emerges. The very nature of these phenomena suggest metaphor shifts in the understanding of reconciliation and healing: they have important features which reframe their meaning and our understanding of their dynamics. Three shifts are particularly prominent and provide a platform useful for our theoretical discussion.

First, we explored the metaphor shift from a line to a circle. By associating circle with our themes of reconciliation and healing through phenomena like containers, mothering, sonic surrounding and repetition, we located images providing constructive frames of reference relevant to both personal and wider social change. Viewed from a linear frame of reference these metaphor shifts are easily written off as irrelevant to programmatic initiatives because they are deemed as not producing anything. Common associations link 'going in circles' as 'not getting anywhere' or portray a repetitious quality of 'going back and forth' and 'not making any progress'. Our inquiry suggests otherwise. Several insights merit mention.

The idea of a *container*, with its bowl-like image of *surrounding a space* and providing *depth*, becomes particularly important to assure proximity of conversation and processes that permit people to *touch* and *feel* a sense of safety and change. In this regard, *voice* as an aural metaphor represents both power and closeness. People feel they are close enough that they are heard and can speak in ways that are meaningful. They can touch the depth and reality of their experience and concerns. They attune, as in a limbic resonance, to the experience of people engaged in a face-to-face conversation. In settings of protracted conflict the reference to 'not having a voice' refers to feeling as if the peace process represents something others are doing. Without a container that provides and holds a space that people feel and interact with in meaningful ways, they experience the change process as distant, removed and untrustworthy. In a similar fashion, the metaphors of *mothering* and *surrounding* create spaces of safety and connection and facilitate the ongoing – one could say lifelong – search for *places of belonging*. In essence, healing requires a womb and a rebirthing.

We noted the prevalent experiences of displacement in the everyday language of protracted conflict. These linguistic metaphors point towards deeper and layered aspects of meaning than might normally be assumed. Displacement functions both internally and externally. A person feels lost; they look for a sense of location and for bearings, thus underscoring the importance of place and belonging as significant components of healing, during and in the aftermath of violence. The search for belonging both during and in the aftermath requires a depth of movement. Internally, this depth moves towards relocating and touching voice and sense of self. Externally, depth metaphorically searches for roots, for connections with people and locations where life acquires a sense of place, where relationships can be trusted, and where voice emerges from meaningful conversation. We noted how these concepts in many regards have spatial and sonic aspects that understand healing and reconciliation as something that must touch a sense of 'being human again'. This may in very real terms capture Guzman's (2009) suggestion that the word 'person' has a connection to the Latin 'sonare'. Here to be a person represents a container that receives and holds the vibrations that make up sound, and provides an almost literal sense of health as staying in touch with self and others.

The notions of *repetition* and *circling* also have significant connections with the image of depth, particularly when metaphorically understood as *ritual* and as creating space for the sacred journey, as expressed in many religious traditions. By recasting phenomena like repetition and circling in the light of an ongoing search for purpose and the meaning of *being* human or, as many put it, 'feeling human again' we find a search for sensing the *depth* of spiritual aspects of wholeness. Again, we note the degree to which many of these metaphors require a capacity to feel, to touch and to sense. Vibration based, sound rises from this level of interactive space and vibration lies below, before and beyond words. *Understanding*, as Watts described it, requires 'feeling it in your bones'. As such the search to find, touch and share voice through repetition and circling, like the flow of music in jazz, the Australian Aboriginal songlines or drumming in Africa, provides space to feel for oneself and to locate place, belonging and purpose.

Second, we suggested a shift from a linear metaphor that views change as a sequential movement described as progress, to a metaphor more in tune with life – as a continuous flow of simultaneous and multilayered experiences. Here we noted the importance of structural and escalated spikes of open violence that do not easily or neatly move from pre- to post- stages, even though they are often described as such for analytical purposes. Rather, violence expresses itself in resilient patterns. Particularly in settings of protracted conflict, violence keeps bouncing back in new forms but plays out old patterns that often reinforce exclusion, creating isolation and enormous pain. For those who live through years, decades and even generations of these patterns, they experience something different from the pre-, during and post-conflict portrayed in our conceptual analyses. They live with an ongoing and simultaneous sense of violence as both *midst and aftermath*.

For many people and communities an extraordinary feature of this experience is found in *temporal simultaneity* in which they must nurture a creative capacity to survive, face violence resiliently and find small doses of human flourishing in the worst of situations. Framed as something much more continuous than a post-conflict phenomenon, temporal simultaneity provides spaces necessary for healing before, during and after the spikes of open violence and in the midst of responding to the structural injustice so prevalent in protracted conflicts. Through metaphors of *sound* and *music* we found parallel examples of temporal simultaneity. Sound creates what Van Morrison sang as the 'eternal now', the lived present as spacemoments creating and re-creating our experiences. While we may usually explain time as falling on a chronological line that runs from the past into the future, lived experience simultaneously holds the past, present and future, all within in a single moment. Through phenomena like music and sound we can in an instant feel transported back and forth across these lived temporal experiences. The spacemoments of lived experience are continuously multidirectional.

Correspondingly, it seems limiting to consider *health* as dependent on moving in a single direction, from past to future though, in essence, sequential progression seems to suggest this movement.

It may be useful to imagine health as the capacity to acknowledge and artistically mobilise *memory and hope* as ongoing features of the unique qualities of being human. This spatial and temporal understanding suggests the importance and potential of the simultaneity of multilayered experience. The journey of health requires a capacity to create meaning from a chaotic past while bringing forward the image of a hoped-for future.

Third, in sonic expression and poetry we noted a metaphor shift from progression as forward moving to maturity and spiritual engagement as evolving and expressing themselves multidirectionally. Quite differently from an image of health as moving uni-directionally forward – in which circling or backsliding is expected but is not seen as progress – sound, poetry and ritual evoke a view of health based on directional metaphors such as *moving inward* and *deepening*. These metaphors suggest the need to envision health as constant renewal. The search for meaning and place as a search for voice share these same qualities. Voice as aural metaphor has moments of great insight and projecting, characterised as *rising, moving outward* and creating *echoes expansively* in social space. Particularly rich, these sonic metaphors provide a basis from which we can explore several definitional contributions suggested through our exploration.

Definitions: the sonic metaphor shift

Protracted conflict and violence destroy human life, divide relationships and create irreplaceable loss. We suggested in our discussion that perhaps underestimated dimensions of this destruction are the loss of voice, sense of self, place and purpose. When deep harm is done, and when it is sustained over time, life loses meaning. Simply put, violence destroys voice, belonging and place. These elements contain important spatial and sonic-specific metaphoric references, particularly in the common use of voice as a way to portray the search for meaning internally and meaningful reconnection externally. In turn, an inquiry into healing requires that we think about how to recoup what has been lost. Our exploration poses the questions of what the definitions of healing, reconciliation and social healing might be from the perspective of an aural understanding of these key concepts, and what those definitions might offer to the practice and pursuit of these ideas in peacebuilding.

Healing

In settings of deep-rooted conflict violence must be understood as collective and systemic even though the suffering falls into the lives of real individuals. Healing as a stand-alone concept faces the important challenge that its micro-quality engages and develops with the individual as a person. Increasingly, research confirms that individual healing, particularly when dealing with deep violation, is enhanced – and perhaps can only be understood – by locating it within the context of the collective. This was further supported in our exploration of the intimate link between the individual and the collective. We suggest that though they are an abstraction, groups or collectives do heal. We add qualifiers to designate the communal nature of healing; qualifiers such as *national*, *community* or in the case of this essay, *social*. However, at its purest micro-level, healing is always a journey faced by and unfolding before the individual. A person heals. People may, and often do, join with others in a similar process that enhances and encourages this journey but each person still faces their own challenging journey. As human beings we don't heal at an equal pace or by similar processes even when we have collectively experienced similar damage. Healing is not a journey for the faint of heart. It takes courage, a process accurately characterised as heroic. With considerable insight many prefer the name survivor over the designation of victim to describe this journey. Surviving violence represents an act of creativity, the artistic rebirthing that must rise from the deadening impact of that which steals life itself.

Given this journey of the individual, the experience of healing, by its very nature, remains unique and highly idiosyncratic and varied. However, by looking at many individual cases, researchers and specialists see common patterns which, when analysed, denote stages, steps and progress that often suggest upwards and forwards metaphors, with directional guideposts marking the progression from harm to health.

From a sonic perspective, however, healing takes on different directional metaphors suggestive of a definition: *Healing represents the journeys to touch, reclaim, name and project voice.*

In settings of violence we noted the wide use of the word and metaphor *voice* as a way to describe the struggle to respond to violence. Finding one's voice and meaningfully projecting voice are keys to change. As directional metaphor, voice suggests more than one movement and none of these movements are linear in nature. The definitional use of 'journeys' in plural reinforces not only that healing requires more than one kind of movement, but that these are repeated over and again as part of a continuous process of health.

We found movement *inward* and *deep*, often conceptualised as the personal inner journey. We also noted the potential of voice to speak out, to *resonate expansively* into a shared social space – considered the outward journey. The sound and echo of this speaking touches spaces and moves in more than one direction. When we associate voice with ritual and health we recognise that seeking voice is not a 'once and it's over' endeavour. The journeys are constantly renewed, built on directional metaphors of circling, surrounding and repeating through which 'staying in touch' with voice and 'sensing' a depth of meaning are elements that contribute towards the construction of purpose in the lived world.

The challenge of sustained, structural and transgenerational violence requires that finding and staying in touch with voice correlates to finding one's bearings while traversing a barren, yet fluid and actively destructive land. Things keep happening that silence voice, destroy place, decimate belonging and pound on the sensitive wounds still raw from recent and long-patterned violence. In these landscapes memory and hope, so necessary for touching voice easily appear as polar opposites, out of reach and out of touch for the traveller.

At one extreme, social and political demands to heal force a forgetfulness that easily overwhelms and submerges memory in order to achieve change. We find this in common phrases and political agendas whether explicit or covert – 'forgive and forget' or 'let go of the past' – as mechanisms of moving on and healing. At the other extreme, hope finds itself diminished by the pragmatic demands of sequential change which, while promising substantial transformation, seems rarely to get beyond minimal steps of political accommodation; a realpolitik of reconciliation.

We return to our definition based on a sonic understanding: healing conceives of memory and hope not as representing opposite ends of a spectrum, or radically opposed horizons, but rather as forming the *container* that, when circled and probed in depth, facilitates the search for voice and makes it touchable. From this container the potential for meaningful conversation and purpose emerges. Necessarily then, healing requires containers relevant and within touch for individual journeys. This need for micro-proximity poses one side of our argument. The completing side requires us to explore how reconciliation may function as sound.

Reconciliation

Within a sonic metaphor we again move beyond a linear understanding of change that suggests a definition: *Reconciliation emerges as the mix of voices finds its natural frequency.*

We recall that physics explains the natural frequency as interacting frictional vibrations which, when connected at the right pace in a given space, rise into sound and resonance. In the context of protracted conflict, such a view again requires a container that holds the mix of voices expressed with the full friction of painful pasts, the idiosyncrasies of their individual journeys, and the jarring realities and commonality of experienced collective violence. From voices mixing and vibrations interacting in a commonly shared space – like the natural frequency of sound – reconciliation rises, creating spacemoments and the echoes of resonance. Contrary to an earlier book title (Lederach 1997) *sustainable reconciliation* is not sonically possible, for sound does not sustain itself independent of the dynamic relational spaces in which vibrations mix, rise and resonate. Reconciliation as sound suggests the need for constant nurturing, circling engagement, mixing and remixing of voices and the repeated deepening of meaningful conversation.

We note here several important themes. First, from a spatial view reconciliation requires proximity of voices; vibrations that create sound must be close enough to touch and interact. The container concept suggests that reconciliation requires some form of face-to-face relationship for voices to meaningfully interact. This suggests that the adjectives all too commonly employed with the term reconciliation – such as national, political or interreligious – are symbolic abstractions and will speak to a space of such grandeur and distance that they may in fact best be described as a void out of which echoes are faintly heard; though at times they may spark and touch individual people's everyday life.

By virtue of the sonic metaphor, reconciliation requires a container, a social space if you will, that holds relationships wherein direct conversation and exchange take place. In other words, a surrounding space is needed wherein voices mix and people feel a sense of resonance. These vibrations may circle and clang, go silent and recede, but when they mix, vibrate and find a natural frequency for a spacemoment, resonance emerges.

Herein we find a second important aspect of the sonic metaphor.

Resonance and sound do not last into perpetuity. There is no 'and-they-lived-happily-ever-after' in the real world of deep-rooted conflict. In fact the rise of resonance may last for fleeting moments only. What can last and remain more permanently available are the elements that permit the creating and re-creating of meaningful conversation, the bases from which resonance may rise, alongside other experiences of dissonance and silence. From this perspective there is the need to nurture the context within which a mixing of vibrations can happen, not as a one-time event but as a continuous engagement, constantly in need of renewal. We return again to a central theme of our exploration. Reconciliation as a sequential process with outcome and product that provide closure does not neatly match the metaphoric meaning structure of voice and sound. Voice and sound suggest the need for containers, the disciplined preparation of spaces that hold the circling, the deepening and the mixing within those spaces, and the commitment to repeat the process in the context of ongoing relationships.

This discussion may well seem absurd from the pragmatic view of political programming and the design and implementation of social projects. But we must remember that projects are constructed mechanisms based on a linear view of change through which agency is pursued to impact complex, fluid and multidimensional realities. This is particularly true of projects that promise social change in settings of protracted conflict and collective violence where reconciliation and healing are often proposed as the results – the outcomes of the project intervention. Projects rarely represent or adequately attend to the complexities they purport to change or deal with.

However, if the metaphoric association for reconciliation is not that of a project but, rather, reflects phenomena as diverse as ritual or spiritual practices and, to provide a vastly different image, democracy, then sound as the point of reference no longer seems absurd. Each of these phenomena requires a repeated practice and a deepening quality of commitment. None of these are assumed to conclude with a single iteration. We do not think of spiritual practices as a project that offers up a product on a one-time basis. We conceive of them as elements of growth, as deepening and touching aspects of human experience that require iterative commitment. The same could be said of democracy. While democracy has clear temporal markers, for example, elections, the fundamental metaphoric structure is one that requires the very foundational elements sonic metaphors highlight: the engagement of voice, the building of spaces for deepening meaningful conversation and the rise of occasional resonance and social echo in the midst of mixing frictions over and over again.

Social healing

What then of social healing? We suggest the concept may best be understood as occupying an intermediary space that touches on the idiosyncrasies of individual healing and the ephemeral promise of fully restored relationships. Following the impulse of our inquiry, from a sonic understanding, we suggest this definition: *Social healing represents the capacity of communities and their respective individuals to survive, locate voice and resiliently innovate spaces of interaction that nurture meaningful conversation and purposeful action in the midst and aftermath of escalated and structural violence.* Social healing sparks collective voice and creates social echo that simultaneously moves inward and out, fostering a sense of belonging and purposeful action.

In part this definition responds to a few of the perplexing questions emergent in settings of protracted conflict. Is it conceptually and practically possible to link the micro-dimensions of healing and the macro-dimensions of reconciliation in settings of protracted conflict? Is reconciliation possible if the original perpetrators have disappeared either because they have died or because they have been submerged under the cover of social amnesia as if they never existed? What if there is nothing to *re-concile*, that is, to bring back together; if there was no real relationship that ever existed? What if relationship is not desired or sought by those who perpetrated or suffered the violence? How do we deal with the transgenerational residue of structural violence where responsibility has been outsourced to earlier generations and little can be done to rectify damages committed a century or five ago, at least according to those who now stand privileged by the flow of history? What if healing is needed but the violence has not ended? What if national reconciliation is offered to those who live under oppressive leaders and forms of governance but with no time for genuine acknowledgement or willingness to provide even symbolic reparations? What of reparation offered as a bribe to move quickly beyond the need to actually engage in meaningful conversation or address the wrongs committed? These are, we believe, the most challenging questions in the healing and reconciliation debate. They also describe the all-too-current state of affairs in the places we described in the opening stories – Colombia, Somalia and West Africa – not to mention the long-ignored plight of indigenous people in many parts of the world.

Social healing offers a modest proposal. It suggests that in settings of protracted conflict the capacity of individuals and communities affected by violence to recuperate and stay in touch with their individual and collective voice creates the platform to build resiliency and foster meaningful conversation. In turn, voice and collective resiliency create significant echo that moves in multidirectional, simultaneous though unpredictable and often serendipitous patterns, touching and constructively impacting individual healing, the potential for reconciliation, and the impulse that mobilises ideas and movements for social change. This may seem like a simple response, given the depth and complexity of the questions just posed. Nonetheless these factors are among the core observations that emerged from our inquiry into a shift of metaphor for understanding aspects of healing and reconciliation and they seem to offer several theoretical inquiries for further work:

1. Based as it is on sound, social healing initiates in shared collective spaces that permit proximity of voices and interaction. As such, social healing proposes a *preferential option for the local community* as the context and level in which meaningful conversation emerges. The local community, often hit hard by violence and experiencing enormous division and survival demands, remains nonetheless the container with the greatest potential to create a mixing of voices. Social healing lodged at the local community level has the innate potential to link the journeys of individual people's voice with the collective rise of resonance and shared purpose perceived as meaningful. In summary, social healing requires conversation based in face-to-face relationships. While not fully understood or studied we are beginning to see the emergence of practice and approaches that take this community level seriously, most often initiated by communities that have experienced sustained violations over time. For example, the recent community-based initiatives aimed at local reconciliation and truth, conducted by Fambul Tok in Sierra Leone and documented by Libby Hoffman (2008), have generated remarkable response and outreach. Key to this process has been the active engagement of local communities as the actors and shapers of their process. The linking of these community experiences then contributes to an echo that resonates more widely.

   We note here that the concept of a 'national' reconciliation when it begins exclusively from the top level down remains one that happens in a space experienced as distant from the local community. While national actions on behalf of reconciliation create echoes that reach the community, these actions remain for the most part symbolic, rather than embedded in real-life relationships. Social healing finds roots in spaces that engage ongoing, real-life relationships. It requires a context of direct interaction that fosters voice, resiliency, meaningful conversation and purposeful action.

2. Social healing *focuses on collective resiliency*, the capacity of communities to find themselves, bounce back from repeated cycles of violence, and continue to respond constructively even in periods of survival. As such, social healing is sphere-like rather than linear in nature. It does not depend on the achievement of full individual healing or a robust reconciliation of enmity as necessary conditions for its practice. Rather it creates opportunities and conditions that prepare the soils, season after season, for the individual life journeys of healing and for the collective narratives of reconciliation. Resiliency may be best understood as generative soil capable of reproducing new growth in both instances.

3. Collective resiliency requires *the search for voice by proactively engaging memory and hope*. In contexts of protracted conflict, trauma and transgenerational violence voice emerges from iterative, ongoing processes through which people actively circle between generationally inherited, lived past experience and the vibrant image of a desired future. We never find a single meaning or interpretation of the past or the future in settings of protracted conflict. The past and the future remain alive, present and available, interacting in a dynamic way in the human community.

4. Voice builds from meaningful conversation *emergent in the discovery of naming, the claiming of new belonging and the framing of purpose-driven action that creates social echo*. In these three ideas we more succinctly define an understanding of meaningful conversation, particularly for those most affected by and living through the unspeakable midst and aftermath of direct and structural violence.

Meaningful conversation requires a circling around, talking over and again about experiences and hopes that are not easy to name and which may come with a thousand legitimate names. This iterative *naming* descends and rises again from the spaces of the unspeakable, feebly finding ways of deepening the understanding of events and experiences that are felt but around which the spoken sound does not easily take the form, shape and meaning of words. Social healing provides a context in which naming, as 'feeling it in the bones' can happen over and again through exchange, ideas and shared experiences.

Claiming suggests that meaningful conversation creates the space for choice and responsibility. Claiming has a real but mixed metaphoric meaning related to the ideas of ground and place. In settings of deep polarisation and protracted conflict, claiming language emerges in the way people talk about 'staking out ground'. The language rises from the divided spaces and relationships that solidify around enemy images and narrowly defined identity groups who feel insecure, their identity eroded by conflict; and a sense of 'losing ground'. The language is instructive. People talk about 'digging in', 'holding fast', 'not giving an inch', or literally 'holding to historic claims'. As the spaces narrow, creating nearly impermeable boundaries of sacred grounds and static (some would argue stagnant) views of self, identity and past, the range of conversation closes in as well.

This deep polarisation tends to create *echo* in the form of classic Greek mythology. Echo was the nymph who talked too much and was then cursed with an inability to originate or express new ideas or thoughts. She had only the capacity to repeat the last sounds that had been said by another and was forced into an interminable exile of meaningless exchange. A claiming discourse that digs in and repeats over and over again the same story that is heard only in narrow spaces of the like-minded has this quality of echo. Deeply divided societies with decades of sharp polarisation and painful experiences of violence on all sides live with hardened and calloused conversation, at times impenetrable. Tough layers build over years that protect the inner pain. In large part the pain is protected by engaging only in echo-like behaviour – finding and engaging in exchange that is already known, with little variation or challenge. In the end echo builds and reinforces mutually exclusive conversation with anyone outside the shared in-group conversation.

Necessarily and paradoxically meaningful conversation has to traverse this land, touch and peel these calluses over and again. For it is only in the context of slow but sure cultivation of trustworthy exchange in sustained relationships that a deeper image of claiming emerges, one that fosters a sense of *place* and the rebuilding of *belonging* capable of generating shared *purpose* that rises from the wider shared spaces inclusive of the diversity co-inhabiting the same geographies. Social healing cultivates the notion that claiming can focus on building mutual respect in a shared space while still living with conflicting narratives of memory and hope, and that this can translate into choice and responsibility for and by individuals and collectives on behalf of their own and a wider common good. Claiming in this metaphor finds new ground, a capacity for a community to say, 'here we stand, together' while respecting differing views of history and continuing to converse about the landscape of the future. It thus moves beyond the curse of Echo to open the interactive space that generates new insight, interpretation and meaning.

Framing suggests that meaningful conversation rises from interactive spaces that foster belonging and purposeful action. In the collective, voice emerges around the sharpening of resilient purpose, the bouncing back to pursue change, in spite of and while carrying the weight of history. With purposeful collective action voice rises into *social echo*. Social echo has a ripple effect like a wave of vibrating sound that expands, touches and impacts on wider spaces, and in turn is impacted by receiving back and feeling the vibration from other voices. In a very real sense, social change ultimately functions by the sonic metaphor of vibrations rising from voices and purposeful action that moves multidirectionally, impacting their immediate locations, while setting in motion ideas and impulses that affect distant spaces. Perceived and real voids are filled with echoes that bounce and reverberate. Ideas emerge, take shape, and move in multiple and usually unexpected directions.

5. Social echo has the *power to touch and impact both the micro individual healing and the macro wider context of reconciliation.* Sound moves multidirectionally. Social echo, based on voice and meaningful conversation, creates impact simultaneously in two directions. On the one hand it has the capacity to touch and be felt by the individual. On the other, it creates waves of ideas, action and impulse that move in and out from the local community. In this sense, voice can be understood as power, inasmuch as it represents the capacity of collective action to touch and move other spaces. This is not power to control process, resource allocation or political positions. Rather, it is power defined as the ability to authentically engage the self, other and social spaces that make possible the very validity of social and political power. In the midst and aftermath of violence, social healing that fosters collective resilience helps create the context, impulse and resonance needed to dynamically build, over and over again, the social contract necessary for a healthy public sphere.

We can visualise a few of these ideas in the following figure that poses the question: what reach and kind of social echo do various types of voice create? (See Figure 4.) Though a two-dimensional figure is not entirely adequate, our aim is to visualise the space affected by a significant violent conflict. Our suggestion is that all voice with purposeful action creates a vibration, a sound with echo that enters this space. On the micro end we find individual action. On the macro we locate action seen at the large group or national level. Across this space we then give consideration to actions aimed primarily at healing and those that purport to reconcile.

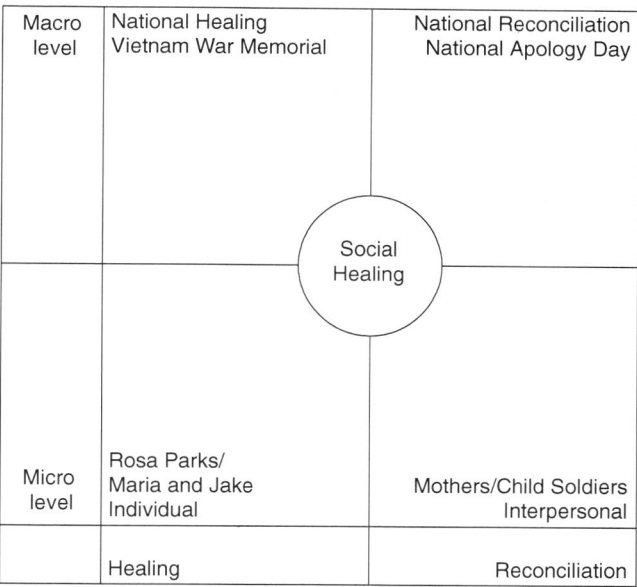

Figure 4. The echoes of social healing.

Starting at the micro healing space we locate the courageous actions of individuals who in the midst and aftermath of violence find ways to move their trauma towards healing. In these spaces this individual process creates a social echo, a sound wave that in all likelihood touches those around them: family, friends and perhaps their community. Often this is limited in scope. The social echo touches but remains in limited space.

In his early work, Robert Schreiter explored a theology of healing and reconciliation, and compared individual with what he referred to as social reconciliation. His work has a distinct parallel with our inquiry into social healing. He specifically refers to the linkage between the micro and macro by suggesting that social reconciliation requires, as he calls it 'a cadre of reconciled individuals' (Schreiter 1998, p. 65). His understanding posits that unless a critical number of individuals as leaders engage and deepen a personal resiliency and healing, then the wider society will not make a transition towards a qualitative shift in public health related to the wider experienced trauma. Here we see that the social echo has the potential for accumulative effect that would reach beyond the micro sphere.

We return for a moment to our opening stories. Maria, in her courageous and resilient pursuit to have the bones in the box named, touched people in her family and community. Though fleetingly and without as much impact, she touched people in the distant national and regional capitals. More importantly perhaps, she created a social echo that helped form a collective that faced economic hardship and pursued the opening of the mass graves. Jake, lost and far from home, found small initial steps for healing. He planted a coconut tree. He made a drum. From his individual space social echo emanated and bounced back as he opened space for others, younger than he, like Morris who arrived ten years later at the refugee camp.

Our attention is of course drawn to individuals who find ways to reach far beyond their immediate space, whose story captivates and touches in such a way that it transcends the normal reach and creates a social echo that can in fact move many people. Rosa Parks, whose action was to sit down in the front of a segregated bus, was a person of resilient health and purposeful action. That action sparked the imagination and touched the core of people far beyond her immediate family, friends or community. So too in the Women of Liberia Mass Action for Peace Campaign, the women lined the streets, sat and raised their voice. Social echo can move widely and quickly even from the action of an individual person, though individual resiliency and healing faces a large, expansive space to touch.

If we move into the quadrant that deals with reconciliation at the micro level we again find many examples. From our stories we found mothers who reached out to returning child soldiers at the Tree of Frustration. Though they were not the birth mothers of these children and in spite of the pain they had suffered at their hands, the women reached out to engage a new relationship with a lost generation. They cut hair and sang them into a new birth. Hand in hand, the women and children walked back into the town. It nurtured an early reconciliation between small numbers of individuals. The social echo, however, vibrated across the community, created new spaces of interaction and touched even hardened soldiers, contributing to healing. The social echo was interpersonal, local and communal.

The paradoxical challenge of social echo is found in the ways micro and macro levels blur. Schreiter refers to the example of Mandela in this regard as a 'reconciled' individual who contributed to wider social healing (1998, p. 65). The relationship of Presidents de Klerk and Mandela provides an example of two men, highly visible, with national platforms and simultaneously an example of two men developing an interpersonal relationship across the lines of historic animosity. Their relationship, finding their voices mixing towards a resonance in the midst and aftermath of the South African journey, created from the interpersonal space a social echo that impacted the imagination, imbuing the context with an ethos of constructive change.

As we move towards the quadrants that focus on macro healing and reconciliation we again face the paradox. The macro level by its very nature has a platform to touch spaces beyond its originating location. However, as we noted in earlier chapters, initiatives purporting to be national in nature are not always experienced by those most affected at the local level by the violence as touching them in ways they can experience as meaningful and relevant to their healing processes. Is it possible to locate events, initiatives and processes which, while symbolic and *national* in nature, affected a wider experience of healing and reconciliation, or what we could refer to as meaningful social echo? Several come to mind as examples that may easily be recognised by the reader.

After the Vietnam War the United States government explored ways of memorialising the events and tragedies of that war. The war had left thousands dead and a country divided. Designer architect Maya Lin was a young student when she submitted her proposal for a V-shaped wall rising up out of the ground of a grassy park. While initially seen by some as inadequate because of its simplicity, the memorial has become perhaps the most interactive and healing of any memorial constructed in the United States. Unlike many other war memorials that are based on massive sculptures which tower over the viewer and create primarily a visual interaction, the Vietnam Veterans Memorial is set at ground level, its wall within reach of the observer. It consists only of highly polished slabs of black granite. Though several sculpted figures are found nearby, visitors are drawn as if by a magnet to the wall with the names of the almost 60,000 soldiers who lost their lives or remain missing in action. The visitors' hands run lightly across the names, looking for family or friends they know. Sometimes they take paper and pencil to rub across the name etched in the stone, creating an imprint of the name to carry home. It is not uncommon to find people, strangers and even those who hold radically different views of the Vietnam War, gathering together, to talk, remember and cry.

Griswold (2007), in his book that explores a philosophy of forgiveness, provides an intriguing description of the history and implications of this memorial on the social ethos and healing in the

United States. Among his primary concerns was the lack of federal government acknowledgement of contrition, of what he calls the 'unfortunate result of silences of the official narrative' that he rightly notes cannot become the habit of nations in these situations where serious mistakes cost the lives of thousands (2007, p. 209). At the same time, in considerable detail, he notes the varied 'therapeutic values' the experience of the monument seems to create for people. He describes this as the way in which people search for names, 'touch' even 'caress' the wall and, inevitably, given the polished face of the stone, see their own reflection as they gaze into the names that seem to gaze back (2007, p. 207). In addition the architect, Lin, indicated in her original proposal that she hoped the scar cut into the earth from which the wall rises would heal with the grass around it (2007, p. 207). His essay finishes with a focus on what he finds lacking in the monument: a more honest public rendering of accountability. His critique, reminiscent of Shriver's *Honest patriots* (2005), suggests the need for greater transparency, for direct and public admission of wrongdoing that should underscore a clear call for national remembrance and reparations.

Our focus here, however, is on the questions of why a monument of this kind has such a capacity to touch a range of people in what they refer to as a healing experience and whether a stone can create a social echo. Several explanations emerge that reinforce aspects of our inquiry, the most specific being that the monument is a mechanism by which the unspeakable becomes touchable and creates echo: the names etched in a way that invites people to touch them, the reflective capacity of the black stone face that inevitably requires people to see themselves as they peer into the names, the touchable proximity of the entire monument that permits direct interaction beyond the purely visual and, in the simple act of touching the names, the moment to remember and speak them silently or aloud, then carry the names home from that place. Something simple – the etching of a touchable name – seems to create an echo that has touched millions.

In Australia a similar though different process emerged around the National Sorry Day and subsequent expressions, in particular the Bridge Walk. While the events of the past years have been varied they trace their roots to a national inquiry into the removal of Aboriginal children and nationally sanctioned separation policies. The process culminated in the Wilson report titled *Bringing them home*.[1] The report was prepared by a seasoned and no-nonsense lawyer, Sir Ronald Wilson, who found himself so moved by the scores of stories he listened to one after the other that what started as an intellectual inquiry, in his words, 'changed me. And if it can change me, it can change our nation' (Bond 2008, p. 310). Six hundred and eighty pages in length, as a report to government, it could easily have disappeared into the archives except that the public yearned to know more. It has sold in far greater numbers than any previous government report (Bond 2008, p. 308). The documented stories echoed and resonated.

Bringing them home recommended that some form of national remembrance and commemoration should be pursued. Nurtured by public interest and formal acknowledgement, the seeds of the National Sorry Day were planted and cultivated. The stories and the large number of them touched people in both populations, the Indigenous who, when they grieve the loss of a loved one, engage in what they refer to as 'sorry business' (Bond 2008, p. 311), and the non-Indigenous. The Federal Government however was not interested in promoting anything official. With the support of Sir Ronald Wilson a small group of 30 people began to meet. In January 1998 this group of Aboriginal and non-Aboriginal Australians proposed that 26 May be National Sorry Day (Bond 2008, p. 311). With the formation of a committee, word spread from the 30 to thousands. Without Federal sanction and promotion the process moved to communities throughout the nation. On 26 May thousands of events took place across the country in local communities and cities, books were launched, money was raised for reparations, and the national news agencies dedicated more than half of their evening prime time to cover the events (Bond 2008, p. 311). The echo, initiating from a national inquiry, back to a small group of 30, and then out again across the nation, created ripples that have reverberated ever since. In subsequent years the national day gained prominence and spawned new events including a massive quarter of a million-person walk across the Sydney Harbour Bridge in 2000. Bond, when writing about these events in the year 2008, posed the question:

> Why did Sorry Day touch such a chord? One of the deepest human pains is that of a mother who loses her child or a child its mother. Yet the gulf between Aboriginal and non-Aboriginal Australians was simply too immense for even this pain to flow across it. *Bringing them home* exposed this gulf, and many Australians were shocked. Sorry Day was a chance to accept blame, and to do something about it (Bond 2008).

We find here a story that intriguingly moved in small ripples and large waves across our figure. Arising as it did out of a national inquiry we suggest that the *Bringing them home* document was a form of national truth-telling, though once published it was not received with interest or acted on at the Federal level. Its echo, however, touched thousands of individuals. The initiative moved down into a small group that began a process that reached back out to and found a home at the community level. The purposeful action emerged from meaningful conversation that launched within and across communities and ultimately became, properly stated, a 'national' day of considerable significance.

We cannot help but notice the metaphors chosen by Bond to

answer his own question; his language finds its way back into our earlier inquiries into the idea of social healing. First, as he framed his question he asked why this event *touched a chord*. Second, he framed the process in the setting of *losing a child*, motherless and childless. Third, he noted the *gulf* was so immense that the pain could not flow across it and no echo was possible. Fourth, he suggested that the *stories* made the gulf visible, creating a sensation of needing to reach across, to bridge and to call out beyond the chasm. Fifth, Sorry Day created an opportunity, a *chance* for meaningful conversation and purposeful collective action.

Conclusion

What our figure explores are ways in which people's experiences, processes and voices create waves, echo if you will, with the capacity to move in more than one direction, touching spaces both within and beyond its initial locality. Among the observations we have made in the preceding chapters is the suggestion that social healing lies between the idiosyncratic micro processes of individuals seeking to heal in the midst and aftermath of violence and the more distant macro processes that purport to provide national reconciliation. In our view social healing emerges at community levels, in spaces where face-to-face relationships and interaction take place. These are micro inasmuch as they refer to individuals and their relationships embedded in local communities. They are macro in that they comprise groups. The ways in which community-based processes emerge have significant characteristics that emulate the movement of sound. In essence, social healing functions sonically in terms of how it impacts people and contexts, which may shed light on the prominence of voice, naming and echo as common metaphors to explain the struggle of how people describe the journey of responding to and rising from experiences and contexts of sustained violence.

In this aural sense local communities form a container within which vibrations interact multidirectionally in that they impact both the individual healing and the wider reconciliation. In settings of protracted conflict, as local communities deal with the need to find ways to address their inevitable interdependence constructively, most commonly as they address immediate need and shared purpose, the interaction of their journeys with myriad frictions as described in the Tibetan singing bowl, creates echo that ripples both towards the individual healing and the wider rebuilding of local relationships. Through our exploration of key metaphors we have suggested that healing and reconciliation can be characterised as having significant aspects that are repetitive, deepening and multidirectional.

Social healing holds the promise of three distinct theoretical contributions. First, social healing creates accessibility. It creates an intermediary space between the individual process and the collective. In this regard social healing sits within touch and reach of daily life for both individuals and the immediate expression of their face-to-face relationships, even those that cross important historic and social divides, given their immediate interdependence at local levels. As such, social healing has a greater opportunity to respond to affected people's more immediate concerns and relationships.

Second, social healing offers multidirectionality of impact through vibration. Social healing ripples. Its contribution lies in the potential to simultaneously impact both the individual finding voice within the healing journey – without prescription as to pace or uniformity – while at the same time it creates, over and again, opportunity for meaningful conversation and exchange in actual relationships and collective action. This multidirectionality suggests a potential to create appropriate spaces for meaningful engagement and the development of proactive purposeful action that touches people with reference to their felt needs. In essence, social healing touches voice in both understandings of the word: the internal challenge of resiliency to stay in touch and the external need for voice as power requiring the collective resiliency to effect the change needed in local settings.

Third, the very context of social healing as an interactive engagement of voice, what we metaphorically call the 'friction creating vibration' gives rise to a ripple effect, or social echo. Social echo requires meaningful conversation, the movement out and back of expressed ideas, needs and hopes. The conditions out of which social echo emerges necessarily contain the movement out and the bounce back, creating as such potential, if not real, impacts in spaces beyond its originating source. Theoretically, social echo has the capacity to touch and move spaces in locations near and far. The dynamics by which this happens, we suggest, may have significant parallel to the movement of sound in space and goes considerably beyond the notion that change happens in purely linear, progressive ways.

We find in these hypothetical musings a number of ideas that suggest the potential and prominence of an aural theory of social change, in particular around the themes of healing and reconciliation. This line of theoretical inquiry proposes that perhaps the base foundation by which change happens is less like a phase-based progression and more akin to the physics and dynamics of sound in space. It moves in multiple directions that appear more sphere-like than linear in nature. The promise of this inquiry may help broaden our notions of how programs and social change initiatives are understood and developed.

CHAPTER 12

Conclusions

I live my life in widening circles
that reach out across the world.
I may not complete this last one
but I give myself to it.
I orbit around God, around the primordial tower.
I've been circling for thousands of years
and I still don't know: am I a falcon,
a storm, or a great song?
Rainer Maria Rilke

We started this book with an invitation to enter an adventurous and experimental journey. We wove through stories, explored Tibetan singing bowls and music, the cutting of hair under a kum tree and the resilient poetry of a child mother. At times it was possible to feel the vibrations in the bones, below and beyond the words. The child poet's voice rang out: 'My body is in my heart'. Her words moving from gut to mouth feebly groped to locate the felt reality of the unspeakable.

We wish that we could say 'and all ended well'. But that would disrespect the heroic journey. Maria died of cancer in 2009 and while their father's bones have been officially named, the children are still displaced far from their *finca* and have received no reparations. The Falui Poets Society buried fellow poet Tom Cauuray in October 2009. Jake and Morris still long for a place to call home. Somaliland is as yet unrecognised while to its south the fighting still rages after several decades. Liberia has a woman president, but the country struggles on a daily basis with the presence of the past and the slow carving of a redefined future. What we can offer are insights into the heroic journey. Three emerge around this initial exploration into a metaphor shift.

First, our explorations suggest that language has significance beyond the scope of definitional meaning. Metaphor matters. The preceding chapters and stories suggest that through examination of underlying concepts and constructs it is possible to locate metaphoric structure that elucidates lived experience and agency. This inquiry suggests that too little attention has been paid to the lived experience of local communities in settings of protracted conflict. The underpinning metaphors rising from that experience offer important insights into the complexity of healing and reconciliation, support the notion of simultaneous temporality, and highlight the critical aspects of locating individual and collective voice, creating echo and building resiliency in the face of direct and structural violence. On the other side, we also find that significant aspects of programmatic agency are primarily guided by a linear understanding of social change that rarely operates as neatly as they are proposed. More importantly, however, is the myriad of unnoticed ways that agency is organised around a linear modality, including a project-based approach to complex change, short-term temporal approaches to reaching goals and funding – a lifeline for many community-based organisations – that views its contribution in terms of logical sequencing of results. At least in this initial level of exploration the metaphors of lived experience suggestive of an aural understanding of change seem to be at a considerable distance from the linear metaphoric structure of sequential change. It raises a useful question about the dominance and power of a project-driven mentality for addressing the complexity of change needed in settings of protracted conflict.

Second, this initial exploration has suggested the importance of proximity with reference to social healing. Specifically, more careful attention paid to communities affected by cycles of violence highlights the importance of meaningful conversation; of recovering and sharing stories that require safety and the deepening of social spaces that respect the complexity of naming unspeakable realities as processes of discovery and the artistic-like expression of resiliency. The metaphoric structure we explore suggests the images of local containers and tangible surrounding love that nurture the space for individuals and collectives which still know full well that the animosity, enmity and violent patterns are still present. This poses significant paradoxical challenges. Social healing requires staying in touch both as a push *into* the individual internal process and *out* towards the building of meaningful conversation that is palpable for local communities. It also requires collective resiliency, the bouncing back time and again in the face of structural injustices and open violence. The key hypothesis suggested: social healing and reconciliation touch a chord that creates meaningful echo in the context of actual, real-life relationships.

Third, considerable evidence emerges through this inquiry that social healing operates on the basis of an aural understanding of change. Key metaphors prevalent in the language of those affected by protracted conflict, particularly around sonic-based notions to locate place, find voice, and create meaningful spaces and conversation, suggest a structure organised around phenomena such as vibration, sound and reverberation of social echo. This would seem to reinforce the insights that containers, circles, ceremony, ritual, artistic process, music and poetry, to mention a few, provide a *central* not a peripheral component of the change process. Not uncommonly the mentioned elements are seen as additives, components that accompany the process of change and healing, while the key to change lies in a capacity to understand and explain it. From an aural perspective these elements create fount and foundation. It is here, as suggested by Watts, that the vibration is 'felt in the bones', that change hits a chord below and beyond words. What is additional and accompanies these aural elements is the retrospective discourse to explain the centrality of the actual experiences, often multiple and repetitious, formed by the many points of friction that gave rise to the resonant experience of change. An aural understanding inverts the notion of what may be central and peripheral, similar to Van Morrison who sang in his inarticulate speech of the heart that he wanted his head to feel and his heart to speak.

The insights also suggest some practical implications, or perhaps in the fine Somali tradition referred to in Chapter 7 we could refer to these as evocations. First, those who use the term 'national reconciliation' widely and increasingly randomly in a political sense would do well to refine their language. Too often what is actually meant is some form of political compromise or accommodation, though not necessarily the end of hostile conflict. This compromise is a laudable goal but it does not approximate or respect the far deeper and more complex process of reconciliation: the word is then diminished significantly in its meaning.

For national political leadership what may be most useful from this study is the careful consideration of two suggestions rising from an aural framework of change. On the one hand it will take considerable creativity and understanding to locate mechanisms that attend to the deeper aspects of widespread collective healing; mechanisms which are rarely reliant on one-time public displays or speeches. The aural approach suggests mechanisms that sustain contact, provide repeated ways of remembering together, with spaces of access and local participation in which to create greater social echo. Efforts such as the National Sorry Day in Australia have created intriguing ways for a national process to link with public access. On the other hand, and perhaps most importantly, is the key role that national political programs can play if they acknowledge that social healing requires safe, protected and local containers for meaningful conversation and the development of purposeful action that attends to the needs of local communities. Too often national programs tasked with peace, justice, truth and reparations agendas follow a form of agency that is very linear in nature. They become distant bureaucracies functioning with a top-down approach in both process and outcome, while at the same time they focus heavily on outreach, which individualises people as 'cases' within a legal structure. Social healing argues for increased acknowledgement of the collective nature of violence. This acknowledgement requires a focus on community-based participation, in other words, local collectives that help shape, develop and participate meaningfully in the national program outreach.

For the wide array of international and national organisations, foundations and educational programs a similar proposal may emerge. An aural approach suggests that in the growing fields of healing and reconciliation the culture of agency – the ways in which programs deliver funding and propose the organisation of activities – has relied too heavily on the promised deliverables in linear modalities of operation. The degree to which their agency organises around the linear view of change inadvertently hides and diminishes other important aspects of social healing. Equally unaccounted for is how much the spaces for healing and reconciliation in settings of protracted conflict can function in frameworks guided by the aural, the circular and the realities of temporal simultaneity. The practical implications are numerous. Social healing suggests a need for much longer-term approaches that work towards assuring that platforms exist locally for sustaining interaction. The aural aspects of voice, music, poetry, ceremony and meaningful conversation open towards more than just counting events, providing training in conflict resolution or creating dialogues. It requires capacity to attend to, notice and encourage the fields and landscapes of change, many invisible to the eye but which, like radio waves, are aural in their touch and reach. Fundamental are the notions of deepening, touching voice and reaching towards resonance and social echo. When people in many settings of protracted conflict note that information and change 'moves by word of mouth' this should be understood in its metaphoric if not literal projection. Programmatic capacity to envision change has been held hostage to a project mentality, and limited by evaluating logical frameworks that accept with little question linear views of change and limit the ability to understand, value and encourage forms of agency that do not operate exclusively by these modalities. The preceding chapters are offered as a starting point, a small contribution to suggest the need to open and explore with greater vigour the recognised but mostly excluded aspects of complexity that do not rely on linear understandings of social change.

We note at the end of this book our own growing admiration for what is perhaps the single greatest unnoticed aspect of social healing which impacts on both the individual and the collective: the presence of surrounding love. We first began to feel this intuition when we were inspired by the women in our stories. Essentialist perspectives would argue that their actions represent little more than a form of feminine outreach and response. As discussed in several preceding chapters, such a view misses the point on several levels. First it tends to overlook and dismiss the extraordinary courage and intentional purpose with which women have interacted at the community levels before, during and after armed conflicts. Second, perhaps more importantly, it overlooks the transformative power of the invisible but tangible presence of love in settings of pain and hate.

Love has not commonly been a topic of much discussion in the literature on healing and reconciliation in settings of deep-rooted conflict. This may be due in large part to the burden experienced by peace studies researchers and authors: that our chosen field represents a 'soft' science struggling for legitimacy among existing disciplines. To directly and openly discuss love enters the slippery slope of the intangibles that lie outside the scientific endeavour. We beg to differ for a number of reasons.

For those whose lens is exclusively scientific rigour and objectivity, we note that members of the scientific community from numerous disciplines – the medical sciences, neurology, psychology and sociology – have made serious inquiry into various aspects of love in recent years (Cozolino 2006; Fisher 2004; Lewis et al. 2001; Siegel 1999, 2007). Perhaps most significant of these inquiries is the book *A general theory of love* by psychiatrists Lewis, Amini and Lannon (2001). They describe clearly the impact and importance of love as a transformative component of healing and its impact on relationships. And, as we mentioned in Chapter 8, neurologist Oliver Sacks (2007, p. 212), describes the way in which Clive (a patient with a severe form of amnesia who had a memory for a fleeting living present only; he was incapable of remembering the past or of envisioning a future) was only truly alive and himself at the piano or in the presence of his wife Deborah, whose unconditional love had been unwavering for the many decades of his condition. Increasingly, some in the scientific community believe that something tangible, though teasingly invisible, exists in the presence of love in human relationships and it has an impact on health at all levels.

John Fetzer, mega-businessman, entrepreneur and former owner of the major league baseball team, the Detroit Tigers, believed the same. Much of his wealth came from the early years of radio. He was fascinated by the notion that something invisible, such as an electromagnetic wave on which sound could travel and whose energy could be harnessed, had constructively changed the way the human community was linked and communicated. How many other things he wondered were invisible but tangible that could change our world for good? He believed the single greatest invisible but poorly harnessed of these phenomena was the power of love. He wrote, 'love is the core energy that rules everything...the one ingredient that holds us all together' (Fetzer Institute 2009). This inquiry became the primary focus of his life in his later years and for him it, of necessity, linked spirituality and science. He endowed the Fetzer Institute with the proceeds of the sale of the Detroit Tigers and his media holdings. Over the decades the Institute has made a significant impact in the areas of holistic and community health. The mission of the Institute 'to foster awareness of the power of love and forgiveness in the emerging global community rests on our conviction that efforts to address the world's critical issues must go beyond political, social, and economic strategies to their psychological and spiritual roots' (Fetzer Institute 2009).

Key to our inquiry is the awareness that rises from the simple recognition that, although not visible, love has a tangible impact, and that love may in fact move in spatial and aural modalities. Our inquiry into an aural theory of social healing and change suggests the importance of felt, experienced vibration that according to 'string theory' lies at the very basis of how life itself is constructed at the subatomic level. As we move out from the quantum level of micro-vibration we have also suggested that these invisible but extraordinary sonic components are the ones that perhaps lie below and beyond words; the terrain of how we respond to the unspeakable which is faced by so many in settings of violence. Their primary need is to feel again. They seek to touch the voice, to gain a sense of self and meaning. This endeavour to re-touch and feel human again happens in a container of safe and meaningful conversation and relationship. The very notion by which such containers are constructed may rely less on the technical aspects of facilitating dialogue and much more on the intuitive feel of safety experienced palpably as an expression of unconditional love. These micro-sonic vibrations, when held within reach, interact in ways that affect well-being, relationships and finding ways to be and to stay in touch. Perhaps key to this invisible but tangible phenomena is precisely what Fetzer called the core energy, and what we described as the surrounding power of love. Such love was courageously displayed by mothers in West Africa; it was found most consistently in the outreached hand, the cutting of the hair, the singing of the child soldiers back into the community they had earlier destroyed.

Finally, it seems particularly illustrative of this point to notice the evolution of insight and thinking over a lifetime of work and writing experienced by people who are formative in the field of peacebuilding, healing and reconciliation. Such was certainly the case of Adam Curle, Quaker conciliator, whose written work spans the 1960s to 2006. His first major book in the field of peace studies, *Making peace* (1971), is a seminal work that influenced theorists and practitioners in the decades that followed. He was the first director of the Bradford Peace Studies degree program (United Kingdom) and author of dozens of formative books and articles. We see an evolution in this pioneer of international conciliation over his more than 40 years of work. In his early years and throughout his career, Adam concerned himself with the conceptual frameworks, theories and technical aspects of his work and experience as a reflective practitioner. Alongside that more technical aspect, a concern emerges as he goes deeper and writes about the spiritual underpinnings of what motivated him to do this work and what sustained him in the midst of enormous violence and chaos; ranging from the Biafran–Nigerian war to the many trips he made well into his eighties to the Balkans.

His final major publication just prior to his death in 2008 carried the most intriguing title, *The fragile voice of love* (2006). In the early pages Adam describes people who choose love even in the presence of hate and animosity. Of these people he wrote the lines we placed at the beginning of this book, they 'simply love and respect us. These are true leaders of humanity, descendants in a direct spiritual line from one or other of the great teachers. They can be recognized by their amazing generosity in both giving and receiving unconditional love' (Curle 2006, p. 4).

In the title of his book we find our primary themes. The fragility of life in facing the overwhelming challenge of violence that is the daily bread of so many who live in the difficult terrains of protracted conflict. To locate their fragile voice, to touch the innermost aspect of feeling human again, reaching below and beyond words, and then to find the strength and courage to reach out towards others and in this to live the life of what Rilke called the 'widening circles'. This incarnates social healing: the vulnerable risk of healing and reconciliation found in the long inner and outer journeys that bounce into social echo; an echo with invisible though tangible waves that emanate and surround us when the fragile voice of love reverberates.

Acknowledgements

We deeply appreciate the many people who inspired this writing and the formative conversations we shared with them over the years. Our gratitude begins with those whose lives have led by example in settings overrun with violence.

These include our dear colleagues and friends in West Africa: Leymah Gbowee and her inspirational work with the Women Peace and Security Network Africa; Emmanuel Bombande and family for their wonderful hospitality; and all the friends at the West Africa Network for Peacebuilding for their unceasing vision and commitment to cultivating healing in West Africa. And for William Saa, William Jacobs, the Reverend Moses Khanu, Haja Kassim, Ebun James and Kadiatu Koroma. We want to extend a particular word of gratitude to Samuel Doe, whose story of wading in the sea and singing the loss of a friend in the early years of the war in Liberia inspired our first connections between trauma and song. We are deeply grateful to Farouk Sesay and carry with us abiding memories of poet Tom Cauuray. A special thanks to Kirsten Rian, poet and peacebuilder, who helped make connections and poetry workshops possible with Farouk, Tom and the inspirational scribes of the Falui Poets Society in Sierra Leone.

From Colombia we wish to thank Father Rafael Cardenas, Father Dario Echeverri, Paul Stucky, Ricardo Esquivia, Doris Berrio, Martha Ines Romero; the inspiration from the community in

La India, especially Donaldo, Mauicio, Llanero and Dámaris Vargas; Jenny Neme and the dear colleagues at Justapaz; and the Mennonite Church and the Secretariat of the Social Pastorate of the Catholic Church.

Gratitude, as well, for those Stateside whose lives have also inspired this writing. Particularly for all our friends at the St Peter Claver Catholic Worker House in South Bend, who provided the space and community of support that helped make this book possible.

At a more formal level we are indebted and very thankful for research and writing funding that came from various sources as this book unfolded. A special thanks to the University of Notre Dame Undergraduate Opportunity Grant that made travel to West Africa possible and to the Kroc Institute for International Peace Studies at the University of Notre Dame for constant encouragement and support for these lines of research. To Elizabeth Hoffman and Catalyst for Peace whose support made more extended and community-based research and practice in West Africa possible, and to Sara Terry and Claire Putzeys for accompaniment. We want to acknowledge with gratitude the Rockwell Lectureship Series at Rice University where the first formal writing emerged on the Tibetan singing bowl and reconciliation. Among our strongest supporters as these themes were developed have been the Fetzer Institute, and in particular a word of thanks to poet Mark Nepo, Tom Callahan, David Addis and Shirley Showalter for their great feedback on early drafts, constant encouragement and support for the development of a paper on resiliency and healthy communities which contributed significantly to Chapter 5 on shifting metaphors. We would also like to thank Happy Trails, in Nederland Colorado, for endless cups of coffee and a creative space that generated much of our writing.

We are deeply grateful for the support, encouragement and constructive feedback we received from our colleagues as we worked through various drafts and efforts to bring this topic together. In particular we wish to thank Scott Appleby, director of the Kroc Institute for International Peace Studies and avid supporter of pursuing music and healing; our always imaginative anthropologist colleagues at the University of Notre Dame, Carolyn Nordstrom and Cynthia Mahmood; the wonderful feedback from Lisa Schirch, Robert Schreiter, Parker Palmer, Patrick Corrigan, Casey Stanton, and Jeffrey Yoder. A special note of gratitude to Ted Grimsrud who first inspired our deeper exploration of Van Morrison and who served as the *de facto* archivist of songs and lyrics we needed to find and understand. To Van Morrison, should you ever read these words, we extend our gratitude for your music and hold open a standing invitation for coffee and a session at our house in the mountains not far from Red Rocks.

The writing of this book, while complicated in its purpose and breadth received continuous and constructive support and feedback from the team at University of Queensland Press. We feel fortunate to have had such an excellent accompaniment that went beyond the call of duty. A heartfelt note of gratitude goes to Kevin Clements, Madonna Duffy, Nikola Lusk and the always artful editing and support from Sybil Kesteven.

Finally, beyond words we are grateful for the support of our family, starting with grandparents, Mary Liechty for giving us constant encouragement, Naomi Lederach for wonderful feedback, and John Lederach whose artistic hand etched the first versions of our graphics; to Wendy, wife and mother, who has always carried music in her heart and soul and whose unceasing support and encouragement kept this book moving even in difficult times; and to Josh, son and brother, who listened to our discussions and gave us great insight on what music mattered.

'Ceremony', from *Ceremony* by Leslie Marmon Silko, copyright © 1977 by Leslie Silko. Used by permission of Viking Penguin, a division of Penguin Group (USA) Inc. Figure 1 adapted from *Turbulent Peace: The Challenges of Managing International Conflict*, Copyright © 2001 by the Endowment of the United States Institute of Peace. Reprinted with permission by the United States Institute of Peace, Washington, DC. 'Tomorrow Is A Long Time', written by Bob Dylan. Copyright 1991 Special Rider Music. All rights reserved. International copyright secured. Reprinted by permission. Extracts from *Van Morrison: too late to stop now*, by Steve Turner. Copyright 1993. Reprinted by permission of Viking Penguin, a division of Penguin Group (USA) Inc. 'Epitaph of a Nation', written by Tom P Cauuray. Copyright 1997. All rights reserved. Reprinted by permission. Extract from Carolyn Forché's anthology *Against Forgetting: Twentieth-century Poetry of Witness*, WW Norton & Company, New York. Copyright 1993. Reprinted by permission. 'I live my life', from *Selected Poems of Rainer Maria Rilke: A Translation from the German and Commentary* by Robert Bly. Copyright © 1981 by Robert Bly. Reprinted by permission of HarperCollins Publishers.

Endnotes

Foreword
1. *Dadirri*, a special quality, a unique gift of the Aboriginal people, is inner deep listening and quiet still awareness. (Miriam Rose Ungunmerr, 1988.)
2. Gnibi: the College of Indigenous Australian Peoples at Southern Cross University, Lismore, Australia.
3. Gnibi, College of Indigenous Australian Peoples, SCU.

Chapter 1
1. This story is based on a series of interviews with William 'Jake' Jacobs and Morris at the Buduburam Refugee Camp.

Chapter 3
1. This story was compiled from personal interviews with Leymah Gbowee, William Saa and Etweda 'Sugars' Cooper, as well as from the documentary *Pray the Devil back to Hell*, released in 2008.

Chapter 4
1. The names and locations have been changed because of the difficulties faced by families like Maria's in Colombia. This story was recounted in the first person; the details emerged over more than three years of work with a displaced community.

Chapter 5
1. WB Yeats. Taken from the poem, 'Woman Young and Old', from section ii, titled 'Before the World Was Made'.

Chapter 7

1. For a film recording of this event see: www.youtube.com/watch?v=3mclp9QmCGs.

Chapter 8

1. The biographies include: Howard DeWitt (1983); John Collis (1985); Steve Turner (1993 and 1995); Brian Hinton (2000); Clinton Heylin (2003); Johnny Rogan (2005).

Chapter 9

1. In Sierra Leonean Krio, 'cool heart' translates more or less as 'peace' or 'inner peace'. A 'hot heart' translates as 'inner turmoil' or 'inner violence'. The language reflects a deep understanding that health and healing are inextricably linked to violence and peace.
2. The Interreligious Council of Sierra Leone included members from the Supreme Islamic Council, the Sierra Leone Muslim Congress, the Federation of Muslim Women Associations in Sierra Leone, the Council of Imams, the Sierra Leone Islamic Missionary Union, the Roman Catholic Church of Sierra Leone, the Pentecostal Churches Council and the Council of Churches in Sierra Leone (Turay 2000, p. 50).
3. Rehn, Elisabeth and Ellen Johnson Sirleaf (2002, pp. 71–2): in Bosnia, international 'peace' workers, including police monitors, peacekeepers, social workers and aid workers, accounted for 30 per cent of all brothel revenue. In Liberia, 6,600 children were fathered by peacekeepers between 1990 and 1998. According to a seventeen-year-old sex worker in Sierra Leone, the majority of her clients were United Nations Mission in Sierra Leone peacekeepers.

Chapter 10

1. Miriam's name has been changed for reasons of confidentiality.

Chapter 11

1. The full report can be found at: http://www.hreoc.gov.au/social_Justice/bth_report/report/index.html.

References

Abu-Nimer, M (ed.) 2001, Reconciliation, justice, and coexistence: theory and practice, Lexington Books, Maryland, USA.

Ali, K 2008, 'The architecture of loneliness', *The American poetry review*, volume 37:6, pp. 13–22.

Arendt, H & Baehr, P 2000, *The portable Hannah Arendt*, Penguin Books, New York.

Assefa, H 1993, *Peace and reconciliation as a paradigm*, Nairobi Peace Initiative, Nairobi, Kenya.

Atkinson, J 2002, *Trauma trails: recreating song lines: the transgenerational effects of trauma in indigenous Australia*, Spinifex Press, Melbourne.

Attali, J 2006, *Noise: the political economy of music*, University of Minnesota Press, Minneapolis, USA.

Augoyard, JF & Torgue, H 2006, *Sonic experience: a guide to everyday sounds*, McGill-Queen's University Press, Montreal and Kingston, Canada.

Bailey, AA 1950, *Glamour – a world problem*, Lucis Publishing Company, New York.

Barkan, E 2000, *The guilt of nations: restitution and negotiating historical injustices*, The Johns Hopkins University Press, Baltimore, USA.

Beah, I 2007, *A long way gone: memoirs of a boy soldier*, Sarah Crichton Books, New York.

Beck, DE & Cowan, C 2006, *Spiral dynamics*, Blackwell Publishing, Malden, USA.

Berger, P & Luckman, T 1966, *The social construction of reality*, Random House, New York.

Bernard, B 2004, *Resiliency what we have learned*, West Ed, San Francisco.

Biggar, N (ed.) 2003, *Burying the past: making peace and doing justice after civil conflict*, Georgetown University Press, Washington DC.

Block, P 2008, *Community: the structure of belonging*, Berrett-Koehler Publishers, Inc, San Francisco.

Bloomfield, D, Barnes, T & Huyse, L 2003, *Reconciliation after violent conflict: a handbook*, International Institute for Democracy and Electoral Assistance, Stockholm, Sweden.

Bloomfield, D, Fischer, M & Schmelzle, B 2006, *Social change and conflict transformation: Berghof Handbook Dialogue Series*, Berghof Research Center for Constructive Conflict Management, Berlin.

Bombande, E 2006, Personal interview, Accra, Ghana.

Bond, J 2008, 'Healing trauma among Australia's "Stolen Generations"' in B Hart (ed.), *Peacebuilding in traumatized societies*, University Press of America, Lanham, USA.

Boreham, P 2007, *Sierra Leone's poems of war*, BBC African Performance, 24 May, Sierra Leone.

Botcharova, O 2001, 'Implementation of track two diplomacy: developing a model of forgiveness' in RG Helmick & RL Peterson (eds), *Forgiveness and reconciliation*, Templeton Foundation Press, Philadelphia, USA.

Bourgois, P 2004, 'The everyday violence of gang rape,' in N Scheper-Hughes & P Bourgois (eds), *Violence in war and peace: an anthology*, Blackwell Publishing, Oxford.

Boutros-Ghali, B 1992, *Agenda for peace, report of the UN Secretary-General*.

Boyce-Tillman, J 2000, *Constructing musical healing: the wounds that sing*, Jessica Kingsley Publishers, London.

Bridgers, L 2005, *Contemporary varieties of religious experience: James's classic study in light of resiliency, temperament, and trauma*, Rowman and Littlefield Publishers, Inc., Boulder, USA.

Brison, SJ 2002, *Aftermath: violence and the remaking of self*, Princeton University Press, Princeton, USA.

Bronkhorst, D 1995, *Truth and reconciliation: obstacles and opportunities for human rights*, Amnesty International Dutch Section, Amsterdam.

Burdette, P 2003, *The power of the spirit: American Indian worldview and successful community development among the Oglala Lakota*, PhD dissertation, Union University, Jackson, USA.

Burns, GW 2001, *101 healing stories: using metaphors in therapy*, John Wiley & Sons, Inc., New York.

Carlson, K & Mazurana, D 2004, *From combat to community: women and girls of Sierra Leone*, Hunt Alternatives Fund, Washington DC.

Cauuray, TP 2007, 'Epitaph of a nation', unpublished, Sierra Leone.

Chatwin, B 1987, *The songlines*, Penguin Books, New York.

Chetail, V 2009, *Post-conflict peacebuilding: a lexicon*, Oxford University Press, Oxford.

Collis, J 1996, *Van Morrison: inarticulate speech of the heart*, Brown Packaging Books Ltd, London.

Cozolino, L 2006, *The neuroscience of human relationships*, WW Norton & Company, New York.

Crocker, C, Hampson, F & Aall, P 2001, *Turbulent peace*, United States Institute of Peace Press, Washington DC.

Crocker, DA 1999, 'Reckoning with past wrongs: a normative framework', *Ethics and International Affairs*, XIII, pp. 43–64.

Curle, A 1971, *Making peace*, Tavistock Publications Limited, London.

———— 2006, *The fragile voice of love*, Jon Carpenter Publishing, Charlbury, UK.

Darby, J & MacGinty, R 2003, *Contemporary peace making: conflict, violence and peace processes*, Palgrave MacMillan, New York.

DeLaet, DL 2006, 'Gender justice' in T Borer (ed.), *Telling the truths: truth telling and peacebuilding in post-conflict societies*, University of Notre Dame Press, Notre Dame, USA.

DeWitt, HA 1983, *Van Morrison: the mystic's music*, Bookpeople, San Francisco.

Doxtader, E & Villa-Vicencio, C (eds) 2003, *Through fire and water: the roots of division and the potential for reconciliation in Africa*, Africa World Press, Trenton, USA.

Doumbia, A & Doumbia, N 2004, *The way of the elders: West African spirituality and tradition*, Llewellyn Publications, St Paul, Minnesota.

Dylan, B 1971, 'Tomorrow is a long time', *Greatest hits Volume 2*, Columbia Records.

Edelman, GM 1989, *The remembered present: a biological theory of consciousness*, Basic Books, New York.

———— 2006, *Second nature: brain science and human knowledge*, Yale University Press, New Haven, USA.

Eichstaedt, P 2009, *First kill your family: child soldiers of Uganda and the Lord's Resistance Army*, Lawrence Hill Books, Chicago.

Elagab, OY 2004, 'The special court for Sierra Leone: some constraints', *International Journal of Human Rights*, 8, pp. 249–273.

Farah, AY 1993, *The roots of reconciliation*, Action Aid, London.

Fetzer, JE 2009, *Our founder, The Fetzer Institute*, http://www.fetzer.org/AboutUs.aspx?PageID=About&NavID=5, accessed 4 July 2009.

Fisas, V 2008, *2008 peace process yearbook*, Editorial Icaria, Barcelona.

Fisher, BS, Cullen, FT & Turner, MG 2000, *The sexual victimization of college women*, US Department of Justice.

Fisher, H 2004, *Why we love: the nature and chemistry of romantic love*, Henry Holt and Company, New York.

Forché, C 1993, *Against forgetting: twentieth-century poetry of witness*, WW Norton & Company, New York.
Fosdick, HE 1945, *A great time to be alive: sermons on Christianity in wartime*, S.C.M, Press, London.
——— 1969, 'God of Grace and God of Glory', in *The Mennonite Hymnal*, Herald Press, Scottdale, Pennsylvania.
Frankl, V 2006, *Man's search for meaning*, Beacon Press, Boston.
Galtung, J 1975, *Peace research education action* volume 1, Christian Ejlers, Copenhagen, Denmark.
Garcia, A 1996, *Hijos de la violencia*, La Catarata, Madrid, Spain.
Gaynor, ML 1999, *The healing power of sound: recovery from life-threatening illness using sound, voice, and music*, Shambhala Publications, Inc., Boston.
Gbowee, L 2006, Personal interview, Harrisonburg, Virginia, USA.
Gordon, D 1978, *Therapeutic metaphors*, META Publications, California.
Graybill, L 2001, 'The contribution of the truth and reconciliation commission toward the promotion of women's rights in South Africa', *Women's Studies International Forum*, 24, pp. 1–10.
Green, P 2009, 'The pivotal role of acknowledgement in social healing' in P Gobodo-Madikizela & C Van Der Merwe (eds), *Memory, narrative and forgiveness: perspectives on the unfinished journeys of the past*, Cambridge Scholars Publishing, United Kingdom.
Greene, RR (ed.) 2002, *Resiliency: an integrated approach to practice, policy and research*, NASW Press, Washington DC.
Griswold, CL 2007, *Forgiveness: a philosophical exploration*, Cambridge University Press, Cambridge.
Guzman, V 2008, *El Arte de Trabajar Las Paces*, paper presented in the Jornadas Aragonesas de Educación.
——— 2009, Personal correspondence.
Hamber, B & Kelly, G 2005, 'The challenge of reconciliation in post-conflict societies: definitions, problems and proposals' in I O'Flynn & D Russell (eds), *Power sharing new challenges for divided societies*, Pluto Press, London.
Harrison, K 2008, *While they slept: an inquiry into the murder of a family*, Random House, New York.
Hart, B (ed.) 2008, *Peacebuilding in traumatized societies*, University Press of America, Lanham, USA.
Harvey, MR & Tummala-Narra, P 2007, *Sources and expressions of resiliency in trauma survivors: ecological theory, multicultural practice*, Haworth Press, Inc., New York.

Hayner, P 2002, *Unspeakable truths: facing the challenge of truth commissions*, Routledge, New York.

Helmick, RG & Peterson, RL (eds) 2001, *Forgiveness and reconciliation: religion, public policy and conflict transformation*, Templeton Foundation Press, Philadelphia, USA.

Herman, JL 1992, *Trauma and recovery: the aftermath of violence*, Basic Books, New York.

Hernández Delgado, E 2004, *Resistencia civil artesana de paz: experiencias indigenas, afrodescendientes y campesinas*, Editorial Pontificia Universidad Javeriana, Bogota, Colombia.

Hernández Delgado, E & Salazar Posada, M 1999, *Con la esperanza intacta: experiencias comunitarias de resistencia civil no violenta*, Oxfam, Bogota, Colombia.

Heylin, C 2003, *Can you feel the silence? Van Morrison: a new biography*, Chicago Review Press, Inc., Chicago.

Hinton, B 2000, *Celtic crossroads: the art of Van Morrison*, Sanctuary Publishing, London.

Hoffman, E 2008, 'Reconciliation in Sierra Leone: local processes yield global lessons', *The Fletcher Forum of World Affairs*, 32:2, pp. 129–141.

Honwana, A 2006, *Child soldiers in Africa*, University of Pennsylvania Press Philadelphia, USA.

Ignatieff, M 2003, 'Reflections on coexistence' in A Chayes & M Minow (eds), *Imagine coexistence*, Jossey-Bass, Boulder, USA.

Jacobs, W 2006, Personal interview, Buduburam Refugee Camp, Ghana.

Jonas, S 2000, *Of centaurs and doves: Guatemala's peace process*, Westview Press, Boulder, USA.

Kaimal, S (project manager) 2008, *Reconciliation*, from International Association for Humanitarian Policy and Conflict Research: Peacebuilding Initiative, http://www.peacebuildinginitiative.org/index.cfm?pageId=1782, accessed 4 July 2009.

Kamanda, Chief Eiah 2007, Personal interview, Sierra Leone.

Kassim, H 2007, Personal interview, Sierra Leone.

Kehayan, VA & Napoli, JC 2005, *Resiliency in the face of disaster and terrorism*, Personhood Press, Fawnskin CA.

Khanu, Moses 2007, Personal interview, Freetown, Sierra Leone.

Kooser, T 2005, *The poetry home repair manual*, Board of Regents of the University of Nebraska, Nebraska.

Koroma, K 2007, 'In my mind', unpublished, Sierra Leone.

Kóvecses, Z 2002, *Metaphor: a practical introduction*, Oxford University Press, Oxford.

Kraybill, R 1995, 'The cycle of reconciliation', *Conciliation Quarterly* 14, no. 3, pp. 7–8.

Kriesberg, L 1973, *The sociology of social conflicts*, Prentice Hall, Englewood Cliffs, USA.

Lakoff, G & Johnson, M 1980, *Metaphors we live by*, University of Chicago Press, Chicago.

Lawley, J & Tompkins, P 2000, *Metaphors in mind: transformation through symbolic modelling*, The Developing Company Press, London.

Lederach, JP 1997, *Building peace: sustainable reconciliation in divided societies*, United States Institute of Peace Press, Washington DC.

―――― 1999, *The journey toward reconciliation*, Herald Press, Scottdale, USA.

―――― 2003, 'Five qualities of practice in support of reconciliation processes' in RG Helmick & RL Peterson (eds), *Forgiveness and reconciliation: religion, public policy and conflict transformation*, Templeton Foundation Press, Philadelphia, USA.

―――― 2005, *The moral imagination: the art and soul of building peace*, Oxford University Press, New York.

Levi, R 2004, 'Group magic an inquiry into experiences of collective resonance: executive summary', doctoral dissertation, Saybrook Graduate School and Research Center, San Francisco.

Levitin, DJ 2006, *This is your brain on music: the science of a human obsession*, Penguin Group, Inc., New York.

Lewis, IM 1994, *Blood and bone: the call of kinship in Somali society*, Red Sea Press, Trenton, USA.

―――― 1998, *Saints and Somalis: popular Islam in a clan-based society*, Red Sea Press, Trenton, USA.

Lewis, T, Amini, F & Lannon, R 2001, *A general theory of love*, Vintage Books, New York.

Lord, D 2000, 'Introduction: the struggle for power and peace in Sierra Leone', *Accord* 9, pp. 10–15.

Lund, M 1996, *Preventing violent conflict*, United States Institute of Peace Press, Washington DC.

Mack, A (ed.) 2005, *Human security report 2005: war and peace in the 21st century*, Oxford University Press, New York. (Also online at http://www.humansecurityreport.info/)

Mariatu, 2007, Personal interview, Sierra Leone.

Mbiti, J 1969, *African religions and philosophy*, Heinemann, Portsmouth, USA.

McCaslin, WD (ed.) 2005, *Justice as healing indigenous ways: writings on community peacemaking and restorative justice from the Native Law Centre*, Living Justice Press, St Paul, USA.

McDowell, R 2008, *Poetry as spiritual practice*, The Free Press, New York.

McSpadden, LA (ed.) 2000, *Reaching reconciliation: churches in the transitions to democracy in Eastern and Central Europe*, Life and Peace Institute, Uppsala, Sweden.

Meintjes, S, Turshen, M & Pillay, A (eds) 2001, *The aftermath: women in post-conflict transformation*, Zed Books, London.

Minow, M 1998, *Between vengeance and forgiveness: facing history after genocide and mass violence*, Beacon Press, Boston.

—— 2002, *Breaking the cycles of hatred: memory, law and repair*, Princeton University Press, Princeton.

Miriam, 2007, Personal interview, Sierra Leone.

Monk, G, Winslade, J, Crocket, K & Epston, D 1997, *Narrative therapy in practice*, Jossey Bass, San Francisco.

Morrison, V 1968, 'Madame George', *Astral weeks*, Warner Bros Records Inc.

—— 1970, 'Moondance', *Moondance*, Warner Bros Records Inc.

—— 1972, 'Listen to the lion', *Saint Dominic's preview*, Exile Productions.

—— 1982, 'Dweller on the threshold', *Beautiful vision*, Warner Bros Records Inc.

—— 1985, 'Evening meditation', *A sense of wonder*, Exile Productions Ltd.

—— 1986, 'Got to go back', *No guru, no method, no teacher*, Exile Productions Ltd.

—— 1986, 'In the garden', *No guru, no method, no teacher*, Exile Productions Ltd.

—— 1987, 'Alan Watts blues', *Poetic champions compose*, Exile Productions

—— 1989, 'Whenever God shines His Light', *Avalon sunset*, Exile Productions Ltd.

—— 1991, 'Hymns to the silence', *Hymns to the silence*, Exile Productions Ltd.

—— 1991, 'Take me back', *Hymns to the silence*, Exile Productions Ltd.

—— 1991, 'On Hyndford Street', *Hymns to the silence*, Exile Productions Ltd.

—— 1993, 'Before the world was made', *Too long in exile*, Exile Productions Ltd.

Nepo, M 2008, Personal conversations.

Nhat Hanh, T 1987, *Being peace*, Parallax Press, Berkeley, USA.

Nordstrom, C 1999, 'Visible wars and invisible girls, shadow industries, and the politics of not-knowing', *International Feminist Journal of Politics*, 1, no. 1, pp. 14–33.

—— 2006, *Vagina monologues* panel speech, University of Notre Dame, Indiana.

Nouwen, HJM, McNeill, D & Morrison, D 1983, *Compassion: a reflection on the Christian Life*, Doubleday, New York.

O'Dea, J 2004, 'Social healing', *Shift,* Issue 3, Institute of Noetic Sciences, http://www.shiftinaction.com/node/106, accessed 22 July 2009.

Philpott, D 2006, *The politics of past evil: religion, reconciliation, and the dilemmas of transitional justice*, University of Notre Dame Press, Notre Dame, Indiana.

Pinsky, R 2008, 'Speaking the unspeakable', *New York Times Review of Books*, 8 June, pp. 1 and 10.

Polchinski, J 1998, *String theory*, Cambridge University Press, Cambridge.

Porter, E 2007, *Peacebuilding: women in international perspective*, Routledge, London.

Pranis, K 2005, *The little book of circle processing: a new/old approach to peacemaking*, Good Books, Intercourse, Pennsylvania.

Pranis, K, Stuart, B & Wedge, M 2003, *Peacemaking circles: from crime to community*, Living Justice Press, St Paul Minnesota.

Pray the devil back to hell, 2008, Dir. Gini Reticker, Fork Films.

Rehn, E & Johnson Sirleaf, E 2002, *Women war peace: progress of the world's women 2002* volume 1, United Nations Development Fund for Women, New York.

Reivich, K & Shatté, A 2002, *The resilience factor*, Broadway Books, New York.

Rian, K (ed.) 2009, *Kalashnikov in the sun: an anthology of Sierra Leonean poets*, Pika Press, Enterprise, USA.

Ricoeur, P 1987, *The rule of metaphor: multi-disciplinary studies of the creation of meaning in language*, University of Toronto Press, Toronto.

Rogan, J 2005, *Van Morrison: no surrender*, Secker & Warburg, London.

Ross, FC 2001, 'Speech and silence: women's testimony in the first five weeks of public hearings of the South African Truth and Reconciliation Commission' in V Das, A Kleinman, M Lock, M Ramphele & P Reynolds (eds), *Remaking a world*, University of California Press, Berkeley.

—— 2002, *Bearing witness: women and the truth and reconciliation commission*, Pluto Press, London.

Saa, W 2006, Personal interview, Accra, Ghana.

Sacks, O 2007, *Musicophilia: tales of music and the brain*, Random House, New York.

Samatar, S 1982, *Oral poetry and Somali nationalism*, Cambridge University Press, Cambridge, USA.

Schapp, A 2005, *Political reconciliation*, Routledge Taylor & Francis Group, New York.

Scheper-Hughes, N 1998, 'Maternal thinking and the politics of war', in LA Lorentzen & J Turpin (eds), *The women and war reader*, New York University Press, New York.

Schirch, L 2004, *Ritual and symbol in peacebuilding*, Kumarian Press, Virginia.

Schreiter, RJ 1998, *The ministry of reconciliation: spirituality and strategies*, Orbis Books, Maryknoll, New York.

Schutz, A 1967, *The phenomenology of the social world*, Northwestern University Press, Chicago.

Scott, C 1933, *Music: its secret influence throughout the ages*, D McKay, Philadelphia, PA.

Senge, P, Scharmer, CO, Jaworski, J & Flowers, BS 2004, *Presence: human purpose and the field of the future*, Society for Organizational Learning, Cambridge, MA.

Sesay, MG & Kainwo, M (eds) 2004, *Songs that pour the heart*, New Initiatives, Sierra Leone.

Sesay, OF 2007, *Salute to the remains of a peasant*, Publish America, Baltimore.

—— 2007, Personal conversations.

Showalter, SH 2005, '"How can I keep from singing?": Seeking the wisdom of sound' in SM Intrator (ed.), *Living the questions: essays inspired by the work and life of Parker J. Palmer*, Jossey-Bass, San Francisco.

Shriver, DW Jr 2005, *Honest patriots: loving a country enough to remember its misdeeds*, Oxford University Press, New York.

Siegel, D 1999, *The developing mind: how relationships and the mind interact to shape who we are*, The Guilford Press, New York.

—— 2007, *The mindful brain reflection and attunement in the cultivation of well being*, WW Norton & Company, New York.

Singer, PW 2006, *Children at war*, University of California Press, Berkeley.

Smith, D 2004, *Towards a strategic framework for peacebuilding: getting their act together: overview report of the joint Utstein study of peacebuilding*, Royal Norwegian Ministry of Foreign Affairs, Oslo, Norway.

Soyinka, W 1999, *The burden of memory, the muse of forgiveness*, Oxford University Press, New York.

Stolen, KA 2007, *Guatemalans in the aftermath of violence: the refugees' return*, University of Pennsylvania Press, Philadelphia, USA.

Storr, A 1992, *Music and the mind*, Balantine Books, New York.

Szabo, LR (ed.) 2005, *In the dark before dawn: new selected poems of Thomas Merton*, New Directions Books, New York.

Terry, S 2005, *Aftermath: Bosnia's long road to peace*, Channel Photographics, New York.

Thompson, J 2005, 'On forgiveness and social healing', panel discussion, *The role of forgiveness in social healing*, 31 October, Harvard Divinity School.

Turay, TM 2000, 'Civil society and peacebuilding: the role of the Inter-Religious Council of Sierra Leone,' *Accord* 9, pp. 50–53.

Turner, S 1993, *Too late to stop now*, Penguin Group, New York.

Turshen, M 2001, 'Engendering relations of state to society in the aftermath' in S Meintjes, M Turshen & A Pillay (eds), *The aftermath: women in post-conflict transformation*, Zed Books, London.

United Nations 2000, *United Nations Security Council Resolution 1325: on women, peace, and security*, United Nations, New York.

United Nations Development Programme (UNDP), 'Evolution of statistics on the armed conflict', *Hechos del callejón*, September 2007.

Ury, W 2004, *The third side*, Penguin, New York.

van der Mark, I 2007, *Reconciliation: bridging theory to practice: a framework for practitioners*, The Centre for Justice and Reconciliation, The Hague, Netherlands.

Villa-Vicencio, C & Doxtader, E (eds) 2004, *Pieces of the puzzle: keywords on reconciliation and transitional justice*, Institute for Justice and Reconciliation, Cape Town, South Africa.

Volf, M 1996, *Exclusion and embrace: a theological exploration of identity, otherness and reconciliation*, Abingdon Press, Nashville, USA.

Volkan, V 1977, *Bloodlines: from ethnic pride to ethnic terrorism*, Westview Press, Boulder, USA.

Watts, A 1968, *Cloud-hidden, whereabouts unknown: a mountain journal*, Pantheon Books, New York.

Webster, D 1998, *Aftermath: the remnants of war*, Vintage Books, London.

Wessells, M 2006, *Child soldiers: from violence to protection*, Harvard University Press, Cambridge, USA.

Wheatley, MJ 2002, *Turning to one another: simple conversations to restore hope to the future*, Berrett-Koehler Publishers, Inc., San Francisco.

Winslade, J & Monk, G 2000, *Narrative mediation: a new approach to conflict resolution*, Jossey-Bass, San Francisco.

Wittgenstein, L 1973, *Philosophical investigations*, Prentice Hall, New Jersey.

Yeats, WB 1996, 'Before the world was made,' in Richard J Finneran (ed.), *The collected poems of W.B. Yeats*, Scribner Paperback Poetry, New York.

Yoder, C 2005, *The little book of trauma healing*, Good Books, Intercourse, Pennsylvania.

Zwiebach, B 2004, *A first course in string theory*, Cambridge University Press, Cambridge.

Index

Abel, 2
Aboriginal Australians
    Bridge Walk for reconciliation, 220–1
    National Sorry Day, 220–2, 229
    significance of land, 59–60, 131
    songlines, 60, 131–2, 142, 164, 200
    taste of songs, 97
    transgenerational trauma, 126
Abubakar, Abdulsalami, 31
Against forgetting: twentieth-century poetry of witness (Forché), 177
agency, 44–5, 55–6
Ali, Kazim, 138
Amini, F, 96, 190, 231
analytic constructs, 46–7, 55–7
anamnesis, 135
Angola, 156
Arendt, Hannah, 137
Arias, Oscar, 81
Arkady, 131–2
'at-homeness', 63–4, 71, 141–2
Atkinson, Judy, 2, 56, 59, 68, 126, 145
Attali, Jacques, 73, 95
Augoyard, JF, 135
aural theory of social change, 224, 227–30

Australia
    see also Aboriginal Australians
    Bridge Walk, 220–1
    National Sorry Day, 220–2, 229

Bailey, Alice, 119
Bangs, Lester, 123
Barre, Siad, 23–4
Basque Country, 84
beauty and healing, 122, 128, 130–1, 133, 143
Beck, DE, 98
Being peace (Nhat Hanh), 135
bell-curve of conflict management, 46–7
'bell of mindfulness', 135
belonging, 59–64, 71, 90, 102, 128, 154–5, 199–200, 202, 205, 208, 211, 213
Berger, P, 13
Between vengeance and forgiveness (Minow), 8
Blake, William, 122, 130
Block, P, 102
Bloomfield, D, 5
Bombande, Emmanuel, 164
Bond, J, 221–2

252 Index

Boroma conference, Somalia, 27, 102–8, 110
Bosnia, 156
Bourgois, Philippe, 185
Boutros-Ghali, Boutros, 47
Boyce-Tillman, J, 120, 124, 127
Bradford Peace Studies degree program, 233
Bringing them home (Wilson), 220–1
Buduburam Refugee Camp, Ghana, 18–19, 21–2, 165
Burdette, Patricia, 94

Carter, Jared, 174
Catalyst for Peace, 181, 186
Cauuray, Tom, 171, 191–3
Chatwin, Bruce, 131, 195
Chetail, V, 48
child abductions, 171, 181–2, 186
child soldiers
    forgiveness for, 19
    girls, 149–50, 155, 157, 161, 186–90
    Liberia, 17–21, 31, 147–9, 153–4, 163–4
    Sierra Leone, 149–54, 157, 161, 186–7
    transformation, 19–20
circularity as reconciliation metaphor, 5–6, 9, 12, 46, 56, 98–100, 103, 109–10, 128, 143
    see also container as metaphor
claiming, 212–13
Cloud-hidden, whereabouts unknown: a mountain journal (Watts), 98, 119
collective resonance, 67–8
Colombia, 34–40
    Autodefensas, 35, 37

desplazados, 36
    population displacement, 58–9, 62–3
Coltrane, John, 120
Communion, 128
community metaphors, 57–68
    place, 58–63, 72
    safety, 63–5, 72
    voice, 65–8, 72, 110
Community: the structure of belonging (Block), 102
Compassion (Nouwen, McNeill & Morrison), 136
'CONFLICT IS LINEAR', 49, 54, 72
conflict management, 47
conflict prevention, 47
conflict resolution
    collective responsibility, 161
    palava huts, 160–2
container as metaphor
    collective voicing, 191
    community space, 10
    holding space, 72, 89, 94, 97
    holding vibration, 100–2, 109
    safety, 64, 68, 71
    social healing, 110, 198–200, 205–7, 223, 228, 229, 233
    surrounding sound, 120, 142
Cowan, C, 98
Crocker, David, 3
Curle, Adam, 49, 233–4

Dadirri, 56
dancing, 21, 30
Davis, Miles, 120
de Klerk, FW, 217
DeWitt, HA, 121
diplomacy, 47
directionality, 94–7

'disappeared', 64, 71
displacement
    Aboriginal Australians, 59–60
    Colombia, 58
    IDPs (internally displaced people), 58
    metaphors, 13
    place as metaphor, 62
    psychological effects, 59–61, 71, 132, 154–5, 199–200
    seeking safety, 63
    sexual violence, 156
    Sierra Leone, 171
domestic violence, 156, 162
Dometz, Faraon, 83
drumming, 22, 100, 120, 125, 200
Dylan, Bob, 85–8, 122

'earworms', 86
echo, 212–14
Edelman, Gerald, 138–40
Ensler, Eve, 184
ETA (Euskadi Ta Askatasuna), 84
'eternal now', 134–6, 139, 142, 201
Ethiopia, 106
evocation, 104–5

Farah, AY, 25–7
Fatura, 30
'feeling human again', 143, 200, 234
Fetzer, John, 231–3
Fetzer Institute, 232
Filipinas, 185
flourishing, 50, 53–4, 138
Flowers, BS, 102
Forché, Carolyn, 177–8
forgiveness, 19, 163, 219
Fosdick, Harry Emerson, 77–9, 83

fragile voice of love, The (Curle), 233–4
framing, 213–14
Frankl, Viktor, 132–3

Galtung, Johan, 49
Gandhi, Mahatma, 77
Gaynor, ML, 112, 120
Gbowee, Leymah, 28–9, 31–2, 149
gender roles, 156, 180
general theory of love, A (Lewis, Amini & Lannon), 190, 231
Ghana
    Buduburam Refugee Camp, 18–19, 21–2, 165
    respect for women, 167
Gilley family, 1
Glamour – a world problem (Bailey), 119
great time to be alive: sermons on Christianity in wartime, A (Fosdick), 77
Green, Paula, 7
Gregorian chants, 120, 125
Griswold, CL, 218–19
Grossman, Allen, 177
Guatemala, 100
Gutierrez, Juan, 83, 85
Guzman, Vicent, 96, 175, 200

hair cutting ritual, 148, 159, 163
Harrison, Kathryn, 1, 66–7, 183
Hart, Barry, 3–4
Hayner, P, 2, 111
'HEALING IS AURAL', 68, 89, 101
health
    importance of place, 61–2
    as metaphor, 10
    multidirectionality, 202

health (cont'd)
    need for safety, 64
    resiliency, 70
hearing, 112–13, 120
Herman, JL, 56
Heylin, C, 134
Hinton, B, 116, 123
HIV/AIDS, 21, 155, 157
Hoffman, Libby, 210
Holocaust, the, 132–3, 137
Holy Sacrament, 128
Honest patriots (Shriver), 219
Human security report (Mack), 99

IDPs (internally displaced people), 58–9
Ignatieff, M, 3
incantation, 123, 126, 130
Institute of Noetic Sciences, 6
interaction, 103–4, 110
international conflict management, 47
iteration, 103, 110, 208
itineration, 103, 108, 110

Jacobs, William 'Jake', 20–2, 53, 165, 216, 226
Jaworski, J, 102
jembe drums, 22, 120
Johnson, M, 43, 49, 54–5
Johnson Sirleaf, Ellen, 33, 183
Jonas, Susanne, 100
Jones, Wendell, 92

Kamanda, Chief, 163
Kassim, Haja, 150–3, 158, 165
Kennel, Ron, 78
Kerouac, Jack, 119
Khanu, Moses, 180, 189

King, Martin Luther Jr, 4
Kooser, Ted, 174
Koroma, Kadiatu, 181–3, 188–9

Lakoff, G, 43, 49, 54–5
Lakota people, 94, 100
Lannon, R, 96, 190, 231
Lederach, Angela Jill, 81
Lederach, John, 78
Lederach, Mary, 76
Lederach, Willis, 76
Levi, R, 67–8
Lewis, T, 96, 190, 231
Liberia
    child soldiers, 17–18, 31, 147–9, 153–4, 163–4
    civil war, 17–18, 31
    cultural practices, 21
    mothers, 147–9, 159–61, 163–4, 166
    peace accord, 31
    rape, 156
    Tree of Frustration, 148–9, 159–60, 162–3, 165–6, 217
    women peacemakers, 28–33, 53, 147–9, 159, 161, 164–5, 167–8
Liberians United for Reconciliation and Democracy, 29–31
life expectancy, 50
limbic resonance, 96, 190
Lin, Maya, 218–19
linearity as reconciliation metaphor, 5–6, 8–9, 12, 42, 44–6, 48–9, 52, 54–7, 72, 127–8, 137, 198, 226–7
love, 230–2, 234
loyal daughters, The (Weisbecker), 186, 189–91
Luckman, T, 13

McDowell, Robert, 177
Mack, Andrew, 99
McNeill, D, 136
Making peace (Curle), 233
Mandela, Nelson, 217
mantras, 120–1, 125, 128
Maria (Colombian woman), 34–40, 45, 51, 53, 59–61, 64, 98, 216, 226
Mariatu (Sierra Leonean woman), 149–50, 155, 157, 159, 161
Max, Cuban, 82
Mbiti, J, 137
memory
    cognitive, 112
    collective, 123
    emotional, 112
    healing and, 166, 188, 190, 205
    hope and, 190, 202, 205, 211, 213
    imagination and, 140
    music and, 129, 132, 164
    ritual and, 163
    social amnesia, 209
    sound and, 134–5
    subconscious, 123
Merton, Thomas, 136
metaphors
    directionality, 42, 94–8, 101, 144
    dominant, 56
    hiding of complexity, 55–7
    linear/sequential, 57
    orientational, 54–5
    role of, 42–4
    spatial, 55, 64, 67, 70, 97, 202
    temporal, 202
    value of, 226
metaphor shifts
    from line to circle, 198–200
    from linear to multidirectional, 42, 93–4, 97, 168, 202
    from linear to simultaneous and multilayered, 200–2
    from linear to sonic, 110, 202–8, 214, 222
    from linear to spatial, 58, 64, 70, 141
metaphors of reconciliation/social healing
    see also community metaphors; sound-based metaphors
    circle or spiral movement, 5–6, 9, 12, 46, 56, 98–100, 103, 109–10, 128, 143, 200, 228
    dominant linear movement metaphor, 5–6, 8–9, 12, 42, 44–6, 48–9, 52, 54–7, 72, 127–8, 137, 198, 226–7
    motherhood, 168–9
    movement metaphor, 5–6, 8–9
    multidirectional, 42, 127, 223
    permanent dynamism, 10–11, 52, 54
    post-conflict as linear concept, 48–9
    ritual and repetition, 22, 56, 95, 100, 103–4, 122–8, 143, 159, 161–5, 200, 207–8, 228, 230
    seed metaphor, 11, 53, 188
    simultaneity, 9–13, 42, 53–6, 60, 65, 109, 126–8, 134–9, 142–3, 154, 201–2, 209, 214
    spatial, 5–6, 9–10, 198, 206
Metaphors we live by (Lakoff & Johnson), 43–4
Mezzrow, Mezz, 119
mindfulness, 135
Minow, M, 2, 8, 111
Miriam (Sierre Leonean woman), 186–90

Mitchell, Christopher, 83, 85–6
Morris (child soldier), 17–21, 150, 159, 226
Morrison, D, 136
Morrison, Van, 112–44
   'Alan Watts blues', 114, 119
   Astral weeks, 115, 117, 123
   childhood innocence, 166
   'Cyprus Avenue', 117, 134
   'Dweller on the threshold', 119
   'eternal now', 134–5, 201
   'Evening meditation', 121
   focus on place, 128–9
   'Got to go back', 117–18, 125–6, 137
   'Hymns to the silence', 117–18
   'In the garden', 117, 134
   The inarticulate speech of the heart, 120, 228
   'Listen to the lion', 121
   'Madame George', 123
   meditative songs, 117–21
   'On Hyndford Street', 119
   poetry, 129–30
   repetition in songs, 122–8
   sonic references, 129
   St Dominic's preview, 121
   'Take me back', 117–18, 123, 130, 132–3
   transcendental wonder, 122, 129, 131, 134
motherhood as metaphor, 168–9, 199
Movement for Democracy in Liberia, 31
Mozambique, 156
Muse, the, 116–17
music, 117–44
   see also dancing; drumming; songs
   emotional memory, 112
   physical effects, 113
   psychological effects, 142, 200
   resonance, 134–5
   social change, 228, 230
Music: its secret influence throughout the ages (Scott), 117
Musicophilia (Sacks), 140

nabad raadin (reconciliation), 24–5
naming, 212
natural frequency of sound, 92–3, 109–10, 206
nature and healing, 122, 128–30, 133, 143
Navajo people, 100
Nepo, Mark, 174, 189
neural Darwinism, 138
New York Times, The, 1
Nhat Hanh, T, 135
Nicaragua, 79–83
   Contras, 79–80, 82
   Sandinistas, 79–80
   US role, 80–1
   Yatama, 79–80
Nordstrom, Carolyn, 51, 147, 155, 157
Norris, Kathleen, 136
Nouwen, HJM, 136

O'Dea, J, 6
Oedipus Tyrannus (Sophocles), 2
Ondarza, Irune, 84–5
Organization of African Unity (OAU), 106–7

Parks, Rosa, 216
peace, stable and unstable, 47

Index 257

peacebuilding
    funding, 55
    as poetic act, 175
    post-conflict, 47–9
Peacebuilding in traumatized societies (Hart), 3
peace conferences, 105–7
    see also Somalia, Boroma conference
peace enforcement, 47
'PEACE IS SEQUENTIAL', 49, 52, 54, 72
peacekeeping, 47
    sexual exploitation during, 157
peacemaking, 47
peace studies, 231
    bell curve of conflict, 46–7
    forms of violence, 49
    peaceful coexistence, 99
phenomenology, 13–14
Philippines, 185
Philomena, 2
Pinsky, Robert, 1–2, 111
place as metaphor, 58–63, 72, 128–9, 131, 142
poetry
    Falui Poets Society, 170–6, 189–90, 192
    limbic resonance, 190
    reconciliation, 25–6
    'social', 177–8
    social healing, 170–93, 228, 230
    Somalia, 25–6
    Van Morrison, 129–30
    voicing the 'unspeakable', 171–91
    of witness, 177
    women's, 178–88
poetry home repair manual, The (Kooser), 174

Politics of Jesus (Yoder, JH), 77
post-conflict
    peacebuilding, 47–9
    sexual exploitation, 157
    violence, 51–2, 168
Post-conflict peacebuilding: a lexicon (Chetail), 48
Presence (Senge et al.), 102
prostitution, 157

rape
    as oppressor of women, 185
    stigmatisation of victims, 179–80
    United States, 156, 185–6
    as weapon of war, 30, 51, 155–7, 171
'rebel babies', 155
reconciliation
    see also metaphors of reconciliation; social healing
    challenges, 209
    defining, 3–4
    funding for, 4, 44–5, 55–6
    justice and, 8
    nabad raadin, 24–5
    'national', 210–11, 215, 218, 228–9
    poetry, 25–6
    relational focus, 4–5
    truth-telling, 178–9
refugees
    child soldiers, 18–21
    repatriation, 47
    sexual violence against, 156
Rehn, Elisabeth, 183
religious rituals, 100, 128
remembered present, The (Edelman), 138–9

Republic of Somaliland, 27, 106–7, 226
see also Somalia
resiliency
    amidst ongoing violence, 11, 53
    children, 69
    collective, 209, 211, 214, 224, 227
    as metaphor, 68–72
    poetry, 176–7
    simultaneity of temporal experience, 138
    social healing, 72
    spatial and directional metaphors, 202
    trauma healing, 68–72
Rian, Kirsten, 171, 181, 189
Rilke, Rainer Maria, 225, 234
ritual and repetition, 22, 56, 95, 100, 103–4, 122–8, 143, 159, 161–5, 200, 207–8, 228, 230
Rodgers, Linda, 112
Ross, Fiona, 179
Rwanda, 156

Saa, William, 29
Sacks, Oliver, 86, 140, 231
safety as metaphor, 63–5, 72
'SAFETY IS CONTAINER', 64
Scharmer, CO, 102
Scheper-Hughes, Nancy, 167
Schirch, Lisa, 95
Schreiter, Robert, 216–17
Schutz, A, 13
Scott, Cyril, 117
Second nature (Edelman), 139
Senge, P, 102
Sesay, Oumar Farouk, 172–4, 176, 189, 192
sex slavery, 155, 180, 186

sex strikes, 29
Shaw, George Bernard, 120
Shriver, DW Jr, 219
Sierra Leone
    child soldiers, 149–54, 157, 161, 186–7
    Civil Defense Force (CDF), 150
    civil war, 18
    displaced people, 171
    Falui Poets Society, 171–2, 175–6, 178, 189–90, 192
    Interreligious Council of Sierra Leone (IRCSL), 151–2
    local reconciliation efforts, 210
    Operation No Living Thing, 149–50, 159, 161
    palava huts, 160–1
    poetry, 170–8
    rape, 156
    Revolutionary United Front (RUF), 18, 149, 151, 157–8, 186
    war statistics, 171
    women peacemakers, 150–3, 158–9, 161, 164–5, 167–8
    women's poetry, 180–4
Silko, Leslie Marmon, 15
simultaneity, 9–13, 42, 53–6, 60, 65, 109, 126–8, 134–40, 142–3, 154, 201–2, 209, 214, 226, 229
Smith, D, 4
social amnesia, 209
social echo, 7, 186, 208, 211, 214–19, 224, 227, 229–30, 234
social healing
    see also metaphors of reconciliation/social healing; reconciliation; sound-based metaphors

circling conversations, 212–13
claiming, 212–13
collective resiliency, 211
community level, 210–11, 227, 229
definitions, 6–7, 208–9
individual healing, 203–4, 210–11, 214–16
longer term approaches, 229
naming, 212
need for play, 166
non-linear, 211
palava huts, 160–2
poetry, 170–93
resiliency, 72
ritual, 163–6
sense of place, 71
song, 32, 164, 166
surrounding and giving voice, 160–3
theoretical contributions, 223–4
'SOCIAL HEALING IS RESILIENT', 72
Somalia
   see also Republic of Somaliland
   armed conflict, 23–4
   Boroma conference, 27, 102–8, 110
   dia payments for deaths, 26
   ergada, 25–6, 103, 105, 107
   guurti gatherings, 25–7
   Hargeisa, 23–4
   poetry, 25–6
   reconciliation, 25–7
   role of elders, 25–7, 53, 103, 105
   women peacemakers, 26
Somaliland
   see Republic of Somaliland
songlines, 60, 131–2, 142, 164

songlines, The (Chatwin), 131
songs, 117–44
   social healing, 32, 164, 166
Songs that pour from the heart (Falui Poets Society), 171
Songs that pour the heart (Sesay & Kainwo), 175
Sophocles, 2
sound-based metaphors, 73–144
   see also music; voice
   directionality, 94–7
   echo, 212–14
   evocative capacity, 141–2
   multidirectionality, 214
   reconciliation, 198
   sense of surrounding, 142
   social echo, 7, 186, 208, 211, 214–19, 224, 227, 229–30, 234
   social healing, 110, 222–7, 230–4
   vibration and resonance, 97–101, 108–10, 200, 205–7, 214–15
South Africa, Truth and Reconciliation Commission (TRC), 107–8, 179
Soyinka, Wole, 116
Spain, Basque resistance, 84
St Benedict's guidelines for monks, 136
St Peter Claver Catholic Worker House, 162
string theory, 96–7, 232
survival
   as resiliency, 53
   simultaneity of temporal experience, 138

Taylor, Charles, 29, 31
temporal simultaneity, 9, 134, 143, 201, 226, 229

therapeutic repetition, 123–4, 143
'third side', 101
Thompson, J, 7
Tibetan singing bowls, 90–110
Tok, Fambul, 210
Tolstoy, Leo, 77
Torgue, H, 135
trauma healing
  resiliency, 68–72
  safety, 68
  story sharing, 68
Trauma trails: recreating song lines (Atkinson), 59–60
Truth and Reconciliation Commission (TRC), South Africa, 107–8, 179
Turner, S, 115, 121, 129
Turning to one another (Wheatley), 24
2008 Peace process yearbook, 156

U theory, 102
United Nations (UN), 31, 105, 151
  Agenda for Peace, 47
United Nations Refugee Agency (UNHCR), 18
United Nations Security Council Resolution 1325: On women, peace, and security, 156
United States
  sexual violence, 156, 185–6
  Vietnam Veterans Memorial, 218–20
'unspeakable', 1–2, 8, 14, 66, 98, 111–12, 154, 180–3, 211
Unspeakable truths (Hayner), 111
Uribe, President of Colombia, 37
Ury, William, 101

vagina monologues, The (Ensler), 184–6
vibration and resonance, 97–101, 108–10, 200, 205–7, 214–15
Vietnam Veterans Memorial, 218–20
violence
  see also rape
  collective, 229
  dehumanising, 133, 143
  direct, 49–52, 54
  gender and, 155–9
  multiple levels, 51
  ongoing, 201, 205
  psychological effects, 63, 180–8, 202
  structural, 49–51, 54, 156, 200, 204, 209
  transgenerational, 126, 204, 209, 211
  against women, 155–9, 178–88
voice
  collective, 32–3, 164
  individual, 111
  loss of, 155, 157, 202
  meaningful participation, 58, 65–9, 89–90, 108–9, 160–2
  resiliency, 71–2
  social healing, 7, 94–5, 97, 110, 170–93, 199–217, 222–7, 230–4
  speaking the 'unspeakable', 170–91, 212
  voicelessness, 58, 65–6, 71, 149, 187
'VOICE IS POWER', 184
voicelessness, 58, 65–8, 71, 149, 187

Watts, Alan, 98, 119–20, 200, 228
Wearing, Clive, 140–1, 231

Wearing, Deborah, 140–1, 231
Weisbecker, Emily, 186
Wheatley, Margaret, 24
While they slept (Harrison), 1
Wilson, Sir Ronald, 220
Wittgenstein, Ludwig, 170
women
    exclusion from peace processes, 158
    exposure to violence, 51
    invisibility, 157
    Liberian mothers, 147–9, 159–61, 163–4, 166
    Liberian peacemakers, 28–33, 53, 147–9, 159, 161, 164–5, 167–8
    poetry of truth-telling, 178–88
    post-conflict violence towards, 51
    rape, 30, 51, 155–7, 171, 179–80, 185–6
    Sierra Leonean peacemakers, 150–3, 158, 161, 164–5, 167–8
    Somali peacemakers, 26
    storytelling, 187–8
    violence against, 155–9, 178–88
Women of Liberia Mass Action for Peace Campaign, 29, 33, 45, 165, 217
Wordsworth, William, 122, 130

Yapo, Monsieur, 96
Yeats, WB, 41, 61–2, 70, 122, 130
Yoder, C, 53
Yoder, JH, 77

Printed in the USA/Agawam, MA
September 20, 2019

aainflight.com